TECHNOPOLS

Published under the auspices of the Inter-American Dialogue
and the Center for International Affairs at Harvard University

Jorge I. Domínguez

TECHNOPOLS

Freeing Politics and Markets in Latin America in the 1990s

The Pennsylvania State University Press
University Park, Pennsylvania

Photographs by Rick Reinhard

Library of Congress Cataloging-in-Publication Data

Technopols : freeing politics and markets in Latin America
   in the 1990s / [edited by] Jorge I. Domínguez.
         p.   cm.
   Includes bibliographical references and index.
   ISBN 0-271-01613-2 (cloth : alk. paper)
   ISBN 0-271-01614-0 (pbk. : alk. paper)
      1. Latin America—Economic policy.   2. Latin America—Politics and
government—1948–   3. Finance ministers—Latin America.
   I. Domínguez, Jorge I., 1945–   .
   338.98—dc20   96-12003
                                                                      CIP

Copyright ©1997 The Pennsylvania State University
All rights reserved
Printed in the United States of America
Published by The Pennsylvania State University Press,
University Park, PA 16802-1003

To Our Families

Contents

List of Tables

Foreword

One evening in 1992, after work at the Inter-American Dialogue, Jorge Domínguez and I invented the term "technopol" over margaritas at the Lauriol Plaza in Adams Morgan. It was that sort of beautiful spring weather that makes the creative juices flow. We wanted a label to describe our friends and colleagues in Latin America that would differentiate them from the "technocrats" of the 1970s pejoratively associated with authoritarian rule but that kept the sense of academic excellence. We sought a label that would capture their ability to function effectively in bureaucratic battles as well as in the rough-and-tumble of political life. We recognized that the term "technopol" carries within it a juxtaposition of opposites—the introspection of the thinker with the sociability of the politician. It is precisely that unusual combination of virtues that bestows upon our leaders the qualities that make for greatness.

Jorge Domínguez and I were convinced that individuals matter in history. Of course structures set limits, but our technopols have indeed altered the course of history—for better and occasionally for worse. Fernando Henrique Cardoso's ability to build a center-right coalition that could identify democracy with financial stability and social advance has placed Brazil back on the road of progress. Alejandro Foxley brilliantly unified macroeconomic stability and democratic coalition building with serious concern for social equity—creating nothing less than a new, genuinely Latin American model of development. Tragically, it was Pedro Aspe's failure to adjust the peso during 1994 that allowed for its collapse and a severe setback for Mexican economic growth.

In early 1993 I left the Inter-American Dialogue to join President Clinton's National Security Council. In that capacity, I had the good fortune to interact with most of the subjects of this volume. Often in life "familiarity breeds contempt," but in these cases my admiration grew as I watched our techno-pols operate in their complex and difficult political milieu. Cosmopolitan rationalists, these intellectuals have had to maneuver within political environ-ments still characterized by patronage, clientism, and in some cases blatant corruption. They have had to deal with parliaments that bear only superficial resemblance to their namesakes in Europe, and with state apparatuses more adept at consuming resources than delivering social services. All five techno-pols have been battered by the storms of political life, some severely. As a result of their experiences, most have become stronger and have maintained their characteristic energy and optimism.

At the NSC I sought to associate the United States with the technopols' projects. It was my great pleasure to choreograph President Fernando Hen-rique Cardoso's April 1995 state visit to the White House and to witness President Clinton praise the Brazilian technopol as "one of the great leaders of the Americas . . . a fighter for democracy throughout his life," and say that he had "every confidence in [President Cardoso's] ability to strengthen Bra-zilian democracy and to advance the visionary economic reforms he began as finance minister." After years of rancor in the bilateral relationship between the hemisphere's most populous powers, that state visit catalyzed a new U.S.-Brazilian partnership around shared values and strengthened Cardoso's standing back home.

The Clinton administration recognized that Domingo Cavallo and Foreign Minister Guido Di Tella were almost magically remaking their country by placing decades of international antagonism and domestic policy error behind Argentina and moving it into the vanguard on issues ranging from monetary management to international peacekeeping. Therefore we consciously placed U.S. prestige—and at critical moments, international financial resources—behind that transformation.

Chile's and Mexico's paths diverged in the mid-1990s, but the Clinton administration sought in both instances to bolster the technopols' vision. President Clinton seconded the Bush administration's nomination of Chile to be the first country to accede to the NAFTA precisely to honor the Foxley trinity of macroeconomic balance, democratic governance, and social equity (even if U.S. electoral politics eventually postponed that project). I did not work directly with Evelyn Matthei, but she was included in the small group of leading Chilean women selected to participate in a dialogue with Hillary Rodham Clinton during her 1995 visit to Santiago. I felt that, despite her past errors of judgment, Matthei could make further contributions to Chile's model democracy. When the Mexican peso collapsed in December 1994,

Pedro Aspe was no longer in government, but in a decision of historic proportions the Clinton administration rapidly assembled a $50 billion financial package to shore up the reforms that Aspe had helped introduce. We did this not simply to salvage Mexico's economic reforms but with the larger purpose of stabilizing the emerging market economies and, we anticipated, the technopol project of open democratic capitalism.

In aligning ourselves in these ways with the best of the hemisphere's technopols, the United States was demonstrating that it, too, possesses their passion and commitment to democratic values and economic efficiency. Here, then, is an instance where politics has followed art (if we can so boldly label this book!).

In a fundamental sense, the 1994 Summit of the Americas was a celebration of the technopol's vision. In Miami, the hemisphere's thirty-four democratically elected leaders committed themselves to making government more efficient and accessible, to rendering their economies more open and productive, and to making their societies less discriminatory and more inclusive. The Miami compact is also a vision of hemispheric integration, not only through trade and investment but in many other spheres as well, as the old conceptions of national sovereignty give way to hemispheric community. In these ways, the Miami summit legitimized and fortified the cosmopolitan philosophy of the technopols. At the leaders' private sessions in the Vizcaya Villa, it fell to President-elect Cardoso eloquently to sum up the significance of the event, declaring it a "true renaissance," with the hemisphere moving beyond zero-sum games to addressing transborder issues collectively. He affirmed that deepening democracy, creating capable states with greater participation by society, was the hemisphere's greatest challenge.

Ideas, like the individuals who carry them, matter in history. For it is not only in Latin America that ideas matter. It is still not fashionable in the United States to proclaim that our foreign policy is based on concepts other than power and interests. Yet my White House years convinced me that, even in the United States, those who most adeptly blend ideas and interests are those who are the most successful in advancing the nation's progress. If that proposition is true, all citizens of the Americas can learn from the triumphs and tribulations of the leading technopols that are the subject of this valuable volume.

Richard E. Feinberg
San Diego, California
July 1996

Preface

How important are leaders and their ideas in economic and political transformations? First Chile, then Mexico, Argentina, and Brazil, replaced state-led economic policies with market-oriented strategies. Each of these countries is also more democratic and more inserted into international markets than a decade ago. Indeed, in the 1990s, elected civilian governments enacted and deepened the liberal economic reforms. How were these changes conceived, designed, and implemented?

This book addresses this question by focusing on "technopols," that is, technically skilled and politically savvy leaders who held key positions during critical periods of change. Five biographical case studies tell the story of these leaders, their ideas, and how they worked to implement them.

One of the people studied, Fernando Henrique Cardoso, is now president of Brazil. He and three of the others—Pedro Aspe (Mexico), Domingo F. Cavallo (Argentina), and Alejandro Foxley (Chile)—have served as finance ministers. The fifth, Evelyn Matthei of Chile, was chosen because she seemed to be heading toward a similar career trajectory. Cardoso, Foxley, and Matthei have also been members of the Inter-American Dialogue.

The idea for the book was suggested by Richard Feinberg, former president of the Dialogue and former National Security Council director for inter-American affairs. We are pleased that he agreed to contribute the foreword to this volume.

The book appears under the joint auspices of the InterAmerican Dialogue and the Center for International Affairs at Harvard University. The editor and the coauthors are grateful to these institutions for their material support and also to the David Rockefeller Center for Latin American Studies at Harvard University for its support in the preparation and publication of this book.

The Inter-American Dialogue's research and publications are designed to improve the quality of public debate and decision on key issues in Western Hemisphere affairs. The Dialogue is both a forum for sustained exchange among leaders of the Western Hemisphere and an independent, nonpartisan center for policy analysis on U.S.-Latin American economic and political relations. The Dialogue's one hundred members—from the United States, Canada, Latin America, and the Caribbean—include former presidents and prominent political, business, labor, academic, media, military, and religious leaders. At periodic plenary sessions, members analyze key hemispheric issues and formulate recommendations for policy and action. The Dialogue presents its finding in comprehensive reports circulated throughout the hemisphere. Its research agenda focuses on four broad themes—democratic governance, inter-American cooperation, economic integration, and social equity. The Dialogue acknowledges general support from the Ford and Mellon Foundations and the Carnegie Corporation of New York. Joan Caivano of the Inter-American Dialogue was the project manager.

Each author, of course, is solely responsible for his or her chapter.

Peter Hakim
President

1

Technopols
Ideas and Leaders in Freeing Politics and Markets in Latin America in the 1990s

Jorge I. Domínguez

"Men make their own history," Karl Marx wrote in 1852, "but they do not make it just as they please."[1] Scholars of Latin America have spent much energy understanding the second half of that sentence, namely, the importance of structures and their legacies. In this book,[2] we are mindful of that second half but call attention to its first half: the conscious choices made by

---

1. Karl Marx, *The Eighteenth Brumaire of Louis Bonaparte* (New York: International Publishers, 1963), 15.
2. This book is a collective project, and as a result, this is not a freestanding chapter. It is

some political actors in the 1980s and the 1990s in Latin America to foster freer politics and freer markets and, in that way, to reinvent Latin American history. We do so not just to record that the ideas, styles, and wisdom of specific leaders make a difference but because the leaders we study have used strategies and tactics that are not just personal or idiosyncratic but also potentially universal in their applicability. Some constraints can be overcome, others cannot. In this work, we are especially interested in how technopols employ some constraints that are difficult to overcome in order to help foster a national consensus on desirable policies to modify the impact of such constraints in the long term. We study these technopols because we think that their approach to politics and economics is "portable"—leaders in other countries can learn from their successes and failures.[3]

In the first half of the 1990s, Argentina, Brazil, Chile, and Mexico each had a more pluralistic political system, a more market-oriented economy, and a more intense and competitive insertion into international markets than had been the case as recently as the mid-1970s. In each, there has been a simultaneous effort to address major economic and political questions. For the first time perhaps since the 1930s, each of these countries is engaged in a far-reaching national project to reshape its future. As the case of Mexico shows, however, market-oriented reforms can be implemented in a nondemocratic political system; and Mexico's December 1994 financial crisis also indicates that the success of economic reforms is by no means guaranteed. Even in the wake of this crisis, however, the extent and significance of the changes enacted during the first half of the decade remain impressive. And just as impressive is the persistence of these countries, including Mexico, on the path of reform.

In this book, we seek to understand the relationship between ideas and leaders, on the one hand, and democratic politics and market-oriented government policies, on the other. We focus on five political leaders who have taken

largely based on, calls attention to, and, to some degree, summarizes themes that emerge in the chapters that follow. There are textual references to the other chapters; at times, a few bibliographic references are given. This approach to writing the introduction to this book has two advantages. The Harvard Center for International Affairs and the Inter-American Dialogue and its funders will find it easier to assert that the views expressed here are mine alone, and the authors will be free to claim, accurately, that all the errors in this draft are mine and that all the insights are theirs. Other authors in this book disagree with some of the specific statements and interpretations in this chapter. Nonetheless, I am especially grateful to my coauthors and to Eva Bellin, Richard Feinberg, Stanley Hoffmann, María Victoria Murillo, Theda Skocpol, Ashutosh Varshney, Jennifer Widner, and Deborah Yashar and to the members of the Sawyer Seminar at the Harvard Center for International Affairs for their comments, criticisms, and suggestions; they too are not responsible for my errors.
   3. I am grateful to Javier Corrales for this and many other insights.

ideas seriously and who have acted in politics and government based in part on these ideas. The chapters that follow analyze five cases: Argentina's economy minister Domingo Cavallo; Mexico's finance minister Pedro Aspe; Brazil's senator, foreign minister, finance minister, and president Fernando Henrique Cardoso; Chile's deputy Evelyn Matthei; and Chile's finance minister Alejandro Foxley.

Four of the five have been finance ministers. Matthei was chosen for this study so that we could focus on a younger technically trained leader who was, at the time the study began, a rising star in her nation's politics, playing a role in the opposition that recalled aspects of the early political careers of Cavallo, Cardoso, and Foxley. All five have been or, in my judgment, are likely to be candidates for the presidency, and Cardoso is president. These five leaders personify the ideas and behavior that concern us. Their actions have made a major difference already. In our biographic approach to the subject, therefore, we focus on the principal agents of change. We call them technopols.

They differ along several dimensions. One is their relationship to democracy. Aspe, Cavallo, and Matthei worked at some point for nondemocratic governments, but Cavallo and Matthei were also able to become prominent political figures under democratic regimes.[4] Cardoso and Foxley never worked for nondemocratic governments. Another dimension of variation at the outset of our project was that three were finance ministers but two (Cardoso and Matthei) were just prominent leaders of the opposition in Congress. Finally, they differ as well on the extent to which they have accomplished the goals they set for themselves; on this account, as of this writing Aspe and Matthei are somewhat less successful than the others.

We address three general questions: Where do ideas that become economic policy come from, and how and why do those ideas become policy? What do these ideas imply about the role of the state in the context of a market economy? And what is the relation between highly technically trained, politically engaged public figures (technopols) and the practices and prospects for democracy?

We argue that those whom we study have taken ideas seriously in their professional careers. The ideas on which they have focused are cosmopolitan and meet normal international professional standards. Moreover, most of these people have themselves contributed to the formulation of the ideas that they eventually come to implement.

---

4. For a powerful argument that Mexico's "technocratic revolution" has not been democratic, see Miguel Angel Centeno, *Democracy Within Reason: Technocratic Revolution in Mexico* (University Park: Pennsylvania State University Press, 1994), esp. chap. 8.

What makes some technopols successful at reaching the goals they set for themselves? Those whom we study are not "mere" technical economists invested with power by politicians.[5] Instead, successful technopols have made economics "political" and, in so doing, have created their own power and have enabled their politician allies to govern more effectively. Technopols have made economic policies acceptable to the public at large in democratic or authoritarian settings. More important, technopols have fashioned economic policies guided by their political analysis of the circumstances of their respective countries at given historical junctures; economic policies must meet requirements that originate in the political sphere. Thus technopols often act in ways that are unfamiliar to many professional economists.[6] Technopols design economic policies by understanding their nations' politics first: the forces of politics are harnessed to fashion economic programs. The unsuccessful cases of economic reform feature "technos" who consciously choose not to be pols or who are not allowed by their presidents to behave openly as pols (see discussion about Mexico in Chapter 3). They disdain political work; they may cherish the majestic beauty of econometrics but not the rough and tumble of partisanship. In the apt phrasing of Catherine Conaghan and James Malloy, such economists wear a "mental shield" to keep out the messiness of politics.[7] In contrast, successful technopols are not mere cooks reproducing the recipes of their foreign instructors, or mere photocopiers of the economic dogmas of other countries. Their discovery of the necessity of politics for the making and the "selling" of sound economic policy in the real contexts of real countries is what makes them pols.[8]

For technopols to be successful in either democratic or authoritarian political systems, they must also build their own teams and institutional bases to provide them with ideas, cadres, and bases of support for their work and, as Javier Corrales emphasizes, to create their own independent power—connected to but not fully representative of the societal actors targeted for reform—from which they can contribute to a wider political coalition and the implementation of change. The strategies chosen by technopols help to

5. Robert Bates seems to hold this view. See his "Comment" in *The Political Economy of Policy Reform*, ed. John Williamson (Washington, D.C.: Institute for International Economics, 1994), 29–34.

6. This is why we part company with John Toye's "Comment" in *The Political Economy of Policy Reform*, ed. John Williamson, 35–38. I am grateful to Javier Corrales for calling this fine article to my attention.

7. Catherine M. Conaghan and James M. Malloy, *Unsettling Statecraft: Democracy and Neoliberalism in the Central Andes* (Pittsburgh: University of Pittsburgh Press, 1994), 174.

8. I am grateful to Jeanne Kinney Giraldo for this and for many other insights.

shape the extent of their influence.[9] They are not the marionettes of other politicians.

We are also conscious, however, that there may be an empirical limit to the replicability or portability of our argument beyond these cases. The political and economic crises in these four Latin American countries in the 1970s and 1980s would in the end open the way for democratic technopols in Argentina, Brazil, and Chile and contribute to political and economic change in Mexico. The rise of these technopols had a structural origin but a voluntarist outcome. It remains for subsequent research to determine whether successful technopols can arise in contexts with less traumatic economic and political antecedents.

What is the relationship between technopols and democratic politics? Worldwide, democracies have been consolidated only in countries with market economies. In the long run, the market has been good for democracy, although markets flourish in many nondemocratic countries, too. In addition, we argue, in the late twentieth century substantially pluralist, and preferably fully democratic, politics can best address the problem of how to shape long-run rational expectations concerning the economies of Latin American countries. Pluralist regimes can give more-credible assurances that today's competent but less intrusive state and its market-oriented economic policies will still endure tomorrow. In Latin America's present and likely future circumstances, democracy is good for markets, although it had not always been so in the past.

Better than many of their predecessors, the technopols we study have understood that there may be in the long run an "elective affinity" between freer politics and freer markets. And where there has been a "democratic deficit" as in Mexico in 1994, the weakness of democratic practices—lack of effective procedures to compel the executive to listen to critics—helps, in part, to explain the eventual failure of economic policy.

Technopols and Technocrats

Technocrats have received much attention in scholarly, policy, and journalistic writings. A familiar definition of technocrats is "individuals with a high level of specialized academic training which serves as a principal criterion on the

---

9. For examples dealing with an earlier era, see William Ascher, *Scheming for the Poor: The Politics of Redistribution in Latin America* (Cambridge: Harvard University Press, 1984). See also Eliza J. Willis, "Explaining Bureaucratic Independence in Brazil: The Experience of the National Economic Development Bank," *Journal of Latin American Studies* 27 (1995): 625–61.

basis of which they are selected to occupy key decision-making or advisory roles in large complex organizations—both public and private."[10]

In the 1970s, important scholars associated the rise and diffusion of technocrats with the rise and consolidation of authoritarian regimes. In perhaps the most important book published in that decade, Guillermo O'Donnell argued that technocrats believe that "the ambiguities of bargaining and politics are hindrances to 'rational' solutions." Technocrats, O'Donnell argued, often studied abroad but could not operate effectively back home until they "constitute[d] the core of the coalition that [would] attempt the establishment of an authoritarian, 'excluding' political system. The usual verbal allegiance to political democracy is apparently the weakest component in their [foreign] role models. It is easily abandoned to promote an authoritarian political system that will (it is believed) facilitate more effective performance by the [technocratic] role incumbents."[11] Scholars have long understood the centrality of ideas for such roles, but have asserted that the ideas are likely to be antidemocratic.[12]

Our views differ from these definitions and arguments. We do not assume that technocrats must always be appointed or selected; some highly trained individuals could be elected to public office. Similarly, an opposition leader could become a shaper of the parameters of fundamental policies. More important, technocrats can and have served under very different political regimes. They can operate in market economies as well as in those that were once centrally planned. They need not be beholden to any one substantive ideology, nor are they inherently "democratic" or "authoritarian." Rather, technocrats offer a methodology to understand social problems that rests on a belief in the ability to arrive at the optimal answer to any problem. Their key criteria for action are realism and efficiency. Their legitimacy, they believe, comes from their appeal to rationality and science in their methodology.[13]

---

10. David Collier, ed., *The New Authoritarianism in Latin America* (Princeton: Princeton University Press, 1979), 403.

11. Guillermo O'Donnell, *Modernization and Bureaucratic-Authoritarianism* (Berkeley: Institute of International Studies, University of California, 1973), 79–89, quotations from 84, 87. For a more recent statement reiterating similar views, see Guillermo O'Donnell, "Democracy's Future: Do Economists Know Best?" *Journal of Democracy* 6, no. 1 (1995): 23-28.

12. See, for example, Magali Sarfatti Larson, "Notes on Technocracy: Some Problems of Theory, Ideology, and Power," *Berkeley Journal of Sociology* 17 (1972–73), 29.

13. This definition benefits from Miguel Angel Centeno's thoughtful analysis in "The New Leviathan: The Dynamics and Limits of Technocracy," *Theory and Society* 22 (1993): 307–35. Centeno appears to be more skeptical, however, about the prospects for reconciling technocrats to democratic politics. For a persuasive argument that the distinction between "technician" and

Though technocrats are often economists, other social scientists (Cardoso) may qualify as well.

Technopols are a variant of technocrats. In addition to being technocrats as just defined, technopols are political leaders (1) at or near the top of their country's government and political life (including opposition political parties) who (2) go beyond their specialized expertise to draw on various different streams of knowledge and who (3) vigorously participate in the nation's political life (4) for the purpose of affecting politics well beyond the economic realm and who may, at times, be associated with an effort to "remake" their country's politics, economics, and society. Technopols so defined may operate in either authoritarian or democratic regimes. Whereas technocrats often rise through bureaucratic ranks (as do some technopols), technopols may have also been outsiders to the bureaucracy—successful economic consultants, prominent academics, or leading opposition figures. Technopols fear politics much less than technocrats because technopols define the "rational" somewhat differently from technocrats; for technopols, a rational policy is not just technically correct but also politically enduring. Rationality thus defined can only be achieved through politics. Technocrats are not new. Authoritarian technopols are not new. Technopols in democratic or democratizing politics are relatively new, however.[14] It is to them that we devote the bulk of our attention.

Cautionary Tales: The Stories of Joseph and Turgot

In order to assess the significance of the cases in the chapters that follow, one may consider aspects of the subject that are as ancient as political systems. In this section, I look at two historical cases to set a baseline from which to make comparisons. I look well into the past and outside Latin America to make the point that the question of technocrats or technopols is timeless and cross-cultural.

The Book of Genesis (chapters 39–41) describes one of the first technopols, Joseph, who rose to become Pharaoh's chief minister. Joseph demonstrated great professional skill and administrative competence in governing Egypt.

"politician" has been overdrawn in the scholarship on Mexico, see Juan D. Lindau, "Schisms in the Mexican Political Elite and the Technocrat/Politician Typology," *Mexican Studies* 8, no. 2 (1992): 217–35, and idem, *Los tecnócratas y la élite gobernante mexicana* (Mexico City: Mortiz, 1993).

14. For the relatively rare example of a book describing democratic technopols (though neither the word nor the concept as such is presented there) who are more effective at advancing the goals of democracy and efficiency than authoritarian technopols are, see Ascher, *Scheming for the Poor*.

(Joseph does not fully qualify as a technocrat or technopol, however, because his initial specialized knowledge—divining Pharaoh's dreams—came from God, not from specialized education.) What made Joseph a technopol, rather than a mere technician, was his ability to connect his evolving practical knowledge and skill to the power of the state. Joseph was an effective forecaster and planner who designed successful programs to store food during seven years of plenty in order to survive through seven years of famine. He applied specialized knowledge to empirical analysis, implemented actions, and sorted through effects well into the future. He combined ideas and implementation with a long time horizon. Joseph was not a populist. He smoothed out the economic cycle at a time of plenty by means of forced savings for the time of famine.

Joseph operated in a constrained international environment. Egypt's survival and power depended on his technocratic success, while his authority derived from his superior. Joseph was not just a captive of these constraints, however; he acted to enlarge his freedom of action. His performance centralized political power in two ways. One was procedural: "I am Pharaoh; without your command no one shall move hand or foot in the whole land of Egypt" (Gen. 41:44). The second was substantive. Joseph's policies centralized the economy and weakened citizen rights: "Joseph, therefore, bought all the land of Egypt for Pharaoh, for every one of the Egyptians sold his field because the famine was unbearable for them. Thus the land became Pharaoh's, and from one end of Egypt to the other Joseph made the people slaves" (Gen. 48: 20–21). Joseph was an authoritarian technopol. He was not "merely" an economist but a master of that expertise needed to reshape the economy, the society, and the polity to serve centralized authority. Joseph foreshadowed the state-aggrandizing economic policies evident in Brazil during much of the 1970s—not every technopol has believed in free markets, and certainly not in free politics.

Many technopols, however, have believed in freer markets and have acted to make them a reality. In 1774, France's Louis XVI recalled the Parlements (sovereign law courts) abolished in earlier decades and appointed a reform government, headed by Turgot, a philosophe and widely respected government administrator. Turgot deregulated the economy by suppressing the guilds, which were privileged monopolies in various trades. He liberalized domestic trade in grain. He took steps to "shrink the state"; he moved to abolish the "corvée"—the annual compulsory peasant labor on France's roads. He launched a tax-reform process. He favored legal toleration for Protestants. However, the Parlement of Paris, supported by provincial estates and the Roman Catholic Church, opposed him, and, in 1776, Turgot resigned.

More clearly than in Joseph's case, Turgot's education and specialized training were his merits. He combined ideas and implementation. His skills were conceptual as well as administrative. He, too, planned ahead in a constrained international environment, as France prepared for war. As with Joseph, Turgot's authority came from the monarch; as with Joseph, Turgot was no "mere" economist; he was also a philosophe. Turgot had a broad agenda to reshape France, even extending to religious toleration. Turgot, too, was an authoritarian technopol, commanding on the king's behalf, but one who believed in freeing markets, a mixture of authoritarian rule and market-oriented policies not unlike those that prevailed in Argentina and Chile in the 1970s.

The stories of Turgot and Joseph illustrate why scholars have been skeptical that technocrats or technopols could foster liberal democracy. To save Egypt, Joseph reduced its citizens into slavery—a metaphor heard at times in southern South America in the 1970s. Turgot's economic reform program was defeated in court, challenging his claim to superior wisdom and showing that constitutional procedures can come in the way of market reforms. These examples suggest why technopols and technocrats have worked for authoritarian regimes: such regimes may seem more capable of adopting "sound policies" than governments that operate under constitutional restraints. Authoritarian Egypt managed well the transition from plenty to famine; independent sovereign law courts in France blocked efficient economic reforms and liberalizing political changes.

And yet, Joseph and Turgot are not alike. There has always been variance among technopols. Joseph was an intentional centralizer. Turgot centralized power to accomplish reform, but many of his policies, if successful, would have devolved state power to the society and economy (deregulation of business relationships, freer labor, wider religious toleration). If technopols are to work for democratic regimes, there must be a large political coalition to empower them to act, to keep them in power, and to keep them accountable to the principle of eventual devolution of power to those outside the state apparatus.

The Tensions Within the Role of Technopol

Technocrats combine aspects of other professional vocations: scholar and administrator. Technopols add a third: politician. Democratic technopols must also operate within two constraints of procedural democracy: unlike Joseph, they must face rules and structures that prevent them from reducing the autonomy of civil society, and unlike Joseph and Turgot, they must work through constitutional government. These roles and constraints pose many difficulties, however. Max Weber has shed some light on the tensions inherent in the role of technopol.[15] I turn to him to show the universality of the concern with such public roles well beyond contemporary Latin America and the tensions that technopols must resolve.

For Weber, three qualities matter in a politician of the sort we seek to understand: passion, a feeling of responsibility, and a sense of proportion. "Passion" means devotion to a cause outside of the self. "Responsibility" need not, for Weber, have a democratic component; it is not whether a politician is responsible before the voters but, instead, whether the politician is responsible to the cause and makes it the "guiding star of action." "Sense of proportion" is what we call pragmatism: the "ability to let realities work upon him with inner concentration and calmness."[16] Politics is born in the heart but is made in the head. Politics seeks power, that is, the means to influence others and shape their behavior.

Scholarship, in contrast, seeks its own undermining: "[T]he very meaning of scientific work . . . raises new questions; it asks to be surpassed and outdated." In that same spirit, scholarship must be nonpartisan: "The primary task of a useful teacher is to teach his students to recognize . . . facts that are inconvenient for their party opinions."[17] Weber therefore doubted that scholars could be political leaders and remain scholars.

The bureaucrat is different yet again. Office holding requires a "firmly prescribed course of training, which . . . [takes] a long period of time."[18] In this "duty," the relationship to others is impersonal; there is no loyalty to any one person but to the procedures of science. Officials should have independence from their superiors and the electorate. Bureaucracy provides for a "rationalist way of life" that has, at best, an ambiguous relationship to democracy.

Weber would doubt that a technopol could exist, because the requirements of "passion" in politics and the "responsibility" to advance a cause require a faith that is at odds with the perpetual questioning of the scholar and the nonpartisan rationalism of the bureaucrat. Weber would doubt that technopols could build

15. I rely on three of Weber's essays: "Politics as a Vocation," "Science as a Vocation," and the sections on bureaucracy in *Wirtschaft und Gesellschaft* in *From Max Weber*, ed. H. H. Gerth and C. Wright Mills (London: Oxford University Press, 1958).

16. Weber, "Politics as a Vocation," 115.

17. Weber, "Science as a Vocation," 138, 147.

18. Weber, "Bureaucracy," in *From Max Weber*, ed. Gerth and Mills, 198–99.

partisan teams and still meet the standards of high technical expertise. A technopol's claim to scientific legitimacy would be flawed because politicians could not meet fundamental tests of scholarship: they have too much passion, they are too responsible, and they are too partisan.

Weber's approach sheds light on the dilemmas faced by authoritarian technopols. The authoritarian technopol acts on a passion to create technocratic policy dogmas to be applied relentlessly through economic policy making independent of popular constraint. Such an official, however, would be likely to lose a sense of proportion and would, in the end, be equally ineffective as politician and bureaucrat: the proposed "efficient reforms" would not be consolidated, because the governed would not have consented. This helps to explain the inherent weaknesses in the economic policies adopted in Argentina and Chile in the 1970s, and some of the problems faced in Mexico in the mid-1990s.

The democratic technopol is more likely to retain the "sense of proportion" necessary to shift policies in response to practical circumstances, not necessarily from personal virtues, but because the procedures of democracy require such prudence from politicians who seek to be effective. The commitment to a sense of proportion and the readiness to change policies explain the policy corrections and adjustments evident in several of the cases we study—a principled pragmatism, not wedded to dogma but also not volatile or capricious. Thus democratic technopols may combine the roles of politician, scholar, and bureaucrat more successfully than do authoritarian technopols. Some democratic technopols may behave as "teachers to the nation," that is, bearers of a more impersonal loyalty to a democratic regime, committed to educate the public about facts that may be inconvenient for their party opinions. Such a technopol is well suited to the politics of opposition, as Cardoso, Foxley, Matthei, and Cavallo have demonstrated at various times.[19]

The Choices of Democratic Technopols in Latin America in the 1990s

Democratic politics in Latin America has been marked in recent decades by instability, policy ineptitude, corruption, and countless other ills. And yet, authoritarian politics in Latin America over roughly the same time period has also been characterized by instability, policy ineptitude, corruption, and countless other ills. No doubt, in 1976, many Argentines viewed the democratically

---

19. Some authoritarian technopols exhibit similar traits—a sense of proportion and action as teachers to the nation—as was the case in Chile in the second half of the 1980s and as has been the case more generally in Mexico.

elected Peronist government then in power as the worst in Argentine history, only to realize a few years later that a military government could perform even worse. Likewise, in Mexico, it was an authoritarian Mexican political system that plunged the country into the economic collapse of the early 1980s. No doubt democratic Costa Rica's economy suffered a severe decline in its gross domestic product (GDP) at the birth of the so-called debt crisis in 1982, but General Augusto Pinochet's authoritarian government in Chile had an even more severe economic collapse that year. By 1984, democratic Costa Rica had surpassed the level of its 1981 gross domestic product (in 1988 constant dollars); authoritarian Chile surpassed its 1981 GDP level only in 1987.[20]

In the 1990s, democracy, Latin Americans knew, was no cure-all for their ills, but their own experience had led them to distrust the claims of would-be authoritarians. Many Latin American democratic regimes remained partial, fragile, and in many ways incapable of delivering on the promise of democracy. But, for a significant portion of technopols and the public at large, the logic of democracy had gained much ground over the logic of authoritarianism.

The influence of technopols in Latin America in the 1990s stems less from the simple presence of the technically skilled at the apex of the state and more from the belated recognition by technopols and by the public that there may be, in Weberian terms, an "elective affinity" between freer markets and freer politics. By this expression Weber did not mean a mechanistic or deterministic connection; he meant, instead, a correspondence ("affinity") of choices ("elective") and institutions in the areas of politics and economics similar to what we highlight in this book: deliberate political entrepreneurship and institutional design can draw upon markets and democracy to reinforce one another.[21]

Democratic technopols in Latin America in the 1990s chose freer markets for both political and economic reasons. In economic terms, freer markets are typically a part of the professional training of most technopols; that has changed little.[22] In politics, democratic technopols have come to appreciate that freer markets permit less room for arbitrary state actions such as those that gripped much of the region from the mid-1960s to the late 1980s. Markets do

---

20. Inter-American Development Bank, *Economic and Social Progress in Latin America: 1991 Report* (Baltimore: Johns Hopkins University Press, 1991), 273.

21. I am grateful to Delia Boylan for this and many other insights.

22. For qualifications on this point, and a fine synthesis of the evolution of economic thought in Latin America, see Albert Fishlow, "The State of Latin American Economics," in *Changing Perspectives in Latin American Studies*, ed. Christopher Mitchell (Stanford: Stanford University Press, 1988).

not ensure civil society against an authoritarian state, but markets can be one important check on the abuse of state power. Markets may not disperse power enough, and in Latin America's small economies market power is often highly concentrated, but markets disperse power more than if it were centralized just in the hands of state decision makers.

Democratic technopols in Latin America in the 1990s chose a competent state (in contrast to the vanishing state in some neoliberal prescriptions) in order to foster consultation with business and labor to create and maintain stable and clear rules by means of the exchange of information and points of view; in that way, they sought to reduce market instability. Democratic technopols also chose the competent state to invest in education and health ("human capital"), both because they considered it ethically right and because it contributes to market efficiency. The competent state can also more readily address market failures and, in particular, can channel resources to enable the poor to overcome their condition.

In the long run, I wish to suggest, the logic of democracy best promises to set the parameters that may ensure the success of the market. That is, a democratic political system committed to a market economy, and capable of delivering on that commitment, is the more effective and stable long-term political response to the problems posed by the rational expectations of economic actors. Rational economic actors look for rules and institutions that endure even as presidents, ministers, and economic cabinets change; authoritarian regimes can provide certain assurances to economic actors for some time, but democratic regimes can provide assurances for the long run, provided government and opposition are committed to the same broad framework of a market economy. In this sense, the opposition gives the most effective long-term guarantees about the continuity of a market economy; when the opposition supports the basic principles and rules of a market economy, then economic actors rationally can expect that a change of government leaders will not imply the overthrow of a market economy. And only democratic political systems embody the compromises and commitments that may freely bind government and opposition to the same framework of a market economy.

To be sure, in a number of East Asian countries authoritarian regimes have managed the economy exceedingly well for several decades. In this book, however, we analyze societies where the extent of political contestation and political participation are already intense and widespread and where military governments were quite unstable. For countries with these political structures, the logic of democracy surpasses the logic of authoritarianism.

Democracy's procedures can restrain the passionate extremism of government officials while permitting more circumscribed forms of commitment. In democratic political systems, moreover, elections provide routinized means for sweeping away failed policies and politicians and starting afresh, which can contribute to the credibility of new, sounder economic policies. Authoritarian regimes cannot get rid of mistaken policies or wrongheaded leaders so readily.[23] In the logic of democracy, to be sure, leaders must elicit the consent of the governed and are thus more likely to consolidate efficient economic reforms for the long run, setting and signaling clear and stable political and economic policy rules that help to shape the rational expectations of economic actors. That has been the long-term experience of Western Europe, North America, and Japan.

Latin America's democratic technopols are also keenly aware of the sorry economic record of democracy in Argentina, Brazil, and Chile at various key junctures during the third quarter of the twentieth century. In these countries, various democratic regimes failed to deliver on the promise of the logic of democracy for markets. The task of democratic technopols in the 1990s has been, therefore, to make the logic of democracy work for its own sake and for the consolidation of market economies in these same countries.

Latin America's democratic technopols in the 1990s sought to turn democracy's capacity to elicit the consent of the governed into an effective instrument for political and economic reform. A broad democratic consensus would help to make and consolidate changes; that consensus would contribute to the credibility of the reforms in the eyes of economic actors precisely because the changes would have been made with the opposition's consent. This was the essence of the strategy followed by Foxley, Cavallo, and Cardoso. In a non-democratic political system, Aspe, too, widened the scope of consultations with societal leaders.

Today's economic policies, economic actors in Argentina, Chile, Mexico, and perhaps Brazil have reason to expect, would endure tomorrow even if the largest opposition party were to win. Today's market-based policies made in a democratic or in a democratizing regime (as in Mexico in the late 1990s), citizens have reason to expect, would make it less likely that dictators or demagogues could imperil citizens' lives and liberties or, in the future, those of their children. That is the hope in all four countries, and certainly the intention of all those whom we study.

23. In the 1990s, this point has been made often by Harvard professor Jeffrey Sachs.

The Making of Technopols

Technopols are made in school, in religious and secular faiths, in teams, on the world stage, and in specific national contexts. These five factors identify their commitment to high standards, their passionate convictions, their mode of professional work, their cosmopolitan vision, and their devotion to their homeland. Together, these factors point to the sources of the ideas and the means of their implementation.

Pedro Aspe's early education was forged in the rigor of a fine Jesuit school, as was Alejandro Foxley's in a Franciscan school. Early on, both combined a Roman Catholic faith with a commitment to academic excellence. Evelyn Matthei's education at a Roman Catholic university resembled the religious schooling of Aspe and Foxley. A more decisive combination of schooling and secular faith developed during their respective university educations.

Even as an undergraduate in Mexico's Autonomous Institute of Technology (Instituto Tecnológico Autónomo de México, or ITAM), Aspe became part of a team that embodied a secular faith: the training of technically skilled young economists who would eventually reshape the nation's economic policy. Overt mentoring and team construction (by Antonio Bassols, Javier Beristain, and Francisco Gil Díaz) were an integral goal of the ITAM Economics Department. The same pattern recurred as Aspe studied at MIT, where Rudiger Dornbusch instilled in him the "passions" for technical sophistication, cosmopolitan breadth, and policy relevance.

A comparable pattern marked Fernando Henrique Cardoso's university life. He, too, became part of a team that embodied a comparable secular faith: the development of sociology as a science with the same rigor as that of the natural sciences. Overt mentoring and team construction (by Florestán Fernandes at the University of São Paulo) were also integral goals. The sociology Fernandes taught to Cardoso was a tropical transplant of what Fernandes had learned at the University of Chicago; thus, while remaining in Brazil, Cardoso's early intellectual training acquired a cosmopolitan dimension that would be reinforced by his subsequent work and residence in other countries.

Foxley and Cavallo followed a path similar to that taken by Aspe, studying economics in the United States (Foxley at the University of Wisconsin-Madison and Cavallo at Harvard), while Matthei's path was closer to that of Cardoso; she studied economics at the Universidad Católica in Santiago, an institution that had come to emulate and adapt the University of Chicago's Economics Department.

The cosmopolitanism of this training would be crucial for their subsequent work. None of these technopols was intellectually or personally parochial. None fell into the trap of believing that "my" country is so different that the international norms of technical analysis should not apply, or that "no foreigner can teach me about my homeland." All were concerned with universal questions; all addressed their work as professionals whose standards and tools were worldwide and universalistic. Cardoso's early studies of race relations, for example, were funded by a grant from UNESCO and addressed universal concerns in the sociology, economics, and politics of race. Aspe, Cardoso, and Foxley wrote doctoral dissertations in economics on topics, and with tools, that were consistent with standard norms in their respective disciplines. Cosmopolitan ideas, understood, applied, and developed according to universalistic professional standards, became parts of their selves.

When these young adults were in school, this cosmopolitan trajectory entailed some professional risks. Two of Latin America's best-known economists of the 1950s and 1960s, for example, denounced this trajectory: "The majority of young economists who go to industrialized countries for training return to their home environment with theoretical schemes that are to a greater or lesser extent divorced from objective reality and from the economic problems of their own countries, and often with research methodologies that have no possibility of being usefully applied."[24] They bemoaned the practice of "copying painfully and without critical adaptations whatever emanates from Harvard" and other such universities.[25] They went on to write that "it would be unfortunate if these new professionals should assume" government posts "with ideas, attitudes, and analytical equipment that are entirely inapplicable and lacking in realism."[26]

Perhaps in tacit reply to this concern, the three who got their doctorates in economics in the United States—Aspe, Cavallo, and Foxley—wrote their dissertations on topics bearing directly on their respective countries. Foxley, for example, did not eschew complex mathematical models but developed one for the Chilean economy. Aspe may have reached the furthest in the attempt to "creolize" economics by studying the history of Mexico with Harvard's historian John Womack Jr.

More important, their cosmopolitan ideas and skills along with their concern with their homelands gave them the professional autonomy needed to

---

24. Aníbal Pinto and Oswaldo Sunkel, "Latin American Economists in the United States," *Economic Development and Cultural Change* 15, no. 1 (1966), 83.
25. Ibid., 80.
26. Ibid., 83.

challenge prevailing orthodoxies back home. Cavallo's doctoral dissertation, for example, took issue not only with structuralist and dependency analyses of Argentina's economy but also with the monetarist ideas that informed Argentine government policy in the mid-1970s. Cardoso's work on race relations helped to puncture the then prevailing myth of Brazil as a racial paradise.

Equally noteworthy, cosmopolitan team building in a national context became an essential task for these would-be technopols early on in their respective professional careers. Their professional autonomy and eventual political clout would be buttressed by creating analytic and policy teams. The teams would have links to government and business but retain their distance from both. The connections helped to generate information and build trust; the distance enabled the teams to formulate their own ideas and recommendations, at times contrary to the wishes of economic, societal, or governmental actors. These teams would embody the secular faith in social science; their mission—in Corrales' characterization of Cavallo—would be to spread the faith.

Soon after Aspe's return from MIT to his intellectual birthplace at ITAM, he became chairman of ITAM's Economics Department. As the critics of training Latin American economists in the United States would have suspected, Aspe realized that the theoretical models and empirical cases he had studied suggested that Mexico's economic policies in the late 1970s were gravely mistaken. To change them became a professional mission; to do so required training a new generation of economists. Aspe reshaped the ITAM economics curriculum and raised academic standards, all the while creating a team of economists that would in due course follow him into government office. He continued to send a steady flow of students to U.S. universities. Aspe, his former students, and his current staff members similarly described to Golob their "shared vision" and Aspe's role in defining that vision; all agreed that this common faith made their team effective. During the Salinas presidency, Aspe's people colonized ministries beyond Aspe's portfolio in Finance—filling senior posts in Agriculture, Social Development, the Central Bank, Education; others became state governors and members of Congress. The ideas shaped the team, and the latter, in turn, became the collective carrier of those ideas in universities and in government agencies.

Cavallo returned to Argentina and founded his own think tank, the Institute for Economic Studies of the Argentine Reality (Instituto de Estudios Económicos sobre la Realidad Argentina y Latinoamericana, or IEERAL); he eventually gained the full support of the Fundación Mediterránea, with which he has remained associated.[27] Cavallo, too, recruited young, highly trained and internationally oriented economists. They shared Weber's "passion" to reduce the weight of the state on the nation's economy and the "responsibility" to foster policies to that end; they also became loyal to Cavallo. Diagnosis, analysis, and prescription built around a faith in a market economy and in the universalistic tools of economics were at this team's core. When Cavallo became Argentina's minister of economy, virtually the entire staff of IEERAL was appointed to key positions in the ministry—for a grand total of nearly three hundred people who had worked at the institute or who were otherwise connected to its staff. The ideas shaped the team, and the team became the collective carrier of the ideas.

A similar story is evident in Foxley's case. Foxley returned to Chile to work in the National Ministry of Planning in President Eduardo Frei's Christian Democratic government in the late 1960s. Upon the defeat of the Christian Democrats in the 1970 presidential elections, Foxley left the government to found an economic think tank that would eventually be known as CIEPLAN (Corporación de Investigaciones Económicas para América Latina [Economic Research Enterprise for Latin America]). As with Cavallo's IEERAL, Foxley's CIEPLAN gave a technical voice to the opposition. CIEPLAN's "passion" was for the market in a democracy; its "responsibility" was to advance both. Its associates needed to demonstrate their command of technical economics, just as good as and preferably better than that of the economic team (commonly known as the Chicago Boys) that worked for General Pinochet's government. CIEPLAN criticized the government's dogmatic refusal to address the costs of opening Chile's economy to international markets as well as the government's technically misguided exchange rate policies of the late 1970s and early 1980s. When Chile's economy crashed in 1981, Foxley's and CIEPLAN's scientific credentials were vindicated. As in the cases of Cavallo and Aspe, CIEPLAN staff followed Foxley in 1990 into the Christian Democratic government of President Patricio Aylwin, colonizing various Chilean government agencies, where they assumed senior posts.

Cardoso's path is consistent with this analysis. In April 1969, Cardoso and his colleagues founded CEBRAP (Centro Brasileiro de Análise e Planejamento [Brazilian Center for Analysis and Planning]); he served as its president and senior researcher until 1982. CEBRAP became a refuge for the intellectual opposition to the military government that had come to power in Brazil in 1964.

---

27. For a detailed account of the circumstances and climate of ideas shaping IEERAL and Cavallo, see Enrique N'haux, *Menem-Cavallo: El poder mediterráneo* (Buenos Aires: Ediciones Corregidor, 1993). I am grateful to María Victoria Murillo for the reference.

It became as well a leading research institute on social, economic, and public policy issues. Like CIEPLAN, CEBRAP was motivated by its passion for democracy and its commitment to research excellence. CEBRAP's role as a source of government officials awaited the return to civilian government in 1985. When Cardoso was appointed finance minister in May 1993, several former CEBRAP scholars became senior government officials in various ministries; months later, upon Cardoso's election to the presidency, many of these colleagues were promoted as well.

Although Matthei did not found or participate in a research-based institution herself, at the Catholic University of Chile she, too, was recruited into a team committed to the vision of economic transformation associated with the Pinochet government in the 1970s and 1980s. She, too, demonstrated impressive intellectual talent and effectively mastered the tools of economics. Miguel Kast was the mentor; the Chicago Boy ideas were the faith. She was schooled in perhaps the best organized and orthodox economic team seen to date in any Latin American country. Matthei never forged, however, a formal institutional tie beyond her government service with the founders of this model in Chile. Unlike others in this book, Matthei entered political life as a somewhat isolated player. This lack of experience with a team and the absence of an institutional base of her own from which to inform her ideas and forge alliances may have hurt her political career, as Delia Boylan's discussion of Matthei's weak institutional base in her own political party suggests. Institutional founders, therefore, were more likely to become successful technopols; Matthei's too different career trajectory may have left her insufficiently prepared for the top of Chilean politics.

All technopols began their careers, therefore, with early experiences that emphasized academic excellence, faith in a cause (religious or secular), the centrality of a cosmopolitan vision anchored in professional competence that met universalistic standards, and deep immersion in each nation's historical context. At the political level, the four more successful technopols founded teams and institutions in opposition to the government policies of the time. The politics of opposition would become "scientific" in response to governments that claimed that their policies were based on economic science. Incumbents would be challenged in the same rational terms on which incumbents wished to be judged: authoritarians would be challenged in terms of their economic policies, democrats in terms of their occasional willingness to resort to rule by decree.

Those teams and institutions would become the eventual vehicles to articulate, develop, and transmit key ideas and to colonize state agencies through the appointments of team members to various ministries. There was a "passion" for a set of ideas and a shared responsibility to seek to implement them. Even before they reached power, these technopols differed from Weber's notion of scholarship: these were politically engaged intellectuals, "partisans" of their ideas through their teams.[28]

The Making of Democratic Technopols: Ideas, Institutions, and Opposition Parties

Democratic technopols are made in the opposition to the government of the moment. They build up a political party as well as a program of government consistent with the ideas that they wish to implement once in power. As seen in the previous section, their initial location in the opposition fosters the team's cohesion and induces a sharpening of their technical skills, thus enabling them to advance their ideas more effectively in public debate.

Cardoso spent much of his adult life understanding and seeking to change Brazil's political and social conditions. As João Resende-Santos notes, Cardoso published a wide array of books and articles in which he developed, refined, and modified his views on democracy, equality, participation, the role of the state, and the place of Brazil in the world. To turn those ideas into reality, institutions were needed beyond CEBRAP: a political party had to embody and carry forward these ideas. In the early 1970s, Cardoso joined the only legally permitted opposition party, the Brazilian Democratic Movement (Movimento Democrático Brasileiro, or MDB), and attempted to turn it from mere reliance on clientelism into a programmatic party. In 1988, Cardoso and his associates founded a new party, the Brazilian Social Democratic Party (Partido da Social Democracia Brasileira, or PSDB); Cardoso became the party's leading intellectual spokesman. Cardoso and the PSDB pressed the new civilian government to move more firmly to install democratic practices and to combat corruption. They advocated replacing Brazil's presidential system with a parliamentary system. The PSDB adopted internal democratic practices to set an example.

---

28. Curiously, scholars often write as if the creation of teams were unique to the countries that they study. Mexicanists write about *equipos* and camarillas, for example, as if they were unique Mexican flowers. For a relatively rare comparative analysis that touches on some of these themes, see Catherine M. Conaghan, James M. Malloy, and Luis A. Abugattás, "Business and the 'Boys': The Politics of Neoliberalism in the Central Andes," *Latin American Research Review* 25, no. 2 (1990): 3–30.

The massive abuses committed by the Brazilian authoritarian regime, and the subsequent failures of the state's economic policies, turned Cardoso and his party toward a wider role for the market than had been the case in their earlier thought and experience: the stronger the market and the more constrained the state, the less likely that the state could exercise arbitrary power or hurt the economy. Cardoso and the PSDB sharply criticized the large, cumbersome, arbitrary, and excessively intrusive Brazilian state but also insisted that the state has an important role in protecting the poor and leading the nation through a viable industrial economic strategy. The policies of both Cardoso and his party differ substantially from socialist programs well to their political left in contemporary Brazil;[29] in particular, Cardoso and his party differ from the Workers' Party (Partido dos Trabalhadores, or PT) in their critique of the state. Nonetheless, the commitment to redress the "social deficit" in education and health and to reduce widespread inequalities remains a centerpiece of their thought.

Cardoso's task, to turn ideas into practice, was made unusually difficult by the nonprogrammatic nature of Brazil's political parties, by their lack of internal discipline, and by the fluidity of party and factional alliances.[30] Much of his energy was invested in constructing vehicles to advance the notions of democracy that flowed from his Brazilianist and cosmopolitan commitments. It was also invested in constructing political coalitions in Congress to the same end. For this technopol, democracy has always been at the center of his thought and political action. His training and his values have been linked from the very beginning.

Foxley's political trajectory is somewhat different. From his youth, he has been a member of Chile's Christian Democratic Party and, as such, has been committed to making democratic politics work in Chile. Unlike Cardoso, Foxley did not have to build a democratic party, because one already existed; the task was to wed Christian Democracy to market-oriented policies and to do so within a wider political coalition to defeat the dictatorship and return Chile to democratic rule. This was not merely a tactical concern. As Jeanne Kinney Giraldo argues, Foxley believed that just as the free market was inadequate to the task of managing the transformation of the economy, so too the political free market was unsuitable to reconstructing democracy. In economics, Foxley believed in greater cooperation among government, business, and labor as well

29. Cardoso has always been sharply criticized by many to his political left. See, for example, John Myer, "A Crown of Thorns: Cardoso and Counter-Revolution," *Latin American Perspectives* 2, no. 1 (1975): 33–48.

30. Scott Mainwaring, "Brazilian Party Underdevelopment in Comparative Perspective," *Political Science Quarterly* 107, no. 4 (1992–93): 677–707.

as in state action to address severe social ills. In politics, Foxley believed that only through concerted actions could agreed-upon limits be set to prevent the polarization that in the early 1970s had destroyed Chilean democracy.

In the 1980s, Foxley labored much of the time to reconstruct Chilean democracy and to retain a largely market-oriented economy. The key effort was to build a political and programmatic alliance between the democratic left and center, mainly between the Christian Democrats and the various democratic socialist parties. As Kinney Giraldo makes clear, one of Foxley's important goals was to fashion both an electoral and a governing coalition, that is, a political coalition that would win the election and remain together to implement an agreed-upon program of government. In so doing, Foxley and CIE-PLAN changed some of the substance of their views and the specific content of some of their critiques of government policy. By 1987, Foxley realized that Chile had successfully transited out of a strategy of import-substitution industrialization (which he had long criticized) and toward an export-oriented strategy and that many entrepreneurs were behaving consistently with the new economic model. Thus the new task was to criticize implementation but also to consolidate Chile's insertion in the international market and to protect the gains in economic efficiency while seeking to add new protections for the weak and the poor. To do so, Foxley the politician assertively led his party and its allies to adopt views more favorable to freer markets than those toward which the parties had been inclined.

Better than the Chicago Boys and the Pinochet government, Kinney Giraldo argues, Foxley and CIEPLAN anticipated an international idea that came to prevail by the end of the 1980s and the early 1990s—that markets should foster "growth with equity." They contributed impressively to the creation of a victorious coalition committed to markets in a democracy that would receive international backing. Indeed, Foxley had warned the Chilean right nearly a decade before its electoral defeat that it had forgotten its own ideological roots: "In the political sphere, [the Chilean government's] model has not been able to solve the inherent contradiction between economic freedom, a basic objective of the model and of [Milton Friedman's] 'ideary', and the political authoritarianism which accompanies it. After all, facing the dilemma, it seems that the Chilean model has certainly chosen capitalism, but has forgotten all about freedom."[31] Sooner than the political right, Foxley understood the power of combining freer politics and freer markets. His party's 1989 electoral victory rewarded

---

31. Alejandro Foxley, "Towards a Free Market Economy: Chile 1974–1979," *Journal of Development Economics* 10, no. 1 (1982), 28–29.

the commitment to markets and democracy on which he had built his professional life.

Matthei illustrates the same principle at a different moment. For her, the key political question was how to salvage the parties of the right for democracy and how to ensure that the nation's market orientation would continue. As Boylan notes, Matthei offered and fashioned a new face for Chile's right. After Patricio Aylwin's inauguration as president in March 1990, the right moved to the opposition for the first time since the early 1970s. There were two tasks for a democrat of the right. The first was to ensure that the parties of the right would remain within the rules of the new democratic regime. The second was to position these parties to do well in elections and eventually to win back power democratically.

Matthei undertook both tasks with clarity and effectiveness. She played an important role in the negotiations over tax reform between her party, National Renovation (Renovación Nacional, or RN), and the government. In so doing, she demonstrated to RN and to the government that civilized politics was possible and that RN was loyal to the democratic regime, though from the political opposition. Toward the longer term, Matthei fashioned a political strategy that emphasized social issues to win cross-class political support. Common crime, the regulation of organ transplants, the defense of the family, the modification of divorce laws, the rights of the unborn, and the improvement of education and curricular change were issues to which she devoted political attention. Her political strategy was to diversify the portfolio of issues on which the parties of the right could win elections, beyond her and her party's long-standing belief in the virtues and utility of the market economy.

Matthei combined this political strategy with impressive communications skills, as Boylan notes. Her abilities to articulate her party's position and to project sincerity and caring for ordinary human beings were noteworthy political assets. Much more than any of the other trained economists in our project, Matthei was able to move her attention successfully to topics and concerns beyond those of the economics profession. Her work toward the transformation of the ideas, practice, and appeal of her party, while remaining true to the earlier faith in markets, contributed to the consolidation of Chilean democracy and has earned her a place among the democratic technopols.

Cavallo came to democratic politics later in life than Cardoso, Foxley, and Matthei. Under the Argentine military government, he served as undersecretary for internal affairs in 1981 and as president of the Central Bank in 1982; the sum total of his government service in these two posts was ten weeks. Cavallo's IEERAL, however, was typically critical of many of the economic policies of both military and civilian governments—a classic role in the opposition. Like Cardoso and Foxley, however, Cavallo soon discovered that more than just a "think tank" was needed to make political change happen. In 1987, Cavallo chose to run for Congress as a Peronist candidate, in opposition to the governing Radical Party, rather than wait for someone to name him again to appointive office.

Aspe's career in the technical niches of Mexico's government foreclosed a role in the democratic opposition, though, as shown earlier, Aspe's professional career began in the "technical" opposition to Mexican economic policies in the late 1970s. Nor did this career pattern enable him to contribute to Mexico's very gradual political opening.

At the outset, these technopols differed in the relative importance that they accorded to the market and to democratic ideas. Democracy was a particularly high value for Foxley and CIEPLAN and for Cardoso and CEBRAP. They would not succumb to the temptations of Joseph or Turgot. Democracy was not a predominant concern for Aspe and his team at ITAM, or for Cavallo and Matthei while they served in military governments. Belief in the market was also a high value for all but Cardoso and CEBRAP, and even these Brazilians, as Resende-Santos makes clear, gradually moved to embrace markets, just as Cavallo and IEERAL, and Matthei, moved to embrace democracy. By the early 1990s, the views of these technopols (though least so in the case of Aspe) had converged to uphold both democracy and markets.

The making of democratic technopols thus begins in the opposition. The technically talented must engage in persuasion to secure funding and to spread their ideas; they must look for allies to advance their cause. In the opposition, they hone their technical skills to improve the efficacy of the presentation of ideas, but to be truly effective in the long term, they must link up with a political party and work to build or to reshape such a party. They learn the utility of democratic behavior in advancing their technical ideas, and they learn to refashion their technical ideas to serve democratic goals.

Much of the professional careers of Cardoso, Foxley, and Matthei was spent in this fashion; at a later time, similar behavior would become evident in Cavallo's career. Cardoso from the left, Foxley from the center, and Matthei from the right moved their associates from their early policy predilections. Cardoso struggled against the Brazilian left's love affair with the state. Matthei fought the Chilean right's Olympian forgetfulness of the politics of daily life. Foxley shifted politicians toward positions supportive of freer markets, while he ensured the bases for political and economic agreement in a fragmented party system. Cavallo, too, struggled against Peronist nostalgia for economic autarchy. As Max Weber's scholars should, all four made a case that, at the time in each instance, was inconvenient for their respective party opinions. Each sought to combine democracy and markets to varying degrees and in different forms, and each was an effective political entrepreneur in so doing. They helped their countries to consolidate or to approach politics consistent with their ideas.

These technopols came to recognize that political pluralism and markets work best if the effort is made to make them work together. The full flowering of these technopols, therefore, occurred (Mexico excepted) in the context of both democracies and markets, in response to the economic catastrophes that befell these four countries and to the harsh dictatorships suffered in the three South American cases.

The Critical Juncture

The historical moment for the technopols we study came when the pillars of the old order crumbled. There was a structural origin to the economic and political changes evident in these countries by the early 1990s, but there was also a voluntarist resolution. The structural crisis helped to provide the opening for the actions of technopols.

Our subjects rose to influence in their respective countries at a specific historical moment, typically when five factors had converged. (1) An economic crisis unequaled in severity since the Great Depression of the 1930s gripped these countries in the early 1980s (in Chile, a severe economic breakdown had also occurred in 1973). (2) When the crisis broke, authoritarian regimes of varying harshness held power in each of the four countries;[32] incumbents were blamed for the economic crisis to varying degrees, which blame helped to discredit or at least to weaken support for authoritarian approaches. Cavallo, in particular, learned that military governments were unlikely to generate or sustain sound and politically viable economic policies. (3) Authoritarian technocrats and technopols held positions of power in each of the four countries, and to some degree they and their style of governing were discredited or challenged. (4) For diverse reasons, including the economic crisis, the political process opened up, though to varying degrees, in

32. For some comparative indicators of repression, see Jorge I. Domínguez, Nigel S. Rodley, Bryce Wood, and Richard Falk, *Enhancing Global Human Rights* (New York: McGraw-Hill, 1979), 93–102.

each of these countries during the 1980s, first accelerating the circulation of elites at the top of the government, and eventually leading to democratic regimes in Argentina, Brazil, and Chile and toward a further easing of Mexico's always less-severe authoritarian regime. (5) Democratic governments pursuing statist economic policies at first proved incapable of resolving severe economic crises in Argentina under President Raúl Alfonsín, Brazil under President José Sarney, and Chile, earlier, under President Salvador Allende, thereby increasing political support for more market-oriented alternatives. The failures of statist policies pursued to varying degrees by the Alfonsín, Sarney, and Allende governments impressed Aspe, Cardoso, Cavallo, Foxley, and Matthei.

In 1982, Latin America's foreign debt crisis erupted, announcing the birth of economic trauma. In that year, Chile's GDP per capita fell 14.5 percent, Argentina's 7.2 percent, Mexico's 3 percent, and Brazil's 1.6 percent; in 1983, Brazil and Mexico each lost an additional 6 percent of GDP per capita. From 1981 through 1989, GDP per capita fell by over 9 percent in Mexico and by over 23 percent in Argentina; Brazil ended the decade at the same GDP per capita as when it began, while Chile's economic recovery during the second half of the 1980s erased the losses of the early 1980s and led to a meager net cumulative gain (1981–89) of just under 10 percent. From the early to the late 1980s, real average wages plummeted in the four countries. During the 1980s, Mexico, accustomed to low inflation rates, suffered from rapidly accelerating inflation. From 1983 through 1988, Argentina and Brazil had annual triple-digit consumer price inflation every year but 1986; both countries had annual four-digit price inflation in 1989 and 1990.[33]

At the moment of economic crisis, there was available an international pool of theoretical and empirical ideas that emphasized the utility of markets; these ideas had become dominant in the industrial countries during the 1970s and the 1980s, precisely when these technopols-in-the-making lived there. These market-oriented international ideas were nested in economics departments, the international financial institutions, and in major private foundations, which fostered and funded the spread of these ideas through the think tanks and teams founded by these technopols.[34] The international context was

33. United Nations Economic Commission for Latin America, *Preliminary Overview of the Economy of Latin America and the Caribbean, 1989*, LC/G.1586, 19–20.

34. For an excellent summary of this ideological consensus, see John Williamson, "What Washington Means by Policy Reform," in *Latin American Adjustment: How Much Has Happened?* ed. John Williamson (Washington, D.C.: Institute for International Economics, 1990). By "Washington" Williamson means not just U.S. government agencies but also "the technocratic

favorable as well because these ideas were supported by the U.S. government, its major allies, and public and private international financial institutions. They "demanded" competence from the economic policy makers of Latin American countries. Technically trained leaders, therefore, would help to generate international and eventually domestic political legitimacy: they knew how to act in accord with "universal" and "scientific" requirements.[35]

From our vantage point, the economic crisis alone did not "cause" the opening of politics, but it facilitated such an opening. The economic crisis permitted technically qualified opposition leaders to criticize authoritarian technocrats on their own terms. The technical criticism of failed economic policies opened a wedge for political liberalization at the elite level, complementing mass protests against prevailing policies. In this fashion, technically qualified people in the opposition derived political legitimacy from the international community to challenge the government and, because they were competent to do so, garnered support for themselves within the opposition and for the opposition in the wider public.

Beginning in the late 1970s, another international pool of ideas became available. It asserted the centrality of democracy as the way to govern and the importance of respect for human rights in the relationship between state and society. The support for democracy and human rights became a part of the worldwide federations of Christian Democratic, social democratic, and liberal parties of special pertinence in Western Europe. The international action of many leaders and parties in the industrial democracies helped to weaken international backing for authoritarian rule in Latin America. In the United States, this idea first reached policy salience during Jimmy Carter's presidency. Though nearly discarded during Ronald Reagan's first term, the centrality of democracy as an organizing principle for U.S. foreign policy gathered support during Reagan's second term and especially during the Bush and Clinton

---

Washington of the international financial institutions . . . and the think-tanks" (ibid., 7). See also his *Progress of Policy Reform in Latin America*, no. 28 (Washington, D.C.: Institute for International Economics, 1990). Thirty years earlier, a narrower ideological consensus had developed in Latin America around the influence of the United Nations Economic Commission for Latin America—another international pool of ideas that was in part implemented into policy. See Christopher Mitchell, "The Role of Technocrats in Latin American Integration," *Inter-American Economic Affairs* 21, no. 1 (1967): 3–29; David C. Bruce, "The Impact of the United Nations Economic Commission for Latin America: Technocrats as Channels of Influence," *Inter-American Economic Affairs* 33, no. 4 (1980); and esp. Kathryn Sikkink, *Ideas and Institutions: Developmentalism in Brazil and Argentina* (Ithaca: Cornell University Press, 1991).

35. For a compatible argument, see John Markoff and Verónica Montecinos, "The Ubiquitous Rise of Economists," *Journal of Public Policy* 13, no. 1 (1993): 37–68. I am grateful to Jeanne Kinney Giraldo for the reference.

presidencies. The U.S. government and the European Union also came to "demand" democratic leadership in Latin America. Cardoso especially, but also Foxley, gained personally from his international standing as a democrat. In Latin America, moreover, normative commitments to democracy have been especially noteworthy among intellectuals and politicians in the 1980s and 1990s.[36] Most cosmopolitan technopols gradually came to incorporate the two international pools of ideas—one favorable to markets, the other to democracy.

The availability of international pools of ideas that emphasized the utility of markets and democracy does not, of course, explain the policy choices and value commitments of the technopols we study. As shown in the previous section, these technopols came to these ideas on their own, in part by "swimming" in these pools of ideas during their time abroad; Cardoso and Foxley, for example, strongly believed in democracy well in advance of the Reagan administration's embrace of democratic ideas in the second half of the 1980s. Having made their own choices to foster markets and democracy, however, several of the technopols we study at first were not listened to by their fellow citizens.

The structural crisis in state and economy opened the wedge for these technopols to be heard and to enter government as carriers of their own ideas. By the early 1990s, these ideas were at last legitimated and reinforced by the changed international intellectual and political climate. (In Mexico, it took a second economic crisis in 1994–95 to make way for a democratizing political system.) Would-be technopols had learned as well as generated ideas of interest to the international community and to their fellow citizens. Technical skills had become widespread and respected enough to legitimate the importance and validity of the teams that these technopols had founded. These technopols and their teams stood ready to fashion government programs to respond to the crisis by means of new ideas and their teams' staffing of the national governments, especially in the wake of the economic policy failures of preceding civilian governments in Argentina, Brazil, and Mexico. They were the idea makers who were about to become idea carriers and policy makers.[37] Unlike technocrats in the past, democratic technopols joined oppo-

36. See Scott Mainwaring, "Transitions to Democracy and Democratic Consolidation: Theoretical and Comparative Issues," in *Issues in Democratic Consolidation: The New South American Democracies in Comparative Perspective*, ed. Scott Mainwaring, Guillermo O'Donnell, and J. S. Valenzuela (Notre Dame, Ind.: University of Notre Dame Press, 1992), 294, 308–12.

37. For the notion of idea carrier and its relationship to leaders and institutions, I am indebted to Peter A. Hall, introduction to *The Political Power of Economic Ideas: Keynesianism Across Nations*, ed. Peter A. Hall (Princeton: Princeton University Press, 1989). See also Emanuel Adler,

sition political parties to ride into government power (Mexico, again, an exception). All five technopols gained power thanks to their association with political parties.

These technopols linked a wide vision, universalistic ideas about markets and politics,[38] and technical skills with a strong commitment to their homelands and to political pluralism. In their careers, they falsified the proposition that those trained abroad, or trained "abroad at home," could not operate sensibly and effectively in government office. They would act to open up markets and politics and, in so doing, remain faithful to the twin cosmopolitan ideas of the age. To the parochialism of some in the past, they responded with an effort to install a patriotic cosmopolitanism, grounding international experience in the empirical context of each country. In such fashion, the structural crises facilitated the voluntarist resolution in favor of markets and democracy.

The Actions of Technopols: From the Fat to the Fit State

A central concern of the technopols we study has been to recraft the state. In so doing, these technopols demonstrate that they are not neoliberals (the usual label applied to all, even, in the mid-1990s, to Cardoso), if by neoliberal one means a proponent of the strategies associated with Ronald Reagan or Margaret Thatcher. Our technopols have sought not to kill the state but to save it, to force the state to shed its "fat" but to ensure that the state will be "fit" to govern and to elicit the consent of citizens. In each case, these technopols have sought to cut back the state's reach into the society and the economy, but they have also sought to increase government revenues and improve the delivery of government services. In several cases, they have sought to redirect the savings from cutting back on certain state actions to redress inequalities or to improve support for the poor.

The Power of Ideology: The Quest for Technological Autonomy in Argentina and Brazil (Berkeley and Los Angeles: University of California Press, 1987), and Sikkink, Ideas and Institutions.

38. For examples, from quite different empirical realms, of the utility of focusing on ideas to understand political and economic changes, see Ashutosh Varshney, "Ideas, Interests, and Institutions in Policy Change: Transformation of India's Agricultural Strategy in the mid-1960s," Policy Sciences 22 (1989): 289–323, and Kathryn Sikkink, "Human Rights, Principled Issue-Networks, and Sovereignty in Latin America," International Organization 47, no. 3 (1993): 411–41.

For Matthei, there have been fewer opportunities to recraft the state, because she has not wielded top executive power. In the 1970s and 1980s, Matthei had supported the Chilean government policies of privatization of state enterprises, and in the 1990s, as Boylan notes, she advocated the privatization of several enterprises that remained in the state's hands. But "state shrinking" does not, in fact, characterize her position. The social policies that she advocated would expand certain areas of state activity. Most important, she was the government's key ally from the opposition, helping to obtain broad enough support in Congress for a tax reform to raise revenues to pay for new social expenditures. Matthei's political career, as Boylan indicates, exemplifies how even certain politicians from the right support the competent state, "fit" but not "fat."

From Congress and the center-left, Resende-Santos notes, Cardoso argued strongly against the bloated and ineffective Brazilian state while also seeking to deconcentrate power in the presidency by means of a constitutional shift to a parliamentary regime. Cardoso is among these technopols also the strongest advocate of government services for the poor and the weak. For Cardoso, the arbitrary state was democracy's worst enemy, and the "fat" state was the main source of corruption, evident most tragically in 1992 with the impeachment and subsequent resignation of Brazil's first directly elected president in three decades, Fernando Collor de Mello. As finance minister, Cardoso raised revenues and protected government services for the poor even as he sought to limit the state's intrusion into society and economy.

As Kinney Giraldo notes, Finance Minister Alejandro Foxley sought to retain and foster Chile's integration into the international economy, to stabilize the economy from its inflationary bout at the end of the Pinochet regime, and to foster social equity. Minister Foxley fostered freer trade agreements while resisting calls for trade protectionism. By institutionalizing free trade, the nation would set clear and stable rules for the future. On the other hand, Foxley understood the need for regulation of financial markets to prevent the reckless inflow of funds that unraveled Chilean economic policies in the late 1970s and early 1980s. But perhaps Foxley's most important accomplishment was his management of macroeconomic policies and the social deficit.

Could Chilean democrats manage the economy? The authoritarian regime's claim to fame had been its ability at last to foster real economic growth by the second half of the 1980s. Nonetheless, rational investors would expect a continued significant "political risk" from operations in Chile because there was reason for uncertainty about future government policies: Could the economic policies of an authoritarian regime elicit enough consent from the governed to endure? If parties of the center and the left were to replace the dictatorship, what economic policies might they follow?

Chile's "Chicago Boys" in their various incarnations could not successfully address this problem of rational expectations so long as the Pinochet regime continued. This rational-expectations problem could best be addressed in a democracy, in which either the renovated right would receive popular endorsement or the center and the left would govern through market-oriented and stable macroeconomic policies. From the perspective of the rational investor, paradoxically, the second of these options would best ensure the future, for it would signal a truly comprehensive consensus on the wisdom of Chile's new economic trajectory: only when there was a democracy committed to markets and governed by the center-left could the rational investor be certain that market norms would prevail no matter which party governed. (Sociologically, of course, most investors typically do not behave this way; they tend to prefer center-right governments. They understand the utility of market-oriented center-left governments only after markets and democracy are consolidated without their active support.)

Foxley understood the utility of democracy for markets and the utility of markets for democracy. Democracy would address the problem of rational economic expectations; markets would generate the growth to consolidate democracy and provide the funds to address the social agenda. This technopol exemplifies the long-term elective affinity between markets and democracy.

Foxley's opening economic policies were austere; public spending was sharply restrained in order to break the late Pinochet regime's inflationary spiral and to stabilize public finances even at the cost of slow economic growth in the short term. These policies set the basis for spectacular noninflationary economic growth in 1991 and 1992 and for continuing good economic growth rates thereafter.

To address genuine problematic social legacies of the Pinochet regime, Foxley led the government to negotiate with the right-wing party National Renovation (prominently including Deputy Evelyn Matthei) over a tax reform whose revenue proceeds would fund government initiatives especially in health and education. Through these technically competent policies, Foxley demonstrated that "growth with equity" was not just a slogan but a feasible policy goal. Foxley also demonstrated that the parties of the center and the center-left had no wish to resurrect the fat state but were more competent to recraft the fit state to address the nation's needs and hopes.

Economy Minister Domingo Cavallo faced a different problem of rational expectations as he sought to govern under President Carlos Menem and the Peronist party. There was "certainty" that Argentina was ungovernable, that the state apparatus was inept, and that the economy would repeat the cycles of decline and decline that had marked it for decades, the best example of a country that had succeeded at becoming "underdeveloped" in the twentieth century. There was a related rational expectation—the "certainty" that the Peronists, given their past record in government, were "closet populists" and incompetent rulers.

If Foxley's opening policy package had to combine a progressive social policy with an austere fiscal policy to become credible, Cavallo's had to be shocking but democratic, for anything less would have been seen as lacking credibility. This policy took the form of the 1991 Convertibility Law, which made the national currency freely convertible into dollars at a fixed and unchanging value. The law ended contract indexation and prohibited the Central Bank from printing money to cover deficits unless new currency releases were backed by gold or foreign reserves. The law had to be shocking to make it clear that hyperinflation would not recur, but this alone would not have made Cavallo so different from some of his predecessors.

The genius of Cavallo's strategy, as Corrales notes, was to use democratic constraints to implement this policy. He chose to act through congressional action, rather than by decree, and in the future to require prior congressional authorization for any change in the exchange rate or printing of more money. Through congressional approval, Cavallo was signaling the commitment of the executive and legislature to alter permanently the course of Argentina's macroeconomic policies. Cavallo induced the Congress to assume responsibility for macroeconomic stability and tied his hands via the democratic process. Self-binding behavior is a long-recognized strategy to demonstrate credibility and to address the problem of rational expectations.[39] Henceforth, the president or the Central Bank would find it much more difficult to change monetary policy; henceforth, the basis for macroeconomic policy would be supported even by Peronists, those who had hitherto been most suspect of recklessness.

Corrales quotes Cavallo's belief that Argentina's past economic problems had not been technical. The technical problems were understood; good technical prescriptions existed as well. Cavallo accurately diagnosed the problem as political; this political problem could only be addressed via democratic procedures. For this technopol, democracy was not an option; it was a neces-

---

39. Thomas C. Schelling, *The Strategy of Conflict* (London: Oxford University Press, 1960).

sity. Only by binding himself, his president, his government, and his party allies to the consent of Congress could Cavallo persuade rational actors to believe that, this time, Argentines, indeed, the Peronists, meant to get their house in order.

The remainder of Cavallo's unprecedented economic program was consistent with his opening salvo. The national government deficit was sharply curtailed; state enterprises were privatized; provincial governments were cajoled into fiscal restraint. Cavallo urged voters to unseat governors who failed to reform. In October 1991, the government adopted a far-reaching program of deregulation. Cavallo also sharply reduced tariffs and other forms of trade protection in order to open up Argentina's economy to the forces of the world market. His search for freer trade agreements was also an effort to use self-binding constraints to institutionalize the rules of an open economy.

And yet, as with the other technopols, Cavallo was particularly interested not in weakening the state but in making it competent. His comprehensive tax reforms sought the inconceivable. As Cavallo has stated (and Corrales quotes), the only miraculous thing his ministry has achieved is to get Argentines to pay taxes. In addition to implementing various tax policy changes, Cavallo strengthened the state's capacity to collect taxes. He also greatly fortified the state's capacity to regulate the markets created through the privatization of state enterprises.

Cavallo's accomplishments, therefore, featured the use of democratic procedures to address rational expectations and transform the state so that it could govern at last. That he was also technically highly skilled was, of course, necessary to the task but not so remarkable. Cavallo is more unusual for his political skill than for his economics, and so he is an example of a democratic technopol.

The "Mexican miracle"—restoring growth while reducing inflation—is more a collective than a personal accomplishment, as Golob reminds us, because Pedro Aspe's role was less singular than those of Foxley and Cavallo. (President Carlos Salinas de Gortari played a far more salient role in fashioning economic policies than did Presidents Aylwin and Menem.) Nonetheless, Aspe played a key role in recrafting the Mexican state, making it "fit" to govern.

As in Argentina and Chile, a far-reaching program of privatization of state enterprises was also undertaken in Mexico under Aspe's general purview. Aspe's ministry also worked in sustained and effective fashion to improve tax collection and to increase the state's revenues. The proceeds from privatization in Mexico were directed to paying off parts of the public debt, thus freeing budget funds to be spent on health, education, housing, and basic infrastructure. Regular tax revenues were also directed to these purposes. The reduction of poverty became an objective of the Salinas presidency; in turn, this goal was made possible by Aspe's successful financial policies. The channeling of public funds to address the social deficit was, as Golob makes clear, an integral part of Aspe's intellectual concerns before his rise through the bureaucracy; as a scholar, Aspe had worked thoughtfully on problems of inequality and poverty.

There was, perhaps, a second Mexican "miracle" that interests us as well, namely, the ability to make significant progress without a Cavallo-like policy shock but also under a politics of elite inclusion in a nondemocratic system. In October 1987, the Mexican stock market crashed more severely than world stock markets did; an unexpected run on the peso sent inflation out of control. At that very moment, Carlos Salinas had been nominated as the ruling party's presidential candidate, and Pedro Aspe had become budget and planning secretary. The ingenious and impressively effective solution to this crisis was a "social pact" of the sort that scholars seem to think never works.

The Economic Solidarity Pact was based on the recognition that the government could not address all problems by decree. The state could not impose a solution; labor and business had to agree to bear some of the burden. And by making policy through negotiations, leading to mutually binding commitments, Aspe and the government increased the likelihood that the pact would be credible at home and abroad. Within a half year of its enactment, the pact had brought Mexican inflation down to just over 1 percent per month; the pact would subsequently be renegotiated various times, but Mexican inflation would remain low through the first half of the 1990s.

As Golob makes clear, little about this pact was truly new. Aspe had learned from the failures of previous inflation-control efforts in Argentina and Brazil and from successes in Israel and Spain; he understood that only fiscal discipline would provide a stable underpinning to price and wage controls. Aspe may have learned a more important lesson from his MIT mentor, Dornbusch; as Golob quotes Dornbusch, "[E]ffective stabilization is, above all, not a technical issue but a political one." Aspe applied this concept to Mexico through negotiation of concerted action among key economic and political actors to avoid shock policies and to succeed in slaying the inflation dragon. Political inclusion was needed, though it fell well short of the democratic politics of Cavallo and Foxley.

By intention and, in the cases of the ministers, by accomplishment, these technopols sought to recraft the state. The state has shed (or is in the process of shedding) its "fat" in order to become more competent ("fit") to tackle a narrower array of tasks that only it can perform. Technopols not only privatize state enterprises in the belief that the state is generally not capable of conducting such business, but they also raise taxes so that the state's public finances are sound. Especially in Chile, Mexico, and Brazil, these technopols take seriously the state's obligations to address the social deficit and have increased government spending on education, health, and basic infrastructure. The support for the competent state is a value shared among these technopols, no matter how much they may differ in other aspects of their politics.

These technopols have also understood that rational investors expect policy continuity. To achieve this fundamental objective, the technopols have followed two strategies. The first harkens back to their founding cosmopolitan vision. They have pursued international trade agreements to "lock in" their country's new, freer market-oriented policies well into the future and thus set the market rules that will meet the rational expectations of investors.

The second strategy has been to foster a political opening in order to ensure that all key actors participate in the shaping of the new policies and, as a result, remain committed to them. In Brazil, where such consent was most elusive, less had been accomplished by the mid-1990s to reorient the economy and secure the bases of democratic politics, though President Cardoso was accelerating the pace of change. Where such consent remained imperfect because transparent democratic procedures had not characterized the polity, as in Mexico, greater uncertainties remained. Nonetheless, the commitment to market-oriented reforms seemed strong by the mid-1990s. Even after Mexico's financial crisis and economic recession of 1994–95 (and a less severe but still noteworthy simultaneous economic crisis in Argentina), whose wider effect was to discourage international investment to varying degrees in Latin American countries, all four governments remained committed to market-oriented policies.

Foxley and Cavallo, therefore, appear as the most successful of these technopols, for their behavior and their policies have fostered freer trade as well as the consent of the governed with regard to market-oriented policies under democratic politics. The democratic center-left parties in Chile and the Peronists in Argentina could demonstrate better than any military governments that the countries' new commitments would endure in the future, and in this way democratic politics responded effectively to the rational-expectations problem.

The Deepening of Democracy

The political actions of the technopols we study have advanced the practice of democracy in each of these countries, though to varying degrees. For the most part, they have acted to deepen democracy because they believe in its values; at a minimum, they have sought to deepen democracy because obtaining the consent of the governed, especially the actual or potential partisan or sectoral opposition, is the most effective way in the long run to consolidate their preferred economic policies.

Foxley and Matthei worked jointly to bridge the gap between parties that had been adversaries in the preceding presidential elections and for the duration of the Pinochet regime. For Matthei, the political risks were higher. She was the daughter of an air force general who had served on the military junta during the Pinochet regime. Her party had just begun life in the opposition. She had barely entered national politics and lacked a strong partisan base. She had to change the right's expectation that it would lack the ability to influence policies under the new government. Even for Foxley, there were risks: would the Christian Democrats in power betray their campaign promises to bring greater fairness to Chile? The Pinochet dictatorship had been accustomed to giving orders as its method of rule. The constitution that President Aylwin and Minister Foxley had inherited vested great powers in the executive branch; instead, they turned to Congress to govern democratically. Led by Aylwin and Foxley, the government reached out to the congressional opposition, led among others by Matthei, to reach an agreement on tax increases and new government expenditures. Foxley repeated as minister the technique that he had first developed within the opposition coalition: the forging of agreements on a sound technical basis to advance policy goals. For her part, Matthei innovated a strategy for her party as the loyal opposition, credible and capable of government. As "teacher to the nation," she communicated a new, caring, democratic image for the parties of the right that should serve them and Chilean democracy well.

Within the government, Foxley spent much time defending his policies before his party and its coalition partners and before the Congress. He fostered the growth of various means for regular political consultation. As Kinney Giraldo reminds us, Foxley also reached out to a dynamic business class that had long distrusted him, his party, and his party's allies, at a time when business was being asked to accept tax increases and labor law changes that they opposed. Foxley also worked to develop fluid conversations with labor, and among business, labor, and the government. Democracy required, above all, that both the political and the economic right remain allegiant; Foxley bargained with the right in Congress and dealt professionally with business.

Foxley also became a "teacher to the nation," using television and other mass media successfully. His public "persona" emphasized sober competence and effectiveness. So, too, as Boylan notes, Matthei had made exemplary use of television and other media to portray a "caring" as well as an always competent image for the right. In Chile, democrats understood democracy required that the "Weberian scholar" hidden within a technopol should surface to consolidate public beliefs in the utility and efficacy of democracy.

Cardoso's central contributions to Brazilian democratic politics have been discussed in an earlier section: the creation of a team, an intellectual institution, a political party, and the sustained effort to insert programmatic ideas into party programs and political discourse. As finance minister and later as president, Cardoso worked with Congress to enact economic reform measures even though Congress was often an obstacle to the adoption of such measures. The 1993 dispute over wage adjustments illustrates Cardoso's approach. In June, the Congress had enacted into law monthly wage adjustments to ensure that workers' pay would remain fully abreast of inflation. Cardoso's Finance Ministry prepared a technical analysis that showed the highly inflationary effects of such a measure, while Cardoso's team lobbied members of Congress. In August, Congress changed the wage law to dampen the inflationary flames. Democracy had to be made to work in Brazil—that had been and remained Cardoso's commitment.

Cardoso has also made three other important contributions to Brazilian democracy. First, he is the peerless teacher to his nation, combining a lively sense of humor and a gift for phrase making with an accessible public demeanor that is unmatched by other technopols we study (except Matthei). His ability to transform important abstract thoughts into more readily understood concepts has helped to deepen mass democracy. Second, Cardoso has been accused by critics of having shifted his views according to prevailing political winds. Resende-Santos discusses in some detail the consistency of the central features in Cardoso's thought while acknowledging that there have been changes of emphasis and substance. That is, of course, what ought to happen in democratic politics. Politicians should shed dogmas in response to new facts; Cardoso has exemplified how this is to be done: in public. Finally, in a political system marked by infidelity to parties, Cardoso has been respectful of his party's discipline, even turning down an early offer to become foreign minister because his party had chosen not to join the president's political alliance. Democratic governance requires party discipline; Cardoso has practiced what he has preached.

As finance minister in a nondemocratic political system, Aspe's role in furthering Mexico's political opening was modest. Nonetheless, as noted earlier, the design of the 1987 Economic Solidarity Pact featured political inclusion within the elite. More important, during the 1980s the Mexican Congress assumed a more active role in questioning government ministers; this role increased once the opposition made major gains in the 1988 national elections. Aspe appeared regularly and often before Congress. Although he occasionally lost his temper, as is the case with the other technopols, Aspe, too, became a teacher to the nation through his congressional testimony.

Cavallo's contribution to deepening Argentina's democratic practice is the most surprising because he had worked for the military government in 1981–82 and because President Menem had demonstrated a penchant for ruling by decree. And yet, as minister, Cavallo, too, made a net contribution to democracy in his country. This process began but did not end with the 1991 Convertibility Law. At times Cavallo was criticized for having compromised too much in his dealings with Congress, but that is of the essence of democratic politics. To secure support from Peronist backbenchers and from the main opposition, the Radical Party, Cavallo permitted the Congress to scrutinize and approve every major step in the reform of the state. Privatizations had been carried out by presidential decree, but Cavallo preferred that those decisions, too, should require congressional approval. He understood clearly that congressional and opposition participation increased the likelihood that such privatizations would be seen as broadly legitimate. Cavallo knew that his democratic predecessors had failed in Congress; it was therefore not just desirable but also efficient to engage the Congress.

In the Economy Ministry, Cavallo built not just a technical team versed in economics but also a political team versed in dealing with Congress, the parties, and the provinces; this team was institutionalized through a new undersecretary's office in the Economy Ministry. Cavallo understood that the making of economic policy was too important to be left to economists alone. Corrales quotes Cavallo's insistence that the economy has to be governed by laws, not by decrees, as a means to ensure endurance of the new rules.

Cavallo became a teacher to his nation by appearing in Congress and on television talk shows, by speaking wherever he had an opportunity to convince his president, his party, the Congress, and the nation at large that the time had come at last to break with Argentina's unstable and undemocratic past, to link democracy and markets in the building of a more secure future. As a scholar, he spoke about things as they were, not about the promises of an imaginary utopia. Cavallo became as well a teacher to the international community—to change the expectation that Argentina would forever be an economic or political pariah. In this fashion, Cavallo redeemed his nationalist credentials in defense of the country's interests.

The time that the four ministers—Cavallo, Cardoso, Foxley, and Aspe— spent in political work also had an economic payoff. By working to improve the government's relations with both labor and business, technopols, through more open politics (and in Argentina and Chile specifically democratic politics), built a consensus behind efficient and realistic policies while reducing transaction costs—fewer strikes, fewer budget allocations for repression, the end of the international isolation of the more authoritarian regimes, and less likelihood of business support for coups. Brazil lagged in the development of this market-oriented policy consensus, but the effort to achieve these objectives began in earnest in 1994. (Mexico's delayed democratization was associated with increased protests demanding greater political opening.) The reduction in transaction costs in Argentina, Brazil, and Chile also probably increased business support for democracy.

More generally, in each of these cases (except Mexico) democratic technopols sought to deepen democracy as an integral part of their task and as a component of their own self-definition in politics. Political openings, and democracy more specifically, moved forward in these countries thanks to the political acts of these technopols.

The Contradictions: Techno Versus Pol

The role of technopol features inherent contradictions, some of which were noted earlier. This book reports not only the successes of technopols but also less fortuitous outcomes. One was Matthei's alienation from her party. Beyond the specifics of her case is the larger problem evident in all the cases, namely, that the skills and predispositions that make for the technical side of the technopol are in some tension with those that make for the political side. To this extent, the themes that have long concerned scholars who have focused on technocrats remain pertinent, namely, whether the technical virtues may undermine the democratic possibilities. We disagree with the extant scholarship in that we believe that it has exaggerated the problem, not that it has lacked a fundamental insight.[40]

Boylan's chapter on Matthei points to three distinct, though related, factors that may account for Matthei's political difficulties. Matthei lacked a team, a think tank, an institutional base of her own that would enrich her ideas and values and temper her political actions. Her technical training had not prepared her for the formation of alliances and the building of institutional bases that are essential for successful political action and that are present to a greater degree in the other four cases. Nor did Matthei have a good sense of timing. To some degree, her meteoric rise in national politics was part of her near undoing; her business background and technical training had not prepared her adequately for the circumspection at times required in political action. Nor did she have enough time to hone the skills for making political judgments in the earlier period of her political career.

The tensions within the role of technopol have had different effects on Aspe. His actions fostered some political inclusion at the elite level, but Mexican politics did not become democratic, and Aspe, unlike the others, did not act in a democratic context. Like Cavallo and Foxley, Aspe, too, could display the arrogance of the flawlessly technically trained, express impatience and disdain for members of Congress, and become too preachy in his approach to the public, the press, and the parliament. Constrained in part by the "division of labor" between economic and political affairs within President Salinas's cabinet, Aspe resolved the tensions within the role of technopol by eschewing the building of democracy, and in so doing, he differed in important ways from the other four technopols.

Golob aptly observes that the "insider" style of Mexico's technopols made it more difficult for them to develop the skills of conciliation and negotiation associated with more openly competitive politics—an observation that echoes Boylan's analysis of some of Matthei's political difficulties. What made Mexico's technopols successful in their country also made it less likely that they would press hard to open up the political system. Aspe was never a member of an opposition political party, unlike the four others we discuss. The unpreparedness of Mexican technopols for democracy may have made them less sensitive as well to the greater readiness of Mexican citizens for democratic politics.[41] Salinas's team of technopols listened too little and too late to the

---

40. For recent thoughtful discussions of these issues, see Conaghan and Malloy, *Unsettling Statecraft*, 220–24; see also Conaghan, Malloy, and Abugattás, "Business and the 'Boys.'"

41. For elaboration, see Jorge I. Domínguez and James A. McCann, *Democratizing Mexico:*

demands for a more open political system; in 1994, those demands were among the factors that would contribute to the unraveling of the economic policies so carefully fashioned by Salinas and Aspe. Salinas, Aspe, and their associates thought that they were more skillful in reforming the Mexican economy than Mikhail Gorbachev was in reforming the Soviet Union's economy. Gorbachev's project may have been undone by the general breakdown of the Soviet system; the Salinas-Aspe project was gravely injured, in part, by its "democratic deficit." A key question for Mexico's future is whether a more democratic political regime can fashion better and more sustainable economic policies.

In economic terms, Aspe is also the least successful of the finance ministers. Mexico's financial panic of December 1994, and the fiscal and monetary policy errors committed by the Mexican government during that year, contributed to a new severe economic recession in Mexico during 1995. The lack of democratic procedures in Mexico to compel the executive to listen to criticism and take it into account insulated top decision makers to an extent unprecedented elsewhere—and at a political and economic cost not found anywhere else on the continent.[42] A short-term political rationality (win the August 1994 election for the governing party) along with this "democratic deficit" contributed to the unmaking of elite economic policies and threatened the decades-old rule of the Institutional Revolutionary Party.

Related problems are evident also in the other cases. Cavallo, Corrales tells us, had little patience for congressional questioning or for delays attributable to mere political factors. This impatience stemmed precisely from the intensity and clarity of his convictions. That is, the more persuaded he became of the technical soundness of his view, the less effective he could be at getting such views accepted politically. This is the Cavallo who lost his temper and shouted at members of Congress; Cavallo the thoughtful "teacher" turned

---

Public Opinion and Electoral Choices (Baltimore: Johns Hopkins University Press, 1996), chap. 2.

42. On economic factors underlying the crisis in Mexico, see Jeffrey Sachs, Aaron Tornell, and Andrés Velasco, "The Collapse of the Mexican Peso," working paper no. 95-97, Center for International Affairs, Harvard University, Cambridge, July 1995. On the closed nature of the policy-making process, see David Wessel, Paul B. Carroll, and Thomas T. Vogel Jr., "Peso Surprise: How Mexico's Crisis Ambushed Top Minds in Officialdom, Finance," *Wall Street Journal*, 6 July 1995. For the most part the crisis was limited to Mexico. Despite a brief initial negative fallout from the Mexican crisis, the economies of Brazil and Chile continued on their high growth path during 1995. Argentina was hit more severely; the country slipped into recession, and in May 1995 open unemployment rose to 18.6 percent. By year's end, however, Argentina's economic crisis was abating. For statistics, see United Nations Economic Commission for Latin America, *Economic Panorama of Latin America, 1995,* 17–31, 41–45, 55–64.

into a shrill "preacher." The same "candid and sincere" Cavallo could make condescending statements in public. There was both an authoritarian streak in the Olympian technical skills and a certain ill-preparedness for the normal rough and tumble of democratic politics that stemmed as well from technical training, orientation, and demeanor.

Institutionally, more worrisome was Cavallo's continued reliance on government by decree to sidestep the Congress because Congress might overrepresent those most resistant to change. This was the reason to deregulate by decree rather than by congressional law. Democratic procedures, then, might be seen as optional tools to be used and discarded in the building of the altar of market-oriented reforms. To this extent, there remained an incompatibility between Cavallo's technical and democratic-political dimensions. And yet, as Corrales reminds us, in reorienting the economy within a democratic polity, Cavallo bested Chile's record under Pinochet and Mexico's under Salinas.

The tensions between techno and pol were evident as well in Foxley's case. As Kinney Giraldo notes, perhaps Foxley's most important political action may have been his veto of the economic program that the technical committees of the opposition parties had negotiated in 1989. In the end, the parties were well served electorally by succumbing to Foxley, but Foxley seemed to expect compliance in deference to expertise. Foxley's occasional flashes of arrogance and extensive use of the mass media could suggest a discomfort with some of the normal conduct of democratic politics.

More seriously, Foxley sought to prevent the Congress, and especially the parties in his coalition, from constraining his technically "correct" policies, because he preferred to retain maximum flexibility. He also continued to see value in the institutional obstacles to party and congressional exercise of power that were inherited from the authoritarian regime, because they forced wide agreements prior to the implementation of major policies. Moreover, Foxley also played on labor unions' fear of the authoritarian regime to moderate labor demands. And yet, Foxley was the first finance minister in Chilean history to succeed at maintaining and developing market-oriented economic policies in a fundamentally democratic context.

Foxley experienced the tensions within the role of technopol more vividly when he became Christian Democrat Party president in 1994. In that new job, he found it difficult to cope with the murky and often personalized nuances of party politics. His commitment to emphasize ideas as the guiding star of politics was at times overwhelmed by the need to attend to egos, jealousies, and interests that palpitate at the heart of politics.

The tensions in the role of technopol also had different consequences for Cardoso, who can be located at the opposite end of the spectrum from Aspe. As Resende-Santos notes, Cardoso never had the "love for the state" evident among so many Brazilians on the political left or in the armed forces, but Cardoso has always been suspicious of the "magic" of the market. With the passing of time and with his growing frustration with the corruption and abuse of the bloated Brazilian state, Cardoso's interest in and respect for markets rose, but Resende-Santos's careful analysis makes evident that Cardoso found it difficult to celebrate a market-oriented economic policy in the manner that came so easily to the others whom we study. Cardoso, in short, resolved the tensions within the role of technopol by emphasizing the primacy of political goals and methods.

Technopols discover ongoing difficulties in reconciling the various dimensions included within this role. In part for that reason, Matthei's political career nearly aborted after a very promising start. Also in part for that reason, Aspe and for a long time Cardoso addressed these internal role contradictions by focusing on one dimension at the expense of the other. Cavallo and Foxley, and eventually Cardoso as finance minister and president, wrestled with these contradictions with far greater effectiveness. By this we do not exempt Cavallo, Foxley, and the latter-day Cardoso from some criticism, but we believe that they should be held to realistic standards in the context of their countries or the region as a whole. No finance minister in Chile and no economy minister in Argentina had pursued market-oriented economic policies in a democratic context as successfully as these two, and no Brazilian president had attempted ambitious and joint democratic and economic reforms.[43] These were historic accomplishments.

Conclusions

"Look at a success story," U.S. undersecretary of state-designate (and former World Bank vice president) Lawrence Summers exhorted his audience at the 1993 Annual Meeting of the Inter-American Development Bank. After having praised the general trend toward "popular, democratic elections and institutions," Summers continued: "Chile is an excellent example of a country that

---

43. See convergent analysis by Alejandra Cox Edwards and Sebastian Edwards, "Markets and Democracy: Lessons from Chile," *World Economy* 15, no. 2 (1992): 203–19.

has implemented far-reaching macroeconomic reforms [and] encouraged the development of the private sector and markets. . . . Now the government can concentrate its resources on the social sector. . . . Chile has demonstrated the political will to make social programs a priority. This is a good example for other countries."[44]

After a decade-long economic decline in most Latin American countries in the 1980s, growth resumed in most countries in the early 1990s. After a legacy of political instability, Argentine and Brazilian civilian governments in the late 1980s and early 1990s survived the sort of hyperinflation that brought European and Latin American governments tumbling down earlier in the twentieth century.

In this book, we argue that there was a structural political and economic origin to the changes evident in several major Latin American countries in the early 1990s but that there has been a voluntarist resolution through the effective use of each nation's institutions. The structural crisis posed the problems; its severity forced elites to consider a wider range of policy options. The fact of an economic crisis does not by itself explain the course of policy adopted in the early 1990s. For example, in the 1980s and early 1990s Brazil suffered a similar crisis but only belatedly did it begin to adopt some policies comparable to those of Argentina, Chile, or Mexico. Similarly, Argentina suffered a severe economic crisis earlier in the 1980s; while it shifted toward democratic politics, it did not at that time adopt the market-oriented policies that it did in the early 1990s. The explanation for the joint adoption of policies that would foster freer markets and freer politics lies in the strategic actions of technopols working with their allies through democratic institutions to formulate new policy designs. They learned from the democratic or economic policy failures (or both) of their authoritarian and democratic predecessors.

The more successful outcomes have been those shaped by political leaders whose ideas were forged in both national and cosmopolitan contexts. They drew on the available international pool of ideas about the utility of markets to legitimate their views and, at a critical juncture, acted to turn ideas into policy. There was a second international pool of available ideas: respect for democracy. Fortunately for the fate of political openings, authoritarian regimes everywhere but in Chile had failed to deliver sound economic policies, depriving them of political support and opening the gates for new political regimes.

44. U.S. Department of the Treasury, *Treasury News*, 30 March 1993, 4–5.

In Argentina, Brazil, and Chile the leaders we study drew upon both sets of international ideas to fashion new market-oriented economic policies and to advance toward and consolidate more open politics rooted in each country's national experience. (In Mexico, the reforms focused mainly on economic issues.) This comprehensive shift was in place only by the early 1990s, ten years after the birth of the economic crisis in most Latin American countries—one reason why the crisis is only an important background factor and not the explanation for the direction and content of the new policies.

These political leaders are not Reagan, Thatcher, or International Monetary Fund "clones." In fact, Cardoso since the 1960s and Aspe and Foxley since the 1970s have spent much time and intellectual energy, in speeches and publications, calling attention to the need for state action to address not just the problems of growth but also those of poverty. These technopols not only drew from but also helped to change the international "consensus" directing greater attention and channeling greater resources to social policies in the midst of economic adjustment and market liberalization. Cavallo's dissertation was a critique of the monetarist policies of Argentina's military government in the late 1970s, a critique—in which he was joined by the others whom we study—of policies once favored by the international community.

From Matthei on the center-right to Cardoso on the center-left, all five leaders we study in this book have advocated or implemented improvements in the state's capacity to tax. "Read my lips, pay your taxes" seemed to be their shared motto. These technopols helped to change the international "consensus" that the state had to be recrafted, not merely reduced, that nations needed competent governments, not puny ones. They are neoliberals neither in their views and policies on the social deficit nor in their views and policies on the state. They forced the state to shed its "fat" not to kill it by starvation but to render it "fit" to serve the nation's interests.

These political leaders learned early on the importance of ideas and of high professional standards. They internalized the norms of their respective technical professions. They returned home to build teams that would seek to conquer the state. They were classic idea carriers who went on to implement those ideas. They were bearers of a "passion" for open politics and open markets, "responsible" for the consequences of those beliefs and guided generally by a "sense of proportion": in these ways, they were classic Weberian politicians. As scholars in Weber's sense, they became teachers to the nation. And though they came to function in bureaucracies, theirs was a more varied career pattern than that of Weberian bureaucrats and, as a result, more open to democratic politics.

As finance ministers, Aspe, Cavallo, Cardoso, and Foxley suffered to some degree Turgot's difficult relations with constitutional government, and Aspe, Cavallo, and Matthei had worked for governments in undemocratic regimes. The trend for them over time, however, was away from the temptations of Pharaoh's Joseph and toward political openings. The tensions inherent in the role of a democratic technopol can never be entirely solved, but these leaders addressed them far better than their predecessors or scholars of "technocrats" have led us to believe.

Their superior performance stemmed less from their technical skill—high as it was—and more from their understanding of the importance of politics for what they wished to accomplish. Our findings are consistent with Conaghan and Malloy's comparative study of Bolivia, Ecuador, and Peru—three cases where elected civilian presidents sought to reorient economic policies in the 1980s. Political craftsmanship was the reason why Bolivia's shift toward a market-oriented economy was much more successful than similar attempts in Ecuador and Peru. "In the final analysis, [Bolivia's president Víctor] Paz Estenssoro's vision—his understanding of the intimate connection between political change and economic change—was what differentiated his administration from those of [Ecuador's president León] Febres Cordero and [Peru's president Fernando] Belaúnde. Paz's accomplishments as an economic policy maker lay in his recognition that neoliberalism required reinventing Bolivia politically as well as economically."[45] In fact, our book's technopols politically outperformed Paz Estenssoro's government. The Bolivian politico-economic team "did not devote much energy . . . [to] how to organize support for their policies once in power." In Argentina, Brazil, Chile, and Mexico, politico-economic leaders spent considerable time explaining their programs and building and consolidating governing coalitions.[46]

In late 1992, Richard Feinberg asked Foxley whether he accepted the label of "technopol." Foxley said he did, and went on to define the term: "First is the realization that to do a good technical job in managing the economy you have to be a politician. If you do not have the capacity to articulate your vision, to persuade antagonists, to bring people around on some unpopular measure, then you are going to be a total failure. . . . Economists must not only know their economic models, but also understand politics, interests, conflicts, passions—the essence of collective life. For a brief period of time you could

---

45. Conaghan and Malloy, *Unsettling Statecraft*, 202 and, more generally, chap. 7.
46. Ibid., 217–18.

make most changes by decree; but to let them persist, you have to build coalitions and bring people around. You have to be a politician."[47]

Speaking for himself and his peers, Foxley sketched the procedural utility of democracy for the implementation and consolidation of market-oriented policies. And so the economists in our study learned much about democratic politics, just as Cardoso, our only sociologist—and now president—learned about markets, jointly narrowing their past differences. Democracy is useful to bring about market-oriented reforms and, above all, to make them last. Foxley's understanding of democracy does not purge it of its "conflicts [and] passions" but, instead, seeks to harness the forces of democracy to set the rules and create the institutions that will shape and respond to the rational expectations of economic actors. Democracy also lowers transaction costs that stem from instability or authoritarian repression.

For these reasons, Chilean democracy accomplished what Pinochet's Chicago Boys never could in an authoritarian context: it bound the nation's future to the market by means of the nation's consent. The Chicago Boys willfully ignored the search for consent and could not institutionalize their policies. Democratic technopols understand the necessity and worth of politics. Cavallo's strategic use of congressional laws to bind himself, the government, and the nation to a new program of market-oriented policies was perhaps the most dramatic example of the efficacy of democratic mechanisms in fostering a healthy market. As Foxley also told Feinberg, the Argentine and Chilean cases show that "democracy can be effective and efficient in producing change."[48] For Cardoso and Foxley always, eventually for Matthei and Cavallo, least so for Aspe, moreover, democratic politics may also be valued for itself. Cardoso and Foxley, in particular, have devoted much of their adult lives to making democratic politics work.

To anchor political openings in markets, all five supported an opening toward international trade, though Cardoso with reservations. Those who served as finance ministers liberalized trade and sought to institutionalize freer trade by means of free trade agreements that would lock in the market reforms abroad just as consensual democratic agreement locked in such reforms at home. In this sense, the foundational cosmopolitanism of their ideas came to be implemented through their market internationalism.

---

47. Alejandro Foxley, interview by Richard Feinberg, in the Washington Exchange's *State of Latin American Finance* (Washington, D.C.: Inter-American Dialogue, 1992), 21–22.

48. Ibid., 22.

Much remains to be done, however. Mexican politics have much room for a further opening; Brazil has barely begun to implement significant changes in economic policies. The near-term future of Argentine and especially Mexican policies remains somewhat uncertain at this writing, even if the overall direction of policy seems settled.

In all four countries, there is already evidence that the privatization of state enterprises has led to the consolidation of certain private and barely regulated monopolies and oligopolies; if this trend continues, privatization may turn out to be market illiberal. And yet, all five leaders seem conscious of the public loss from such concentrated private power, holding the hope that democratic governance and institutional transparency committed to markets may induce even alleged capitalists to welcome capitalism. As Golob quotes Aspe, in the long run market policies will only work if the private sector itself is privatized and becomes less dependent on state protection, subsidies, and contracts. Democracy will prosper best if private economic power is not so concentrated. The search for market liberalism, not just for the private ownership of the means of production, will serve the rational expectations of democrats who expect such policies from democratic technopols.

Moreover, as Golob also calls to our attention, the Mexican case reminds us that there is no easy and no instant correspondence between market-oriented economic reforms, on the one hand, and political democratization, on the other. Mexican leaders attempted the first, while at the same time limiting the second. It remains possible, however, that Mexico, too, will feature a market-oriented economy and more democratic politics as the new millennium begins.

"The philosophers have only *interpreted* the world, in various ways," wrote Karl Marx in his eleventh thesis on Feuerbach. "The point, however, is to *change* it."[49] Our technopols would agree. For them, too, the point has been to "change the world" in their respective countries and, they hope, to succeed more than Marx did.

---

49. Karl Marx, "Theses on Feuerbach," in *Marx and Engels: Basic Writings on Politics and Philosophy*, ed. Lewis S. Feuer (Garden City, N.Y.: Anchor Books, 1959), 245; italics in the original.

2

Why Argentines Followed Cavallo

A Technopol Between Democracy and Economic Reform

Javier Corrales

In Europe during the interwar period, the concurrence of overwhelming debt, economic recession, income decline, price instability, and internal strife culminated in the demise of seventeen democracies and the rise of a new class of dictators. In Argentina in the 1990s, similar ills culminated in the rise of Domingo Felipe Cavallo. Dr. Cavallo was not a dictator; he was not even the

In addition to newspaper and archival research, this chapter is based on interviews with more than a hundred Argentine political and economic leaders, including various conversations with Domingo F. Cavallo. Most interviews were conducted during three trips to Buenos Aires (summer

president of Argentina. Yet, he was one of the most powerful—and revolutionary—ministers of the economy that his country had ever seen. His accomplishments, together with his commanding style, have made him one of the most talked-about political figures in the country, at times more so than his former boss, the flamboyant president Carlos S. Menem.

There are indeed some similarities between Cavallo and the European dictators of the 1930s. Like them, Cavallo sees himself as a messiah destined to solve his country's economic calamities once and for all, even if this entails waging a ruthless political battle against the bulwarks of the status quo. But unlike the European dictators, Cavallo conducted this political battle, not by abolishing democratic institutions, but often by engaging them. In stark contrast with his predecessors and even his own boss, who often have attempted to supersede democratic institutions, Cavallo involved the Congress, parties, elected officials, popular sectors, and elites in his unprecedented effort to reform the state. In doing so, Cavallo was at times forced to compromise. But to him, the gains, in terms of consensus and credibility obtained by working with the system, compensate for any loss in dogmatic purity.

During his tenure as minister of the economy (January 31, 1991 to July 26, 1996), Cavallo mastered the art of maneuvering in a democratic polity. In fact, he used democratic institutions to conduct one of Latin America's most unexpected economic about-faces. Cavallo spent considerable time pondering the technical details of his policies. But he devoted equal time to pondering ways to make his ideas politically viable and irreversible. And he has demonstrated—ironically for a man who collaborated with Argentina's military regime—that the most reliable way to ensure irreversibility is to have his policies sanctioned by democratic institutions.

"Successful" Technopolitics

Even by admission of his own detractors, Cavallo was exceptionally successful. A country that throughout most of the 1980s was unable to approve a budget,

1991, summer 1992, and fall 1994). Funding for this research was provided by the National Science Foundation, the Inter-American Dialogue, and the Ford Foundation. I am especially indebted to numerous individuals who facilitated my research in Buenos Aires, including Wenceslao Bunge, Gustavo Ferrari, José Luis Tagliaferri, and Enrique Zuleta. I am also grateful to Richard Feinberg, Merilee Grindle, Deborah Yashar, María Victoria Murillo, Atilio Borón, and the other authors of this volume for their comments and suggestions. All translations from Spanish sources (including interviews) are mine, unless otherwise indicated.

control inflation, collect taxes, impede capital flight, and win the confidence of the international and domestic financial community became a model of economic adjustment under Cavallo. By early 1995, Argentina proclaimed four consecutive years of remarkably stable currency, year-end fiscal surpluses, high economic growth, rapid increase in gross national product per capita, and the lowest inflation since 1969 (lower in fact than that of Germany). And rather than succumb to the 1995 regional crisis created by the December 1994 devaluation of the Mexican peso, Argentina seemed to have weathered the crisis, defying the predictions of many experts. In sum, Argentina under Cavallo went from one of Latin America's most notorious economic "basket cases" to one of the developing world's most respected reformers.

But Cavallo's most impressive successes occurred on the political front. First, there was his own survival in office (and hence that of his policies)— longer than any of his predecessors since the 1970s. This is all the more remarkable given the enormous pressures for Cavallo's departure since his first day in office: during uncertain times (early 1991), when most Argentines doubted his ability to tame the country's finances, during good times (late 1991–94), when resurgent populist forces questioned the need for further austerity, and during bad times (1995), when many Argentines blamed Cavallo's inflexibility for the country's recession.

But his most important political accomplishment was the homogenization of economic thinking in Argentina. Before 1989, Argentines were deeply divided between advocates of statism (the stronger and more vocal majority) and those of free markets (a weaker and less self-persuaded minority).[1] Today, a consensus exists in Argentina, even among the left, that Cavallo's harsher version of economics—free convertibility, free trade, privatized public services, simplified tax systems, fiscal austerity—ought to be indelible features of the new Argentina. Even some of the most successful government opponents (e.g., Chacho Álvarez) have stated that they would gladly incorporate numerous Cavallo policies and "Cavallo boys" in their governments.[2] In short, Cavallo in the 1990s was the bridge that brought to Argentina the 1980s international consensus in favor of economic liberalization.

To be sure, Cavallo is not the first minister of the economy to promise glory for Argentina, or the first to advocate market liberalization as the means to that end. But he is no doubt the one who reached the farthest. Even compared

1. See Edgardo Catterberg, *Los argentinos frente a la política: Cultura política y opinión pública en la transición argentina a la democracia* (Buenos Aires: Editorial Planeta, 1989).
2. *Noticias,* 10 July 1994, 60–65.

to the accomplishments of the man once considered a miracle maker, José Martínez de Hoz, Argentina's minister of the economy (1976–81) during part of the military dictatorship, Cavallo's record is far more impressive. Economically, Martínez de Hoz never fully controlled inflation, balanced the budget, or privatized key state-owned enterprises (SOEs), all goals of his program. And politically, he never really persuaded the public—and his military bosses—of the wisdom of his ideas. Cavallo, on the other hand, did everything that Martínez de Hoz failed to do and much more—all in a democratic setting. The question is, therefore, why did a country that was a textbook case of monetary chaos and reform resistance attain stability with growth under Cavallo?

This chapter explores the origins of, and reasons for, the "Cavallo surprise." It provides an alternative to the two most commonly accepted explanations for Argentina's turnaround. The first is that this occurred because Argentina finally hit bottom in 1989. Based on the idea that economic crises create the conditions for reform implementation,[3] some argue that Argentina's two hyperinflations (1989 and 1990) were sufficient to demolish opposition to reform. A second explanation attributes the turnaround to the executive's concentration of power, what Carlos Acuña calls the "Hobbesian strategy," and Guillermo O'Donnell, "delegative democracy."[4] This chapter argues, on the other hand, that before Cavallo, despite two severe hyperinflations and extensive use of decrees,[5] Argentina's reform process remained precarious, at best. In fact, before Cavallo, the willingness of economic and political actors to cooperate with the reforms was remarkably absent, short-lived, or increasingly thin. Policy reversal, muddling through, and even regime breakdown (such as in Peru in 1992 and Russia in 1993) were plausible scenarios for Argentina before Cavallo.

Cavallo's success in avoiding these scenarios is reason to consider him a "successful technopol."[6] It is clear that Cavallo epitomized the qualities of a

3. See, for example, Allan Drazen and Vittorio Grilli, "The Benefit of Crises for Economic Reforms," *American Economic Review* 83, no. 3 (1993).

4. Carlos H. Acuña, "Politics and Economics in the Argentina of the Nineties (or Why the Future No Longer Is What It Used to Be)," in *Democracy, Markets, and Structural Reform in Latin America: Argentina, Bolivia, Brazil, Chile, and Mexico,* ed. William C. Smith et al. (New Brunswick, N.J.: North-South Center/Transaction, 1994). Guillermo O'Donnell, "Delegative Democracy," working paper no. 172, Helen Kellogg Institute for International Studies, Notre Dame, Ind., 1992.

5. For a discussion of the use and abuse of decrees by the Menem administration, see Delia Ferreira Rubio and Matteo Goretti, "Gobierno por decreto en Argentina (1989–1993)," *El Derecho* (Universidad Católica Argentina) 32, no. 8525 (1994).

6. This is not a normative judgment, that is, an evaluation of the moral desirability of the changes introduced by Cavallo. It is not a judgment on the economic soundness of the changes that he has introduced either. It is instead an empirical observation of economic "governance," defined

technopol as described by Domínguez—a highly trained, cosmopolitan social scientist engaged in the "reshaping" of politics. However, not all technopols succeed at reshaping politics the way Cavallo has (see Chapter 5). In this chapter I argue that an important "independent variable" of successful technopolitics is the concept of "linked independence": a situation in which the reformer is neither fully autonomous nor fully representative of the societal sectors that are targeted for reforms. This accords the technopol some degree of independence and simultaneously some degree of trust from targeted sectors. In this chapter I explain this concept and apply it to the Cavallo case.

In addition to linked independence, a second feature of Cavallo's politics was to engage democratic institutions, especially Congress, in the task of economic reforms. In and of itself, this does not make Cavallo a "democratic technopol," in the strict terms proposed by Domínguez. In fact, Cavallo's adherence to democratic practice has been far from absolute. Nonetheless, the extent to which Cavallo has engaged democratic institutions in the process of implementing far-reaching reforms is unprecedented in Argentina as well as in the region. It was also an important reason for Cavallo's success in transforming the economy.

After a brief account of Cavallo's economic thinking and political career, this chapter presents a discussion of his performance as a member of Menem's cabinet, first as foreign minister (July 1989–January 1991), then as minister of the economy (February 1991–July 1996). Various aspects of Cavallo's economic reforms are then treated—the components of the package, the reasons for their success, and some problem areas. The chapter concludes with an assessment of how Cavallo may have transformed Argentina's politics and the stress points of his reforms.

The Making of a Mind (and a Career)

From Córdoba to Harvard

Unlike most contemporary political elites in Argentina, Cavallo was not yet available for political socialization during Argentina's first Peronist period. Cavallo was born in 1946, the same year in which Juan Domingo Perón, the founder of the movement that Cavallo would later help to transform, was first elected head of state. Also unlike one third of his compatriots, Cavallo was

---

as the capacity of state leaders to accomplish their self-declared goals.

born in a province of the interior (Córdoba) rather than in greater Buenos Aires. But it is precisely this detachment from two of Argentina's strongest political forces—Peronism and life in the capital—that explains, to a large extent, Cavallo's eventual embrace of liberal economics. As Cavallo likes to put it, "It is in the provinces, away from Buenos Aires, where one most easily noticed the pernicious effects of an overexpanded, rent-granting and arbitrary economic system."[7]

Cavallo's rejection of statism occurred therefore early on. But it was at Harvard University during the 1970s that Cavallo formalized this dissent. Studying with economists such as Martin Feldstein, Benjamin Friedman, and Stanley Fisher, Cavallo devoted himself to the study of Argentina's "persistent inflation." What made this inflation so intractable, Cavallo argued, was the fiscal irresponsibility of Argentina's leaders. Their eagerness to intervene in the economy at any cost, what Cavallo calls "exaggerated political voluntarism," clearly went far beyond what any serious Prebischist economist would recommend.[8] Such practice was based on unsound economic principles and, most important, on an illusion of state grandeur long out of touch with Argentina's reality. Fighting inflation, thus, required defeating this pathologically outmoded mentality.

However, in his 1977 doctoral dissertation, Cavallo advanced a serious indictment of monetarism, the economic doctrine in vogue among the military rulers of the Southern Cone at that time. Cavallo predicted—accurately—that monetarist stabilization programs would fail because they were radically at odds with the logic of private enterprise: by severely curtailing working capital, monetarist contraction kills the only engine of inflation-free growth while disregarding the real source of inflation—fiscal undiscipline. Cavallo would continue to criticize monetarism throughout his writing, distancing himself from the economic experiments in Argentina of the late 1970s.

Cavallo was thus not a pure neoliberal. Although a strong advocate of market economics, he was never a believer in the invisible state. Instead he believed in the specialized state: modest enough to engage exclusively in whatever it does best, but strong enough to excel in those tasks. Rather than be reduced, the state must be submitted to a rigorous fitness program: it must shed its unnecessary fat (through privatizations, spending control, operational streamlining, deregulation), but also grow muscle (new bureaucracies, new regulations, fiercer taxation).

7. Domingo F. Cavallo, interview by author.
8. Domingo F. Cavallo, *Volver a crecer* (Buenos Aires: Editorial Planeta, 1991), 32.

What must the state be made fit to do? Cavallo clearly shares the neoliberal conception of the state as a greenhouse: rather than choose which plants to grow, the state should simply provide the right lighting, temperature, and humidity to foster the healthy growth of the private economy. Rather than a structural transformation, this requires an institutional revolution: "Argentina needs an integral reformulation of its economic institutions. . . . This means a more . . . competitive private sector with less casuistic intervention from the state, that makes its own decisions with responsibility, and that receives the rewards and suffers the punishments of its wrongful decisions."[9] Economic governance is thus about building institutions that foster the rational functioning of the markets. This is only possible insofar as institutions are stable, transparent, and nonarbitrary.

Cavallo was also contemptuous of those who attributed Argentina's problems to international vulnerability. For Cavallo, *dependencistas* were mere scapegoaters. He coauthored *La Argentina que pudo ser* to argue that Argentina's economic decline in the twentieth century had internal, rather than external, sources. Phenomena like declining terms of trade, a favorite culprit of *dependencistas,* ought to have been an incentive for export expansion and diversification, as was the case among the Asian Tigers.[10] The greenhouse state must make creative use of external light, not block it out.

But Cavallo has also always believed in the "paramedical" state. The act of growing should not be left unassisted: whenever crucial institutions come under stress, the state should be prepared to restore order. An interventionist state is not a neoliberal concept or a particular novelty in Argentina. But what Cavallo advocated—and herein lies his distinctiveness—is that this assistance be neither arbitrary nor preferential. The state should be ready to restore health, without providing a licentious insurance protecting reckless economic behavior (i.e., "moral hazard," in economic jargon).

Few state builders have succeeded in creating the highly complex state envisioned by Cavallo. One might even argue that this greenhouse-paramedic state, which is indiscriminate yet restrained, which requires both downsizing and upsizing, is quixotic and self-contradictory. But Cavallo always disagreed. And ever since he left Harvard, he has been engaged in a lifelong mission to prove his point.

    9. Domingo F. Cavallo, *Economía en tiempos de crisis* (Buenos Aires: Editorial Sudamericana, 1989), 196.
    10. Domingo F. Cavallo, *El desafío federal* (Buenos Aires: Editorial Sudamericana/Planeta, 1986), 159, and idem, *Habla Cavallo: Mensajes de su campaña electoral* (Buenos Aires: Impresiones Gráficas Tavaré, S.A.I.C., 1987), 12.

The Missionary Life

Cavallo was trained to be an academic. But more than teach or do research in the field of economics, Cavallo became an activist of economics, or, more precisely, "Cavallonomics." This sense of intellectual mission was almost religious—a fight against economic heresy. After Harvard, Cavallo eagerly accepted the invitation by a Córdoba businessman to launch an economic think tank under the auspices of the Fundación Mediterránea—the Instituto de Estudios Económicos sobre la Realidad Argentina y Latinoamericana (IEERAL).[11] The IEERAL virtually became Cavallo's religious order—the launch pad for his attacks against the economic status quo. In a matter of years, the IEERAL became one of Argentina's most important research organizations.[12]

Being president of an important think tank allowed Cavallo to recruit a cadre of disciples—young, highly trained and internationally oriented economists. Loyalty to antistatist ideas was a requirement for recruitment; but loyalty to Cavallo was a soon-to-come by-product of recruitment. It is this mixture of faith in both the man and his ideas that is salient about these "Cavallo boys." Later on, these "Cavallo boys" would prove to be among Cavallo's most significant political resources.

Soon after the restoration of democracy in Argentina, Cavallo published his own "catechism," *Volver a crecer,* in which he provides a reader-friendly summary of his thinking. Paraphrasing a colleague, Cavallo argued that the problem in Argentina is the coexistence of "a socialism without plans and a capitalism without markets."[13] Like Machiavelli's *The Prince,* the explicit intention of *Volver a crecer* was to enlighten the republic's new government. Cavallo personally delivered a copy of his book to the newly elected president, Raúl Alfonsín. But the president paid little attention to it.[14] It would not be long before Cavallo's impatience with the government would push him into politics.

Cavallo the Politician

In 1987, Cavallo took the decisive jump into politics when he accepted an invitation from the Córdoba branch of the Peronist Party to run for the National

11. The Fundación Mediterránea was established in 1977 by two immigrant businessmen, Piero Astori and Fulvio Pagani, as a small fund-raising institution committed to support economic research.

12. The Fundación also expanded, opening branches in most of Argentina's major cities and obtaining the support of approximately five hundred business firms.

13. Cavallo, *Volver a crecer,* 26.

14. Cavallo, *Habla Cavallo,* 44.

Congress. The sudden affiliation of IEERAL's president with Peronism came as a brutal shock to both Peronists and Cavallo's friends. Peronism, more than anything else, symbolized the type of economic philosophy that IEERAL sought to discredit. Yet, this political marriage reflected more a nascent internal change within Peronism than a change in Cavallo. As a result of their unexpected 1983 and 1985 electoral defeats, the Peronists split between a more populist wing and a more fiscally conscious democratic wing, the so-called *Renovación*. It was this latter wing that persuaded Cavallo to resign from IEERAL and join the party's ranks. By a narrow majority, Cavallo became a congressman in 1987.

Cavallo the congressman was a somewhat frustrated politician. In Congress he watched Alfonsín's Plan Austral and Plan Primavera decay. These plans collapsed, Cavallo would say, because the government failed to create a political coalition on their behalf. Alfonsín's main saboteurs were of course the Peronists, who thought that Alfonsín was going too far. Cavallo joined these Peronists in criticizing Alfonsín, but only because he thought that Alfonsín was not going far enough.[15]

Cavallo the congressman was also a lonely politician. As a newcomer with rather "foreign" ideas, he was resented by many of his Peronist colleagues. And as an outspoken critic of the government, he obviously shunned the Radicals. Nonetheless, Cavallo's congressional interlude proved to be crucial, since it was there that Cavallo concluded that one of Alfonsín's principal shortcomings was his disregard of Congress: "One of the first things I noticed as a member of Congress is that the budget, the supposed 'law of laws' . . . is handled with very little seriousness. In part, this is due to the legislators' lack of interest, but in large measure, to the lack of respect on the part of the executive power to the role that corresponds to Congress."[16] Cavallo may have been referring to the fact that Alfonsín's minister of the economy since 1985, Juan Sourrouille, seldom visited Congress, even when the Radicals held a majority in the lower chamber. For Cavallo, this disregard of Congress was one main reason that Congress proved so hostile to Alfonsín. And this hostility was not confined to the Peronists: on one of the few occasions that Sourrouille visited Congress, the Radicals joined the Peronists in booing the minister.[17]

15. There are widespread rumors that Cavallo became so disappointed with Alfonsín that he traveled to Washington to lobby officials against extending credits to Argentina, alleging that the government would be unable to meet its obligations. Cavallo has adamantly denied these charges; see Cavallo, *Economía en tiempos de crisis*, 12.

16. Ibid., 176.

17. For a discussion of the Radical Party's response to Alfonsín's economic policies, see

In the 1988 Peronist primaries, the then populist Menem defeated the *Renovación* candidate, Antonio Cafiero. This came as another shock to Cavallo's sympathizers. Nevertheless, Cavallo managed to become a close friend of Menem and accompanied him throughout the presidential campaign, surprising Cavallo's followers once again.[18] The next shock came soon after the May 1989 elections, when Menem unabashedly revealed his market-oriented economic program—in many ways, a carbon copy of Cavallo's ideas. But in this sequence of shocks, the one with the most impact, at least for Cavallo's friends, was Menem's 1989 decision not to appoint Cavallo as minister of the economy.

In making this decision, Menem might have noticed a very dark spot in Cavallo's curriculum vitae: Cavallo had served in the military government, first in 1981 as undersecretary of internal affairs (sixteen days) and after the Falklands War in 1982 as president of the Central Bank (fifty-three days). In Argentina, affiliation with a military regime is seldom an immediate disqualifier, but what was controversial about Cavallo was his policies while in office. Many Argentines, especially prominent neoliberals such as Álvaro Alsogaray,[19] blamed Cavallo for triggering (if not founding) the crisis of the 1980s.[20] Cavallo

---

Marcelo Cavarozzi and María Grossi, "Argentine Parties Under Alfonsín: From Democratic Reinvention to Political Decline and Hyperinflation," in *The New Argentine Democracy: The Search for a Successful Formula*, ed. Edward C. Epstein (Westport, Conn.: Praeger, 1994).

18. In Argentina, it is customary for presidential candidates to campaign with their ministers-to-be. However, the Menem-Cavallo duo was clearly recognized as an odd couple right from the start. A mutual acquaintance once argued that a Cavallo-Menem relationship had no future: after all, Cavallo was not a tennis fan, a womanizer, or a social butterfly. How this friendship came about remains unclear and a matter of comic speculation. Some say that Menem felt impressed by Cavallo's economic competence and his uncanny skills to entice audiences. Others say that Menem was simply impressed by Cavallo's "phenomenal" English. For these and other stories, see Gabriela Cerruti and Sergio Ciancaglini, *El octavo círculo* (Buenos Aires: Editorial Planeta, 1992), and Daniel Santoro, *El hacedor: Una biografía política de Domingo Cavallo* (Buenos Aires: Editorial Planeta, 1994).

19. President of the conservative party Ucedé, Álvaro Alsogaray became Menem's adviser on the foreign debt (1989–early 1991).

20. Specifically, Cavallo was blamed for, first, the "statization" of the private debt. By providing a *seguro cambiario* (i.e., a promise to protect the exchange rate from devaluation), the military government had created incentives for private firms to accumulate liabilities. When the government was forced to devalue (by 30 percent), this private debt became overwhelming. Cavallo inherited this crisis as well as the government's prior commitment to these private debtors. He thus created the conditions for his successor to take over the private debt, burdening the Central Bank with 90 percent of the total foreign debt. Cavallo was also blamed for the *licuación de pasivos*. Appearing on national television, an uncharacteristic move for a Central Bank president, Cavallo announced a major reduction in interest rates intended to alleviate Argentina's internal debt burden. This announcement led to an unexpected dramatic inflationary surge (the

always defended himself against these accusations. He explained that in those days the state had no options and that, unlike other *licuaciones,* his was "generalized" rather than selective (i.e., it benefited every sector rather than just a few). For Cavallo's critics, it was the indiscriminate scope of this *licuación* that was reproachable; for Cavallo, it showed his aversion to *amiguismo*.[21] However, many neoliberals never forgave Cavallo, which may explain Menem's 1989 decision.

Instead, Cavallo was appointed foreign minister, a post traditionally assigned to a jurist.[22] For Cavallo, however, becoming foreign minister was all for the better; after all, he also believed that Argentina's international relations were in desperate need of serious overhauling.

Reintroducing Argentina to the World

Shortly after taking office, Menem announced a major realignment of Argentina's foreign relations. At least since the late nineteenth century, Argentina's foreign policy had consisted in demonstrating independence, if not superiority, vis-à-vis its hemispheric neighbors.[23] Aspiring to be a "Third Force," Argentina's leaders (often regardless of ideology) believed their country to be, if not a regional power, at least a "moral leader" in the Third World.[24] Even Alfonsín espoused these policies and rhetorical positions.[25] Menem was seen as a champion of these views.[26]

---

demand for money skyrocketed as a result of people's expectations that inflation would be higher than the announced interest rates). While a major debt crisis was postponed (the real value of the debt was reduced approximately 40 percent), Cavallo gave Argentina its first taste of a quasi-hyperinflation. See William C. Smith, "State, Market, and Neoliberalism in Post-Transition Argentina: The Menem Experiment," *Journal of Interamerican Studies and World Affairs* 33, no. 4 (1991): 47, and Santoro, *El hacedor,* 144.

21. Cavallo, *Economía en tiempos de crisis,* 126.

22. This appointment was also criticized, prompting Menem to defend it: "[I]t is the logical possibility for today's world. . . . So many more commercial or economic cooperation agreements are written among nations than border treaties." Carlos S. Menem, *Estados Unidos, Argentina y Carlos Menem* (Buenos Aires: Editorial CEYNE, s.r.l., 1990), 31.

23. See, for example, Carlos Escudé, *Realismo periférico: Fundamentos para la nueva política exterior argentina* (Buenos Aires: Editorial Planeta, 1992).

24. The means used to obtain this foreign policy goal have varied, however. In general, military governments have been associated with emphasizing glory and military activism (e.g., supporting the Nicaraguan contras in the 1980s); the Radicals have emphasized a more moral, humanistic, and legalistic discourse; Peronists stressed economic nationalism and nonalignment.

25. Joseph S. Tulchin, *Argentina and the United States: A Conflicted Relationship* (Boston: Twayne Publishers, 1990), 175.

26. For instance, Menem is known to have said: "[W]e should recapture the Malvinas with fire and blood."

Nevertheless, Argentina's international standing was in shambles in 1989. Even the World Bank, whose greater leniency toward Alfonsín had put it at odds with the International Monetary Fund (IMF) in the 1980s, declined to back Alfonsín's last stabilization effort.[27] The hyperinflation that ensued was thus as much a symptom of international discredit as it was of internal disarray.

Once in office, Menem declared that Argentina's policy of "projecting power without power" was absurd. He therefore moved quickly to realign Argentina's foreign relations more closely to the West. But unlike in his economic reforms, Menem was successful in this "foreign relations reform" from day one. It may not be coincidental that Cavallo was the person in charge of this task.

Cavallo was indeed the right man to handle Menem's international public relations—if for no reason than his curriculum vitae. Cavallo, more than most *Menemistas,* epitomized the image that Menem wanted Argentina to project abroad: serious about business, economically competent, fiscally responsible, and internationally linked—everything that Menem himself was not. Indeed, when Cavallo became foreign minister, he was one of the most internationally connected figures in the government, having developed these connections since his days at Harvard. It was there, for instance, that he met and became good friends with Pedro Aspe, Mexico's finance minister under President Salinas de Gortari; Alejandro Foxley, Chile's finance minister under President Aylwin; and Jeffrey Sachs, a Harvard professor of economics and adviser to Russia and other countries, then a classmate of Cavallo.

But what qualified Cavallo the most for this task was his firm belief in Argentina's global integration. Cavallo always criticized Martínez de Hoz for failing to achieve a convergence of international and domestic prices, and Alfonsín for keeping "a greater confinement of the economy" than necessary.[28] If Argentina was ever to escape chronic decline—Cavallo reasoned—it needed to reenter the global community, preferably side by side with the First World.

Cavallo began by focusing on the United States. In less than a year and a half, Cavallo visited the United States at least four times, meeting everyone from high government officials to prominent business leaders, achieving one

---

27. Mario Damill and Roberto Frenkel, "Restauración democrática y política económica: Argentina, 1984–1991," in *La política económica en la transición a la democracia: Lecciones de Argentina, Bolivia, Chile, y Uruguay,* ed. Juan Antonio Morales and Gary McMahon (Santiago: CIEPLAN, 1993), 62.

28. Cavallo, *Economía en tiempos de crisis,* 99.

public relations success after another. He then globalized his effort. He persuaded the IMF to extend credits to Argentina at a time when domestic reforms were precarious, reestablished diplomatic contacts with the United Kingdom, normalized the situation in the South Atlantic, committed Argentina to the Gulf War, further liberalized trade relations with Chile, launched the Mercosur (a customs union with Brazil, Paraguay, and Uruguay), and reined in Argentina's nuclear projects.

For Cavallo, this doctrine of "rejoining, rather than resisting," the West was a matter of principle: "Latin America wants to join the club of economically developed nations. And if you want to become a member of any club, you have to follow the rules of the other members."[29] But seducing the West also brings practical payoffs—not just much needed foreign trade and investment but also an improvement in Argentina's beleaguered international leverage. As one high-ranking World Bank official remarked: "Because of his knowledge of English, his familiarity with the rules, and his international contacts, it is easier and more pleasant for us to deal with Cavallo. But it is also because of these factors, that it can also be difficult to deal with him—Cavallo just knows too much."[30] By staying in touch with his friends, Cavallo stays on top of what other countries are negotiating, and this gave him an edge in international dealings.[31]

In sum, Cavallo's role as foreign minister was to acknowledge the "smallness" of his country, not an easy task for an Argentine. Smallness precludes pretensions of economic independence and autarchy, but it does not preclude economic growth and international leverage. Yet, for these objectives to obtain, smallness calls for international opening and conciliation rather than romantic recalcitrance. Some argue that the smaller states of Europe learned this lesson after World War II, hence their subsequent prosperity.[32] As foreign minister of Argentina, Cavallo's accomplishment was to teach this very same lesson to his fellow citizens.

29. *LatinFinance* 35 (March 1992): 19.

30. Anonymous, interview by author.

31. Cavallo's "internationalism" proved especially useful, for instance, during the regional financial crisis that followed the 1994 Mexican peso crash. Whereas his Mexican counterparts were hard-pressed to assuage the fears of international investors throughout 1995, the more internationally connected Cavallo proved to be a public relations hit on Wall Street, convincing investors of the reliability of Argentina's public finances (even though his economic numbers were not especially supportive).

32. See, for example, Peter J. Katztenstein, *Small States in World Markets* (Ithaca: Cornell University Press, 1985).

Please Come and Help Me

While Cavallo was achieving unprecedented success abroad, Menem faced serious trouble at home. In January 1991, Menem's economic package, and indeed his administration, were in jeopardy. Menem's first three economy ministers could claim many accomplishments (e.g., inflation was reined in at approximately 10 percent per month, key privatizations were carried out, the domestic debt was tamed, foreign reserves reached a record of U.S.$2.8 billion). Yet, these accomplishments were gained through highly restrictive monetary and fiscal policies, which plunged the country into a hyperrecession—as predicted in Cavallo's dissertation. Meanwhile, the prospects of hyperinflation continued to linger. One reason for this was that provincial governors and managers of SOEs continued to extract money from the Treasury. Congress was also less cooperative than anticipated, and thus, the use of decrees was rising (by early 1991, Menem had issued 100 decrees of the approximately 130 decrees since 1858).[33]

Argentina in early 1991 thus continued to be a case of reform noncredibility and societal noncooperation. The public had come to believe—in fact, confidently expect—that the state would never succeed in curtailing inflation. This lack of trust was not a figment of the Argentines' imagination. Rather, it was the result of historical experiences with unfulfilled promises. At the onset of the Austral Plan in 1985, for instance, Alfonsín promised in a public speech that the Central Bank would not print any money to finance the public sector.[34] At first, Argentines believed the president. Inflation declined, and Alfonsín's popularity surged. But the government did not keep its promise. By late 1986, the government was once again printing money.

As a result of this credibility gap, even actors who had gains to realize from a successful reform program were reluctant to cooperate with the government by early 1991. These actors feared "the sucker's payoff"—the possibility that their counterparts would cheat on them.[35]

---

33. Menem's *Decretos de necesidad y urgencia* are technically different from *decree laws*. The latter consist of laws mandated by the executive in the absence of a congress. Menem's authority to make decrees was not only sanctioned by Congress, but can also be reverted by a congressional veto. This veto, however, must be exercised in a matter of days. See Ferreira Rubio and Goretti, "Gobierno por decreto en Argentina."

34. Roque B. Fernández, "What Have Populists Learned from Hyperinflation?" in *The Macroeconomics of Populism in Latin America,* ed. Rudiger Dornbusch and Sebastian Edwards (Chicago: University of Chicago Press, 1991), 122.

35. For a discussion of state-society tensions and their impact on reform governability at this stage, see Javier Corrales, "From Market-Correctors to Market-Creators: Executive–Ruling

Consequently, in January 1991 the austral plummeted almost 27 percent, in part because of well-founded rumors that the government was printing money.[36] Collective panic was fueled by important defections from the government (Álvaro Alsogaray), charges of high-level corruption, and cabinet infighting.[37] The country came close to a third hyperinflation. As one leading economic news magazine observed: "Argentina's history was repeating itself."[38] Menem reshuffled his cabinet and asked Cavallo to assume control of the Ministry of the Economy.[39]

Cavallo's critics were expecting audacity—and they got it. In a matter of months, Cavallo announced one of South America's most extreme financial stabilization programs ever—the Convertibility Law. This congressionally sanctioned law obliges the Central Bank to convert australes freely into dollars at a fixed rate of 10,000 australes to a dollar.[40] The law also ended contract indexation, historically a principal culprit of inflationary inertia in Argentina, and it prohibited the Central Bank from printing money to cover deficits unless new currency issues were backed by gold or foreign reserves. From then on, the government would have to seek approval from Congress to change the value of the currency or print more money.

The law was a stunning and immediate success. Inflation plummeted from a 27 percent monthly rate in February to less than 1 percent a few months later. For the first time in generations, Argentina experienced macroeconomic stability. Cavallo's political stature and popularity surged, and the country experienced an economic boom that continued until 1994. Why did this plan, unlike many others in the past, succeed in placating exchange rate volatility in Argentina?[41]

Party Relations in the Economic Reforms of Argentina and Venezuela, 1989–1993" (Ph.D. diss., Harvard University, 1996).

36. The Economist Intelligence Unit, *Argentina Country Profile, 1992–93*, 10.

37. In particular, the government was beset by the "Swiftgate" scandal: the U.S. ambassador, Terrence Todman, accused officials in the executive office of demanding kickbacks from U.S. firms seeking to participate in the privatizations. Menem and many of his advisers were tempted to respond in a hostile manner. Ultimately, Cavallo succeeded in placating Menem's anger and diffusing the tension between the two governments.

38. *Carta Económica* 8, no. 91 (1991).

39. Cavallo was not yet a "popular" cabinet figure: fewer than 25 percent of the public had a positive image of him.

40. In 1992 the name of the currency was changed back to "peso," equivalent to 10,000 australes.

41. For instance, Menem's second minister of the economy, Néstor Rapanelli, attempted to uphold a fixed exchange rate regime—to no avail.

El Problema es Político

Using Democratic Institutions to Deliver Stability

In designing the Convertibility Law, Cavallo was aware of the limits of technical ingenuity. As a student of the history of Argentina's inflation, he knew that almost every stabilization idea had been attempted (more than twenty packages since 1980). He also knew that stabilization packages generally entail a common set of measures (a visit to the World Bank Bookstore is sufficient to get an idea of the necessary recipe). Cavallo, therefore, knew that previous failures were not due to technical incompetence, as he remarked while campaigning for Congress in 1987: "If everything is so clear, if the solutions exist, why doesn't the government put them into practice? Is it a technical problem? . . . No, it is not a technical problem. The government, too, has good professionals and they are aware that many of these things that I have conveyed to you could solve the country's problems. *It is a political problem.*"[42] By "political problem," Cavallo probably meant, first, that previous administrations failed to make stabilization packages politically acceptable and, second, that they succumbed to *cortoplacismo,* trading commitment to reform for sectoral support. Rather than poorly conceived, previous plans were poorly backed. More than technical acumen, Cavallo concluded, the solution necessitated political savoir-faire. The ingenuity of the Convertibility Law lies in how faithful it is to this rationale. Specifically, the law's effectiveness stems from (1) its solid organizational grounding, (2) its irrevocable congressional support, and (3) its reliance on a clever bargaining technique.

Conquering the State: The Search for Organizational Grounding

Although Cavallo became minister of the economy in late January 1991, the Convertibility Law was not launched until three months later. Most people assume that Cavallo spent this interlude working on the law; in reality, he was working on capturing the state.

First, he consolidated enormous organizational power by finalizing the merger of the Ministry of Public Works (which was in charge, among other things, of privatizations) with his own ministry. Second, the "Cavallo boys" were brought in. Virtually the entire staff of IEERAL was appointed to key

---

42. Cavallo, *Habla Cavallo,* 42; emphasis added.

positions in the ministry. Some of these "Cavallo boys," such as Joaquín Cottani, who at the time was working at the World Bank, left well-paying jobs to go to work for Cavallo. In less than two months, close to three hundred "Cavallo boys" settled in at the ministry; the personnel, the ideas, and the loyalty of Argentina's key economic bureaucracy were instantly transformed. With a monolithic economic bureaucracy, the probability of policy inconsistencies and internal sabotage, which had proven so detrimental to previous stabilization programs, was reduced.[43]

Seducing Congress (and Peronists): The Search for Seguridad Jurídica

A few days after becoming minister of the economy, Cavallo launched an effort to seduce Congress. Executive-legislative relations were dismal. Peronists controlled the Senate, but not the House. And the Peronists had yet to become true friends of Menem's reforms. Cavallo experienced this sour state of affairs firsthand during his first visit to Congress as minister of the economy. Legislators (especially Peronists) refused to listen and even insulted Cavallo, who was trying to explain his policies. Enraged, Cavallo shouted back: "If you don't like what I am doing, go to the President and ask him to appoint another Minister."[44]

Realizing the futility of these outbursts and the dangers of sour executive-legislative relations, Cavallo returned to Congress with a more conciliatory tone. This time, his package was approved. But Cavallo did more than subdue his temperament. He agreed to allow Congress to scrutinize and approve every step of the reform of the state. Privatizations, which were virtually at the exclusive discretion of the executive, henceforth required Congressional approval. What Menem had worked so hard to obtain, the ability to reform the state by decree, was disposed of by Cavallo in one day. Some pro-reform forces criticized Cavallo's action as "a threat to the whole Menem plan."[45]

What few observers realized then was that Cavallo was trying to obtain what eluded most ministers of the economy in the past—congressional consent for the

---

43. For a description of how stabilization packages throughout the Southern Cone in the late 1970s and early 1980s were undone by policy contradictions, see Vittorio Corbo, Jaime de Melo, and James Tybout, "What Went Wrong with the Recent Reforms in the Southern Cone," *Economic Development and Cultural Change* 34, no. 3 (1986).

44. *Review of the River Plate,* 15 February 1991, 70.

45. Ibid., 28 February 1991, 92.

reforms. The last thing that Cavallo wanted was a repetition of Sourrouille's infamous relations with Congress. He feared that Menem's growing penchant for decrees was bringing just that. Cavallo sensed that the Congress—and the public—were beginning to find these decrees disturbingly excessive.

Cavallo's overture to Congress was more than just an effort to correct the government's image. It was mostly the result of Cavallo's conviction of the political necessity of *seguridad jurídica*—the rule of law. Cavallo opens the second edition of *Volver a crecer* with an explanation of this concept: *"As I have said on repeated occasions, we have to run the economy by laws, and not by decrees or resolutions and memos, as has been done before."*[46] Whether this was a long-standing belief or a recent lesson is unclear, and so is whether "done before" refers to previous presidents or his own boss. But what is unquestionable is that the need to pursue *seguridad jurídica* became a guiding principle for Cavallo as minister of the economy.

For Cavallo, *seguridad jurídica* is worth its risks because it can enhance the credibility of public policy. First, it reduces the chance of congressional sabotage. By approving laws, Congress gets a stake in the reforms and thus an incentive to ensure their success and to minimize criticism during their implementation. Second, *seguridad jurídica* protects the reforms not only from future administrations but, even more important, from Cavallo's own. (After all, Menem's whimsicality, especially during election time, was well known, and 1991 was an electoral year.) Finally, and most important, *seguridad jurídica* makes policies harder to revoke. One significant flaw of presidential decrees is that they are as easy to reverse as they are to enact—all it takes is a presidential announcement. A law, on the other hand, can only be changed by Congress, and this makes policy reversal more arduous and, hence, less likely.

With *seguridad jurídica,* Cavallo was therefore adapting a lesson from economic theories of rational expectations to politics: laws are equivalent to market signals about policy continuity. And signals of continuity, he believed, were the missing ingredient of Argentina's previous economic packages.

The Convertibility Law: Using *Seguridad Jurídica* to Kill Inflation

The Convertibility Law epitomizes—and, some contend, exaggerates—Cavallo's concern for *seguridad jurídica*. By March 1991, foreign reserves were at an all-time high, the deficit was in decline, the ministry was under control, Con-

---

46. Cavallo, *Volver a crecer,* 6.

gress was seduced, and the global community was on Cavallo's side. A young lawyer on Cavallo's team, Horacio Liendo Jr., convinced Cavallo that the time was right for a currency board (pegging the currency to a foreign currency). Cavallo agreed, thereby taking the riskiest gamble of his career.

The Convertibility Law was approved by Congress in less than four days. That this reform-skeptic Congress would approve so swiftly the most classically neo-liberal monetary regime possible had much to do with Cavallo's public relations acumen. To sell the law in Congress, Cavallo's team argued that they were not following IMF recipes but rather Argentina's history, that is, the 1899–1914 period, in which Argentina adhered to the gold standard and experienced growth and stability.[47] The nationalistic flavor of this argument appealed to most legislators. Cavallo also argued that congressional control of the Central Bank was a highly Peronist institutional arrangement because it secured state prevalence over (exchange rate) markets. Peronists loved this argument. Antonio Cafiero, one of the government's most serious challengers inside Peronism and a notorious reform-skeptic, declared: "With these decisions, Domingo Cavallo has restored the prestige and power of the state over markets."[48]

Many economists criticized the Convertibility Law for being—simply put— bad economics: fixing the value of the austral to the dollar was not only wrong (since the chosen value was deemed unrealistic) but also foolish, since no one can really anticipate the future value of a currency, especially in a country as susceptible to international market fluctuations as Argentina. But to most observers, the main problem with the law was that it entailed a precarious risk: by relinquishing control over the exchange rate, the state was not only risking its hard-earned reserves but also denying itself a policy instrument, which, however distorting in the long run, came in handy during short-term crises. Few Argentine economists would have ever pursued such a self-limiting law. Many argued that Cavallo backed himself into a cage and threw the keys away.

But for Cavallo, self-binding was the only antidote to Argentina's credibility deficit. When politicians face uncertainty, that is, the possibility that opponents will undermine their "policies and creations," they normally respond by creating "insulating regulations,"—rules and restrictions that protect public agencies and policies from their potential saboteurs.[49] The uncertainty faced by Cavallo

47. By 1913, Argentina had the sixth largest reserve of gold in the world. The gold standard was suspended one year later, at the outbreak of World War II. See Roberto T. Alemann, *Breve historia de la política económica argentina, 1500–1989* (Buenos Aires: Editorial Claridad, 1990).
48. Quoted in *Ámbito Financiero*, 10 April 1991, 40.
49. Terry Moe, "Political Institutions: The Neglected Side of the Story," *Journal of Law, Economics, and Organization* 6, special issue (1990): 227–28.

was the inflationary expectations and noncooperative proclivities of Argentines, which were threats to exchange rate stability. Cavallo knew that he needed to "insulate" his stability anchor. But he also knew that mere regulations would not do the job. Previous attempts at fixing the exchange rate through regulation (the most recent one in 1989 under Minister Rapanelli) had failed. Cavallo knew that in Argentina mere regulations, in addition to generating economic inefficiencies, were easily disregarded by Argentina's ferocious rent-seekers.

Cavallo's solution to uncertainty was not more regulation, but rather self-binding, a tactic that has long been recognized as perhaps the most effective, albeit risky, means of securing an optimal outcome in a bargaining situation (from the point of view of a bargainer). Thomas C. Schelling illustrates this.[50] He argues, for instance, that if a buyer in a bargaining situation conveys an inability to pay a higher price, the buyer reduces the range of indeterminacy down to the point most favorable to the buyer. The Convertibility Law epitomizes this bargaining trick. It conveys to speculators that the executive is unable to tinker with the exchange rate. Together with the large volume of reserves, the law unambiguously conveys that the government is legally banned from altering the currency's fixed value. In Argentina, there have never been fewer reasons to doubt this than after the law was approved.[51]

Few politicians would be so willing to bind themselves this tightly. But the IMF has recommended Argentina's currency board to other nations. Estonia decided to take the advice: in 1992, it pegged the kroon to the deutsche mark and banned the Central Bank from printing money.[52] Not unlike Argentina

50. Thomas C. Schelling, *The Strategy of Conflict* (Cambridge: Harvard University Press, 1980), 24.

51. In resorting to Congress to bind the government, Cavallo was making a double bet. First, he was counting on the notion that parliaments are less likely than other state institutions to alter policy (in this case, the fixed exchange rate) once implemented. In some ways, he was right: for legislators to change policy, they must overcome collective-action problems. However, these collective-action problems are not insurmountable. In Argentina, if Peronist legislators ever decide to change the exchange rate, a change in the Convertibility Law is likely. This would undermine Cavallo's self-binding policy and the expectations of stability that the law has generated. Thus, Cavallo's second bet in resorting to Congress to stabilize the exchange rate was that the Peronist Party would cooperate (i.e., refuse to tinker with the fixed exchange rate). Thus far, this cooperation has endured. In short, the success of the Convertibility Law has had two sources in addition to Cavallo's ingenuity: an institutional factor (the lesser probability of congresses to change policy, compared to that of other state institutions) and a political factor (the cooperation of Peronist legislators). For a discussion of the latter factor, see Corrales, "From Market-Correctors to Market-Creators."

52. Peter Restsinki (Commercial and Business Adviser, Embassy of Estonia), interview by author, Washington, D.C., 9 July 1993.

under the Convertibility Law, Estonia went from having a monthly inflation rate of 25 percent to being one of the most stable countries of Eastern Europe. Lithuania (in 1993) and El Salvador (in 1995) established similar regimes.

Cavallo's successes in Congress did not stop with the Convertibility Law: ten major reform-related laws were approved in 1991. Ultimately, it was this set of laws that brought about Argentina's stabilization and opened the way for the rest of the reforms. More than technical finesse, these laws sent an important political message: the Ministry of the Economy and the Congress were finally working together on behalf of Argentina's economic transformation, a sign of executive-legislative economic cooperation unknown in Argentina since the mid 1970s.

The Rest of the Package: Erecting a New State

With inflationary expectations successfully defeated, Cavallo embarked on his downsizing-upsizing reform of the state. On the downsizing side, Cavallo set serious brakes on state spending, launched a fierce attack against provincial squandering (one of the largest drains of the state),[53] and in October 1991 introduced a sweeping deregulatory measure (Decree 2284) aimed at simplifying Argentina's byzantine system of regulations.

In trimming the state, Cavallo had to resist enormous societal pressures. Pensioners were one source of pressure. From 1982 to 1990, pensioners lost 50 percent of their purchasing power. They were one of the sectors most adversely affected by the 1989 freeze in state spending. In late 1991, a group of angry pensioners unexpectedly barged into Congress, where Cavallo happened to be present. The pensioners confronted the minister with their plight and made him cry. Despite his tears and the television cameras, Cavallo responded with his typical resoluteness: he begged for patience and explained that meeting their demands would bring back inflation. The pensioners retreated, and Cavallo continued to say no to social demands.

Nothing reflects Cavallo's obsession with a lean state more than his privatizations. Cavallo not only expanded Menem's original number of firms to be privatized (Table 2.1) but even dared to touch Argentina's sacred cows—the oil

---

53. What is ironic about this attack on the provinces is not just that Cavallo comes from a province but that he had been considered until then a champion of provincial rights. In *El desafío federal,* he argues that part of Argentina's economic calamity stems from the gigantism of Buenos Aires, which absorbs and distorts most of the country's resources. In retrospect, Cavallo explained that this critique of centralism never meant condoning provincial abuse (interview by author).

Table 2.1   Number of Enterprises Privatized

	1990	1991	1992	1993	1994	1995
Argentina	6	13	30	34	34	4
Bolivia	0	0	6	19	0	19[a]
Brazil	0	5	15	6	12	5
Chile	4	2	0	0	5	1
Colombia	7	10	4	3	4	0
Ecuador	0	0	0	0	8	2
Mexico	90	70	28	21	12	0
Panama	1	1	2	3	1	0
Peru	0	2	10	15	26	30[b]

SOURCE: Economic Commission for Latin America and the Caribbean, *Preliminary Overview of the Latin American and Caribbean Economy, 1995* (Santiago: United Nations, December 1995).
[a] Includes privatizations and capitalizations.
[b] Includes leasing and concessions.

company (Yacimientos Petrolíferos Fiscales, or YPF) and the pension system. In privatizing YPF, Cavallo did more than vaporize a traditional symbol of Peronist glory (the nationalization of the oil sector was one of Perón's best-known legacies). He also showed that, for him, privatizations are more than just a practical response to fiscal crises. Unlike most privatized companies in the Third World, YPF was not losing money at the time of its privatization: Cavallo had turned YPF's U.S.$576 million deficit in 1990 into a U.S.$747 million profit in 1993.[54] Moreover, at the time of YPF's privatization, the economy was in "good" shape. Numerous Radicals and Peronists were opposed to this "less necessary" privatization. Cavallo thus could have saved himself a lot of trouble by yielding. But Cavallo chose to fight because, for him, privatizations are more than just a solution to fiscal drains—they are the right thing to do, not because the state is incapable of running a business (he showed that the state too could manage YPF well), but because the state should not be running businesses.

It is wrong, however, to think that Cavallo just shrank the state; in some areas, he enlarged it. For instance, he criticized Menem's first privatizations for lacking a prior regulatory framework and made sure that his privatizations were accompanied by new regulations, with expanded congressional participation and new public regulation-enforcing bureaucracies. Moreover, Cavallo launched one of South America's most far-reaching efforts to raise revenues. His first act as minister of the economy was to raise the value-added tax

54. *New York Times,* 28 June 1993, D1; *U.S./Latin Trade,* October 1995.

(VAT). And during bad times (1995), Cavallo's response has not been to lower the VAT rate (as supply-siders would recommend) but to increase it. Cavallo has focused on the VAT not because he is enamored with its technical merits but because it is easy to enforce and does the job of fortifying the state. Cavallo has also created one of the most competent tax bureaucracies in Argentina's history. By early 1996, tax collection in Argentina was approximately 21 percent of GDP (up from 15 percent in 1989–92).

In creating a stronger and more fiscally sound state, Cavallo outdid most of his neoconservative predecessors. But by insisting on taxes, new regulations, and new bureaucracies, he distanced himself from the Reagan-Thatcher supply-side view of economics that many detractors attribute to him.

After Stability, Then What?

The Problem of Keeping the Pax Cavallo

The return of economic good times (late 1991–94) did not mean a return to economic confidence. Insecurity about the fate of the program spread even as macroeconomic indicators were rising. By mid 1992, most experts expected the package to "explode" at any time.[55]

The problem was that stability became its own enemy by paradoxically becoming the source of new instability, for at least two reasons. First, while the end of inflation is initially welcomed by the public, in countries with long-standing inflationary histories, stability generates the impression of economic loss in the medium term. With stability, citizens gain purchasing power but simultaneously lose the illusion of rapid social improvement. During inflation, wage earners may be willing to accept a "bad" salary today because they hope to negotiate a better one in the next round. But stability freezes the status quo, and this can generate discontent. And in Argentina, discontent was more prevalent because inflation did not disappear completely (average retail-price annualized inflation was around 20 percent in mid-1992), creating a deterioration in real wages.[56]

---

55. There were numerous signs of uncertainty. For instance, in the Buenos Aires congressional elections of June 1992, the Radical candidate, Fernando de la Rúa, defeated the Cavallo-supported Peronist candidate. Shortly thereafter, the stock exchange began a 40 percent precipitous decline.

56. In some sectors (e.g., real estate, entertainment) inflation continued to be substantial.

Second, the more progress the government made in stabilizing the country, the harder it was to convince the public to continue to make sacrifices. Once the country was perceived as "normal again," economic groups found it harder to understand the need for austerity. Consequently, sectoral claims and challenges to Cavallo resurfaced with a vengeance in mid-1992. Cavallo confronted a serious dilemma: the more his reforms worked, the more difficult it was to convey that a state of emergency persisted, and hence, the harder it became to justify Cavallo's adamant "no" to social pressures.

All this explains why the task of imposing stability is trivial compared to the task of preserving it. That is one reason that most stabilization packages collapse, not in the beginning, but halfway into their implementation. Argentina in 1992 faced the same risk. This is how Cavallo avoided it.

The Triangular Campaign

To fight what he called the "volatile emotivity index" of Argentines, Cavallo mounted a far-reaching public relations campaign that targeted three sectors: (1) the elites (intellectual, political, and business leaders), (2) the public at large, and (3) the Peronist rank and file. The strategy consisted in entrusting each targeted sector to a different part of the government. He and his boys took charge of the country's elite. More than is customary for economy ministers, Cavallo participated in public forums explaining his projects. Cavallo thrives on public debates, an activity for which his pedagogical skills serve him well. Cavallo also enjoys public appearances, especially television and radio talk shows (to which he often calls in if he happens to have a strong opinion about the discussion in progress).

But Cavallo is aware of his limitations: his sophisticated discourse is intelligible to the elites (including the opposition elites), but it may appear esoteric to the masses—at least, that is what Cavallo thinks. He thus relied on Menem to do the job of talking to the masses.[57] Cavallo explained: "In the area of communication, Menem and I fulfill complementary roles; I reach certain specific sectors, whereas Menem reaches the public at large."[58] And indeed, Menem, unlike Alfonsín with Sourrouille, has remained an ardent propagandist of the economic plan of his minister. Cavallo therefore appre-

---

57. Cavallo admits to relying on another person—Sonia, his wife. "She is my wire to earth; she transmits to me the comments of the taxi driver, the butcher, and the tailor. Ultimately she represents me in different meetings, and besides, before making any speech, I let her read it" (*Noticias,* 2 August 1992, 71).

58. Domingo F. Cavallo, interview by author.

ciated the utility of a populist-appealing president in a structural reform program.

Finally, there remained the task of converting the Peronists. The relationship between Cavallo and the ruling party has been complicated. Politicians and *técnicos* in general tend to mistrust each other. Peronists, in particular, never got along with market-oriented *técnicos*. Cavallo, however, managed to establish a working relationship with the party throughout most of his tenure. He attempted to portray himself as a friend of Peronism, especially its electoral goals. He also made significant overtures to the party: congressional participation in policy making, Peronist access to public funds, consent to the nonliberalization of labor laws, and so forth. Nevertheless, the relationship between Cavallo and the party was always rocky. Cavallo implemented reforms that went far beyond what even the most pro-reform Peronists had ever intended, often directly hurting the party's natural constituency. And Cavallo was often impatient with Peronists and dismissive of many of their proposals.

Aware of these limitations, Cavallo relied on a number of old-time Peronists to conduct his relationship with the party (e.g., Minister of Labor Rodolfo A. Díaz, another intellectual-turned-politician, mounted a massive campaign within the party on behalf of the economic program). More important, in mid-1992 Cavallo established the Secretaría de Relaciones Institucionales, a branch within the Ministry of Economy entrusted with conducting Cavallo's political relations. The Secretaría's staff consist of well-respected Peronists—thus they have the credentials to talk to Peronist legislators. The staff are also career politicians rather than economists—thus they are more comfortable compromising than Cavallo is.

Cavallo's triangular campaign, especially his Secretaría, seemed to have worked. Peronist endorsement of the reforms, including support from the labor unions, became surprisingly high.[59] Labor strikes declined after 1991 (Table 2.2). After meeting with the head of the Secretaría (Guillermo Seita) at a moment of state-labor tensions (October 1992), a leader of the General Confederation of Labor (Confederación General de Trabajo, or CGT), Oscar Lescano, argued that "the Ministry of the Economy treats us better than the Ministry of Labor."[60] With this triangular campaign, the Peronist party overcame one of its primary historical predicaments: although enjoying a

---

59. Díaz points out that the eventual acquiescence of Peronist unions exceeded the government's expectations. Díaz explained this: "The Peronist party still enjoys a socializing capacity that few other parties in Argentina possess" (interview by author).

60. *Clarín,* 30 October 1992.

Table 2.2   Annual Labor Conflicts, 1980-1995

Year		Number of Protests
1980		432
1981		378
1982	(Falklands War)	128
1983	(democratic transition)	348
1984		368
1985	(Plan Austral launched)	288
1986		725
1987		764
1988		949
1989	(Menem takes office)	751
1990		864
1991	(Plan Cavallo launched)	581
1992		279
1993		224
1994		250
1995	(recession)	454

SOURCE: Centro de Estudios Unión para la Nueva Mayoría.

large mass following (by virtue of the sheer size of the Peronist working sector), the party had never appealed to every sector of the population. With Menem, the party finally reached almost every popular sector; with Cavallo, the country's elites. Cavallo therefore provided the party's missing link, and he often reminds Peronist leaders of this debt to him. The benefits that this triangular campaign afforded to each of the "angles" of this triangle placed Menem, the party, and Cavallo in a situation of mutual dependence, which explains why this otherwise incompatible trio stayed together longer than most experts ever imagined.

Keeping Up with Congress

Cavallo's quest for laws required enormous lobbying. Always a skillful pedagogue, Cavallo was well suited for this task. But lobbying also required tact and diplomacy. Cavallo's abrasive personality was a liability here. Aware of this, Cavallo sought help in his lobbying efforts. Initially he relied on some Peronist friends he made while in Congress (e.g., José Luis Manzano), but soon discovered that this was also an uncertain arrangement.[61]

61. For instance, Manzano quit Congress to become minister of the interior in 1992 and later quit the government amid accusations of corruption.

Cavallo's response was to delegate relations with Congress to the Secretaría. From little details, such as halving the ministry's response time to congressional petitions, to more onerous ones, such as actively lobbying Congress, the Secretaría shares much of the credit for Cavallo's congressional triumphs.

Another response has been to mobilize specific interest groups in order to pressure Congress. Cavallo's 1992 agreement with the provinces is an example. Then, Cavallo faced two problems: Congress was reluctant to approve some laws, and the provinces were reluctant to share some economic burdens. Cavallo's solution was to launch negotiations with the provinces regarding the budget issue, but linking them to the impasse in Congress. The final agreement, although closer to the original demands of the governors, committed them to assume more responsibility for health and education expenses and to pressure their respective congressional deputies to support the stalled projects in Congress. This was a double victory for Cavallo.

Despite these successes, it should be clear that Cavallo-Congress relations were often stormy. In part, this was the result of Cavallo's explosive personality. In part, it was also due to the fact that legislators (especially Peronists) love to show their constituents that they can pick a fight with the Superminister. Albeit grudgingly, Cavallo learned to accept these fights as the necessary transaction costs of reforming the economy.

The Reform of the Private Sector

One of Cavallo's major problems since 1991 has been that the economy did not grow as he had hoped. Cavallo knew that the economic boom of the first year and a half of the program was "artificial," stemming from the impressive return of capital and an overexpanded domestic demand.[62] Yet, growth of internationally competitive sectors was not forthcoming. Cavallo realized that Argentina's only hope was a surge in productivity, which was only possible through heightened private-sector competition. Consequently, the centerpiece of Cavallo's private-sector reforms was to introduce intensive market forces. But in a highly rent-seeking country, inducing the private sector to compete is not easy.

Before Cavallo, Argentine governments attempted to promote private-sector competition through "industrial policies," which were invariably captured by the already-well-off and the incorrigibly inefficient entrepreneurs.

---

62. Having seen its purchasing power restored as a result of stability, the public began to purchase high-priced commodities.

Table 2.3 Cavallo's Numbers

	1989	1990	1991*	1992	1993	1994	1995[a]
GNP growth (%)	-6.2	-0.1	8.9	8.7	6.1	7.4	-2.5
Consumer price variation (annual)	4,923.3	1,343.9	84.0	17.6	7.7	3.9	1.8[b]
Urban unemployment	7.6	7.5	6.5	7.0	9.6	11.5	18.6
Average real wages (1990 = 100)[c]	95.5	100.0	101.3	102.7	101.0	102.0	100.9
Public-sector surplus (% of GNP)[d]	-3.2	-3.8	-1.6	-0.1	-0.1	-0.1	-0.4
Disbursed external debt (U.S.$Billions)	63.3	61.0	63.7	65.0	74.5	82.0	84.0
Disbursed external debt (% of exports)[e]	538	412	443	439	473	439	346

SOURCE: Economic Commission for Latin America and the Caribbean, Preliminary Overview of the Latin American and Caribbean Economy, 1995 (Santiago: United Nations, December 1995).

[a] Preliminary estimates, subject to revision.
[b] Corresponds to variation from November 1994 to November 1995.
[c] Average total wages in manufacturing.
[d] National nonfinancial public sector (does not include provinces and municipalities).
[e] Includes exports of goods and services.
* Cavallo assumes Economy.

Cavallo has sought instead to rely on implementing a constraining institutional framework. This tactic has consisted in foreclosing the various channels through which the private sector managed to escape adjustment in the past: (1) pressuring for exchange rate manipulation, (2) seizing public spending, and (3) capturing the regulatory process. With the Convertibility Law and the freeze on state spending, Cavallo managed to foreclose the first two escape avenues. He has been less successful, though more than his predecessors, in foreclosing the last avenue.[63]

Cavallo believed that most Argentine firms had the capacity to adjust if forced to do so. He tried to confront the private sector with a sink-or-swim choice, gambling, of course, that many firms were capable of choosing the latter. At one level, these institutional pressures worked: for the first time ever, Argentina experienced price wars, a surge in productivity (4 percent per year), specialization in some sectors, and a reduction in major structural components of the "Argentina cost" (e.g., financial-sector costs were halved between 1991 and 1993).[64]

Yet, the trade deficit that surfaced in 1992, reversing an eleven-year record of trade surpluses, has yet to subside. Exports expanded dramatically, but not as fast as imports. At first, the government blamed the 1990–91 world recession. Then it blamed Brazil, which up until late 1994 violated its Mercosur macroeconomic obligations, placing Brazilian exporters at an advantage vis-à-vis Argentina. But Brazil did not deserve all of the blame; the trade deficit with the United States was always larger.

In addition to placing pressure on public finances, these deficits also raised political pressures. As a coeditor of a major industrial magazine put it: "This massive influx of imports is forcing many firms to close down; the shrinking of the private sector is more impressive than that of the public sector."[65] The cries for help from many of these firms became too compelling.

Perhaps remembering that inflexibility in similar circumstances proved fatal for Martínez de Hoz, Cavallo relaxed his open-door policy in October 1992: he announced (again on national television) the restitution of a tax credit to the exporting private sector.[66] Critics contended that this was a de facto devaluation and hence a renouncement of the plan. Cavallo replied that

63. Javier Villanueva (Instituto di Tella), interview by author.

64. *Latin America Weekly Report,* 4 February 1993, 60.

65. Luis Leibas, interview by author.

66. This consisted of a rebate of the 18 percent value-added tax and all other taxes related to exports. This rebate is a common European practice and was permissible under the rules of the General Agreement on Tariffs and Trade (GATT).

because there was now greater competition, the effects of the tax relief were neither a devaluation nor a subsidy, but rather a reward for performance. Cavallo also slowed down trade liberalization in the auto parts industries and in 1994 imposed some restrictions on trade with Brazil.

Thus, Cavallo showed that he too was willing to intervene in the economy and to fine-tune his policies according to political circumstances. This has paid off. While the trade imbalance remains unresolved, Cavallo generated an expansion of productivity and exports. But more important, he left the industrial sector in relative peace, even though this sector was subjected to the most intensive economic opening since the 1930s.

Cavallopolitics

Cavallo has meant for Argentina more than economic miracles. Politics under Cavallo have acquired new and colorful dimensions. Cavallo had a tumultuous but nonetheless straightforward relation with the popular sector, a hard-line but nonetheless collegial rapport with the private sector, and a not-so-constant but nonetheless high commitment to work with democratic institutions. How did Cavallo, the technopol, manage to achieve these political results? This section argues that three features of a technopol—(1) personality, (2) linked independence, and (3) attitude toward political regime—play a role in determining the success of technopols.

Cavallo and His Personality: The Pitfalls of a Candid Mouth

Cavallo loves to argue, so much, in fact, that he would not let the need to avoid confrontation get in the way of a good debate. Cavallo is always prepared to talk to his opponents, as long as his opponents are equally willing to contend with one of Argentina's most candid mouths. This candor contributed to an image of sincerity never enjoyed by previous ministers. In fact, Cavallo seemed tailor-made for Argentina's politics: his deepest flaw, arrogance, is not a trait that Argentines find repulsive, whereas his trademark, sincerity, is one that they welcome as a refreshing anomaly.

But often, this candor got Cavallo into trouble. Cavallo simply does not react well to criticism and dissent. The skillful politician, the magical diplomat, the masterful negotiator, was also capable, paradoxically, of the most startling acts of tactlessness. For instance, responding to heightened social demands, Cavallo is rumored to have uttered: "If they want bread, they should go to a bakery." In late 1992, responding to criticism arising from revelations that his salary was supplemented by close to $8,000 per month in wages from the Fundación, Cavallo said: "Do you think that living where I live, sending my kids to the Colegio San Andrés, and with all the meetings I hold at home, that I can live on less than $10,000?"[67] This comment was made three days before the scheduled CGT general strike demanding a raise in the minimum wage to $530 per month. In October 1994, he told some (female) fellows of the state-funded science research institute (Consejo Nacional de Investigaciones Científicas y Técnicas, or CONICET) to quit their jobs and "go wash dishes." He has also accused members of the press of using a "Nazi-like system of propaganda," and some judges of being accomplices in the "lawsuit industry racket."

For the press (and Cavallo's critics), statements like these were a feast; for the government, an embarrassment. At times, Cavallo had to be "coached" by his advisers and boss before making public statements. The minicrises that Cavallo's tongue sometimes engendered, however, have yet to teach him the importance of being a diplomat even when he is not around diplomats. For the most part, he continues to criticize his political opponents, and democratic politics in general, for putting a premium on demagoguery. By 1996, when almost every sector of civil society had been the target of the minister's invectives, tolerance for his linguistic and personality excesses dramatically declined.[68]

Cavallo and the Business Sector: The Benefits of "Linked Independence"

Like few other Argentine ministers of the economy, Cavallo managed to introduce impressive pressures on the private sector. To be sure, he was not inflexible (e.g., the October 1992 export tax relief). Moreover, Cavallo's economic program also generated business sweets such as an immediate economic boom, a reduction in the risks of and barriers to domestic participation in privatizations, and some serious efforts at reducing labor costs. These initiatives no doubt earned Cavallo many allies within the private sector.

Nonetheless, Cavallo's attack against corporate subsidies, tax evasion, inefficiency, rent seeking, and protectionism has had no match in Argentina's history. And his liberalization policies, despite their recent relaxations,

67. *La Nación,* 8 November 1992, 28.

68. Cavallo is not oblivious to this. When asked by a reporter about the possibility of running for president in 1999, Cavallo responded: "According to what one reads in newspapers, Argentines will be pretty fed up with my personality by then" (quoted in *Clarín,* 16 October 1994, 2–3).

hurt inefficient industries. Martínez de Hoz, who was even more accommodating to the private sector than Cavallo, was practically unseated by disaffected protectionist business leaders. Yet, business resistance to Cavallo was meek in comparison to that faced by his predecessors and in comparison to the magnitude of Cavallo's reforms.

Political theories on both state reform and democratization would have a hard time explaining this phenomenon. On the one hand, his challenges against business-sector privileges, according to the literature on democratization, are a recipe for instability, since they constitute a dangerous provocation of a sector that is potentially disloyal to democracy. On the other hand, Cavallo's extensive links with the private sector should have precluded him, according to some state-reform theorists, from implementing meaningful private-sector reforms.

The "Cavallo case," therefore, reaffirms the notion that democracies need not be prone to paralysis and that "autonomy" in and of itself need not be a precondition for change. Instead, a precondition for successful technopolitics in democracies may be "linked independence": a situation in which the leader is neither fully divorced from nor fully representative of the societal sectors targeted for reforms.[69] Much of linked independence must be present in the reformer's résumé before assuming office—having a professional background that is respected by the targeted sector is crucial. Coming from an academic setting such as IEERAL, which was not beholden to any particular firm or political party, was ideal. IEERAL often embraced (and made more scientific) many of the complaints that business firms had about the economy (hence its ability to command business's respect). But IEERAL was also relatively independent of business preferences: rather than echo some of the solutions proposed by the business sector (e.g., free exchange rate with trade protection), IEERAL often advocated policies that contradicted even the preferences of its benefactors. Had Cavallo come from a specific business firm rather than a business-respected but still independent organization, he would have been more susceptible to accusations by business groups of favoring "his own firm." Likewise, "his own firm" would have felt that it "owned" the minister

---

69. Equivalent concepts, but ones that are applied to states rather than individuals, are "embedded autonomy," proposed by Peter Evans, *Embedded Autonomy: States and Industrial Transformation* (Princeton: Princeton University Press, 1995), and the "state-in-society" approach, developed in Joel S. Migdal, Atul Kohli, and Vivienne Shue, eds., *State Power and Social Forces: Domination and Transformation in the Third World* (New York: Cambridge University Press, 1994).

and, hence, was justified in dictating his policies. This was the problem that ultimately overwhelmed Rapanelli but that Cavallo eluded.[70]

Another source of linked independence might be future career plans. A technopol who is interested in a future career within the business sector might be reluctant to pursue business-hurting reforms in fear of closing future career opportunities. Cavallo, on the other hand, repeatedly claimed that he had no intention to pursue a business career after leaving office; instead, he would be "perfectly fulfilled" by returning to research. Because Cavallo was never interested in future employment in business, he was less trapped by business preferences.

Linked independence can also be gained while in office. Developing an institutionally grounded team of collaborators (the Cavallo boys) provided an independent power base. Cultivating close exchanges with entrepreneurs is helpful as well. For instance, each month Cavallo attended a business luncheon with high-level representatives of the Fundación's private sponsors. The luncheons were run like town meetings: the business executives took turns questioning, even admonishing, Cavallo, who then responded, often followed by loud applause. In addition to continuous dialogues, Cavallo managed to exhibit transparency and nonbias in the formulation and implementation of his policies. A cohesive team, constant dialogue, and transparent hard posturing allowed Cavallo to achieve linked independence vis-à-vis business groups while in office.[71]

In sum, full autonomy makes the targeted group mistrustful of the reforms; full representativeness encourages the targeted sector to "colonize" the reforms. A completely autonomous minister, such as Sourrouille, proved unable to rally the private sector. A completely representative one, such as Rapanelli, was unable to resist the pressures from the private sector. And a

70. Before becoming minister of the economy (July–December 1989), Rapanelli was a top executive in one of Argentina's leading business conglomerates (Bunge & Born). Throughout his short tenure as minister, Rapanelli was pressured by Bunge & Born to avoid policies that would hurt the firm. At first, Rapanelli resisted, prompting Bunge & Born officials to accuse the minister of betraying his "benefactors." In the end, Bunge & Born's pressures led to Rapanelli's resignation.

71. In many ways, this is Cavallo's variation of what Chalmers Johnson, in reference to Japan, describes as "administrative guidance": the authority of the government to issue directives, requests, warnings, and encouragements to the enterprises or clients within a particular ministry's jurisdiction. For Johnson, administrative guidance is a key ingredient of Japan's effective state-business relations. See Chalmers Johnson, *MITI and the Japanese Miracle: The Growth of Industrial Policy, 1925–1975* (Stanford: Stanford University Press, 1982), 265.

completely dogmatic one, such as Martínez de Hoz, was unable to uphold the trust of the private sector. Only Cavallo succeeded in cornering the private sector and still elicit its trust and cooperation. Cavallo's linked independence (provided by his background, career goals, and efforts while in office) explains much of this outcome.

Cavallo and Democracy: The Ambiguities of a Technopol

It is hard to assess the extent to which Cavallo saw himself as explicitly engaged in the task of consolidating democracy, or even how much he cherished this goal per se. After all, Cavallo participated, albeit briefly, in Argentina's military regime. And despite his professed loyalty to democracy and his efforts to engage Congress, Argentines often wonder whether Cavallo is a truly committed democrat.

Indeed, Cavallo understood that there was a limit to what he could accomplish through democratic processes. First, there are the problems of his personality—compulsive, irascible, obdurate—which, he is the first to recognize, are not amenable to consensus building. Then there are the problems of Argentina's political style—impatient, incredulous, inclined to criticize—which are not amenable to long-term projects. And finally, there are the problems of democracy itself—delays, compromises, and overrepresentation of sectoral interests—which pose grave obstacles to any state-reform effort.

At times, therefore, Cavallo neglected, even violated, some democratic institutions. Cavallo continued to believe in decrees. He argued that the *vía expeditiva,* as he calls this prerogative, is sometimes necessary because democratic institutions tend to overrepresent those most resistant to change. It was precisely out of fear of these overly represented antireform lobbies that Cavallo deregulated by decree in late 1991.[72] For Cavallo, decrees can be legitimate and market-friendly as long as they conform to the "democratically mandated" spirit of reform, that is, as long as they seek the elimination of privileges and monopolies. In addition, he argues that his decrees were congressionally endorsed—at least tacitly—since Congress seldom exercised its right to veto them. This veto option, however, was less significant than Cavallo claimed, since Congress was given only very few days to exercise this veto, a time constraint that effectively canceled out congressional scrutiny. Nevertheless, Congress rarely reversed Cavallo's decrees.

72. Domingo F. Cavallo, interview by author.

Cavallo's aggressiveness toward some institutions has also been criticized. Often, Cavallo used the threat of issuing a decree as a device to force Congress (or others) into action. And his tendency to burden Congress with an excessive amount of enormously complex projects can be construed as a tactic to preempt close scrutiny of his measures, which in turn provided Cavallo with an opportunity for Congress bashing, since he then blamed Congress for the inevitable delays.

Cavallo does find some democratic institutions to be a real nuisance. In 1992, he stated that he wished there would no elections in Argentina until October 1993 because, "each time there are elections, the opposition embraces a demagogic discourse, forcing the government to compromise on some issues."[73] And indeed, judged against strict Western standards (after all, the standards against which the government wishes to be judged), Cavallo's resort to decrees, his pick-and-choose commitment to democratic procedures, and his firm-hand approach to many institutions appear undemocratic.

However, Cavallo's critics may be confusing his disdain for electoralism (the mother of economic incorrectness, according to Cavallo) with nondemocratic ideas. They may also be mistaking ruling style for political values, or at least failing to compare his style with that of the government he joined.[74] Cavallo and his boys emerged as an oasis of probity and institutional respect in a government tarnished by corruption and capricious ruling. And as argued, Cavallo successfully used democratic institutions to bring about economic change, which was unusual by Argentine standards. The 1985 Plan Austral, for instance, which established a new exchange rate and a new system of price controls, was not as democratic, because it was a decree rather than a law, a difference from the Convertibility Law that Cavallo loves to reiterate.

Indeed, Cavallo's resort to democratic institutions was high not just for Argentine but also for regional standards. For instance, whereas Cavallo's reform of the pension system took more than one year of negotiations with political sectors and entailed major concessions (e.g., Cavallo's acquiescence to a state-owned pension alternative within the new privatized system), the 1995 Mexican reform of the pension system under President Ernesto Zedillo

73. *La Nación,* 11 July 1992.

74. In addition to his penchant for ruling by decree, Menem has tried to personalize, bypass, and trivialize some of Argentina's democratic institutions. For instance, in 1990 he packed the Supreme Court with new appointees after obtaining congressional approval by using unelected clerks to fill the seats left vacant by dissenting Radical legislators. He is the Argentine president who has intervened the most in the provinces. He has also launched attacks against journalists who ventured into any of the numerous corruption charges that surround his administration.

got less than twenty hours of debate in Congress and few modifications.[75] Thus, unlike two of the region's most far-reaching reformers (Chile in the 1980s and Mexico to this day), Argentina has conducted a 180-degree change without the "benefit" of an authoritarian regime and with the "inconvenience" of checks from Congress, the parties, and the media.

The Dilemmas of Technopolitics and the New Argentina

The ultimate test of a successful technopol is creating new economic institutions that will outlast his or her tenure in office. By insisting on governing with *seguridad jurídica* and international credibility, Cavallo hoped to achieve this. Nevertheless, it is not yet clear whether the restored confidence of Argentines in their country is the result of the stable and transparent state institutions created by Cavallo or of "Cavallomania," the belief that only Cavallo the person, not the institutions, is what holds everything together. The statement "Without Cavallo, Argentina goes to hell" was as common among Buenos Aires kiosk attendants as it was among Wall Street investors.

This raises doubts about the capability of Cavallo's reforms to survive Cavallo's departure from office. Essentially, it shows a dilemma that successful technopols cannot easily escape: the more they succeed in creating effective institutions, the more they risk personalizing them. By doing his job, Cavallo could very well have undermined the entire enterprise of technopolitics.

This problem is perhaps more serious in the long term than in the short term. In fact, in the short term, Cavallomania was an asset for Cavallo, since it gave him a wide margin for maneuvering. Precisely because Cavallo was in charge, he made changes in the system without undermining stability.

Fears of devaluation have lingered in Argentina since the very first day of the Convertibility Plan.[76] That loans in pesos pay almost twice the interest as loans in dollars attests to these fears. Yet, the government successfully resisted

---

75. *Latin American Economy and Business*, January 1996, 11.

76. Almost since the launch of the Convertibility Law, numerous experts have argued that the Argentine currency is overvalued. By the end of 1995, some local economists argued that the peso was overvalued by as much as 40 percent. The IMF argued that if productivity gains were taken into consideration, the overvaluation would be less serious (between 12 and 17 percent). Still others argued that as long as exports were rising, the overvaluation of the currency would be a nonissue. However, not even the government is persuaded by this last argument.

the pressure to devalue. This pressure reached crisis proportions on two occasions. The first, in November 1992, was contained by doing exactly what the Convertibility Law mandated—the Central Bank sold the demanded number of dollars, almost U.S.$300 million in a matter of days.[77] The Central Bank's counterattack was so successful that, in the end, it had to buy back some U.S.$22 million.

The second and more serious pressure occurred in the aftermath of Mexico's December 1994 peso crash. Before this crisis, an increasing number of international economists (e.g., Rudiger Dornbusch, Paul Krugman) publicly expressed deep concerns about overvaluation of the Argentine peso. When the Mexican crisis erupted, almost everyone expected Argentina to devalue, if not at the moment, then certainly after the May 1995 presidential elections. Indeed, Argentina was the perfect candidate for devaluation; although foreign reserves were at an all time high, Argentina's trade deficit continued, and public finances were experiencing some difficulties.

Not surprisingly, dollar purchases ballooned dramatically. Exchange houses began to add 0.001 to 0.003 pesos to the value of each dollar. The stock market retreated to its 1989 level (approximately a 35 percent drop). By late February, Argentines withdrew an estimated U.S.$2 million from banks. Various financial institutions were suspended from operating after their holdings in Argentine public debt papers fell sharply in value while the interbank interest rate rose to 40 percent. The country plunged into an economic recession.

However, the Convertibility Plan survived. And the 1995 economic recession, although painful, was mild (an estimated 2.5 percent decline in GDP) relative to Mexico's and even Argentina's historical record of steep downturns produced by external shocks. In fact, before 1991, a comparable international shock would probably have brought down the government (as in 1982 and 1989). This time, however, Argentina seemed to have weathered the crisis—and still managed to keep a stable exchange rate and minuscule inflation rate—which is all the more remarkable given the lack of a foreign bailout for Argentina.

Placating the hysteria of domestic and international economic actors, however, did not occur by accident. The Argentine government's reaction to the Mexican crisis was swift, unambiguous, and backed by more than just slogans about the exceptionality of the Argentine case. Soon after the announcement

77. *Clarín,* 15 November 1992, 2–3.

of Mexico's devaluation, Menem walked across the street from the Casa Rosada toward the Ministry of the Economy, where Cavallo was giving a press conference. This was a symbolic reminder of presidential backing. A series of televised news conferences followed, where both men underlined their determination to defend the currency. Cavallo took a series of domestic measures (e.g., requiring the Central Bank to hold sufficient reserves to meet the demand for large sums of dollars, allowing banks to hold smaller cash reserves in U.S. dollars). He also took various trips to the United States to persuade foreign investors of the economic soundness of the country. The government also provided funds to the U.S.-directed bailout of Mexico as a way to signal Argentina's solvency and commitment to hemispheric stability.

Cavallo thus reacted to the Mexican crisis the way Mexican officials should have reacted: by signaling control of the situation, producing information, and reiterating policy commitment. More than anyone, Cavallo was aware that the exchange rate regime was the vortex of his program, but it was also the most panic-prone; hence the swiftness of his moves.

Defending the exchange rate required repeated fine-tuning. This fine-tuning, as argued in this chapter, is a hallmark of technopolitics. But it can also be a source of institutional erosion. It is not clear how many more exceptions, corrections, and ad hoc agreements the country's institutional framework can tolerate before its credibility begins to erode. Every time that there was a rumor of Cavallo's resignation (rumors that recurred at least twice a year since 1991), capital markets trembled; once those rumors were dispelled, tranquillity returned. The status of "Cavallo-Menem relations" replaced "Central Bank actions" as the index that was most closely watched by Argentine speculators. This raised doubts about the institutionalization of Cavallo's policies.

Only a Beginning

Far from solving all of Argentina's economic calamities, the Cavallo Plan has actually left unattended a series of problems and even helped to create new ones. A crucial omission was the failure of provincial governments to replicate at home some of the reforms carried out by Cavallo at the national level. As a result of the 1992 agreement with the federal government, the provinces accepted the main responsibility for the provision of health, education, and social assistance services. While this devolution solved a major drain on the national budget, it left the provinces with too much responsibility and too little supervision. Numerous provinces not only have reneged on carrying out needed reforms but even have diverted social spending and investment to meet current-account expenditures. Between 1992 and 1994, provincial spending rose 26 percent. The combined fiscal deficits of all the provinces in 1994 was estimated at U.S.$2.7 billion,[78] most of which was financed through public debt (reaching U.S.$12.5 billion for all twenty-three provinces in 1995).[79]

As a result, a number of provinces underwent economic recessions and lags in social service provision even before the overall recession of 1995. In December 1993, thousands of people rioted in Santiago del Estero, protesting the failure of the highly corrupt local government to meet wage obligations. Comparable unrest has occurred in other provinces (e.g., Salta, La Rioja, Córdoba).

Cavallo's initial response to the provincial question was to admonish publicly those provinces that failed to make adjustments and to call voters to "punish with their votes" the nonreforming incumbents. Cavallo even encouraged voters from La Rioja to vote against the Peronist governor, an old-time friend of Menem. While daring, these steps seem extraordinarily naïve coming from a man who understands the impact of clientelism in determining local voting and the notion that economic actors need more than tough words and moral exhortations to alter their behavior. While more promising steps have been taken recently (e.g., the government has offered debt relief in exchange for provincial spending cuts), the fact remains that Cavallo's failure to provide a broad structure of incentives for local-level reforms constituted one of his program's principal shortcomings.

In addition to the trade deficit, the Cavallo Plan also has been accompanied by the new curse of unemployment, which in 1995 reached an all-time high of 18.6 percent. What is most alarming about this rise in unemployment, which began in 1992, is that it occurred even while the economy was growing. For the opposition, it is a symptom of everything that is wrong with the current regime. For Cavallo, it is an "understandable" result of the increase in the number of new job seekers who previously had given up hopes of finding a place in Argentina's labor markets, and of Congress's unwillingness to relax labor laws.

While the Convertibility Law helped secure Argentina's stability, it also curtailed the country's ability to deal with external shocks, such as the 1995

78. *Latin America Weekly Report,* 2 February 1995, 39.
79. *Latin American Economy and Business,* December 1995.

Tequila effect. Cavallo's only options during this crisis were to allow the country to fall into a recession, to increase foreign borrowing, and to tighten austerity. The "pains" that these responses bring are familiar to Argentines and to Latin Americans in general. Cavallo also began to abandon some of the practices that contributed to his earlier successes (e.g., he asked Congress in late 1995 for special powers to deal with the crisis, a reversal of the 1991 policy of congressional engagement that served Cavallo very well). But Cavallo's refusal to seek an easy solution (i.e., devalue) was a hallmark of Cavallopolitics and a novel phenomenon for Argentine ministers of the economy. It also seems that this aspect of Cavallopolitics will endure. In fact, Cavallo's resignation in July 1996 is possibly the first change of minister of the economy in Argentina that did not come with a change of policy. The day of Cavallo's resignation Menem not only described Cavallo as "the best minister of the economy that Argentina ever had," but also declared that he would continue the economic plan launched at the onset of the Tequila Crisis (1994).[80]

Argentina's new and old problems, however, were insufficient to undermine the government politically in the 1995 presidential elections. They did not undermine Cavallo's popularity significantly either (on inauguration day, Cavallo was the most-applauded minister). Proportionally speaking, Argentina's problems pale in comparison with the magnitude of Cavallo's accomplishments. Nevertheless, these problems are a reminder that for all its glory, the Convertibility Plan is only the beginning of a new and still troublesome era in Argentina's political economy.[81]

Conclusion

In a March 1993 forum at Harvard University, Cavallo declared: "Perhaps the only truly miraculous thing that we have done in Argentina is to have the Argentines pay their taxes."[82] Without minimizing the magnitude of this accomplishment, it seems that Cavallo was being too modest—for a change.

80. Early reports about the reasons for Cavallo's departure suggest an intensification of Menem's (and the Peronist Party's) impatience with Cavallo's personality rather than a serious disagreement over policy course.

81. For a more detailed, reader-friendly overview of the economic gaps of the Convertibility Plan, see Felipe A. M. de la Balze, *Remaking the Argentine Economy* (New York: Council on Foreign Relations, 1995), 123–68.

82. Domingo F. Cavallo, Rudiger Dornbusch, and Jeffrey Sachs, "Argentina's Economic Reforms: A Model for the World?" (panel discussion, Harvard University, Cambridge, 1993).

That the country that defined "transition to underdevelopment" and "monetary catastrophe" should experience five consecutive years of economic stability, four of which had economic growth, is nothing short of the ultimate Latin American surprise. To be sure, getting Argentines to pay their taxes is one reason for this miracle. But it is only part of the answer, and one that is subsumed under the overall role played by Cavallo.

A person like Cavallo was not needed to figure out what economic measures were necessary to stabilize the Argentine economy; these answers were readily available in the World Bank Bookstore. But a person like Cavallo was indeed needed to make such ideas politically viable. Cavallo's ability to maneuver the entire political system on behalf of his ideas distinguished him from most of his predecessors. It is the attribute that justifies the suffix "pol" when we call him a technopol.

Cavallo's tactics seem somewhat counterintuitive, at times undemocratic, and always very risky. He first consolidated organizational power, only to transfer part of it to Congress. He worked hard to raise foreign reserves, only to risk them by tying them to a foreign currency. He showed humanity by crying in public, but reverted to stoic recalcitrance in resisting social demands. He settled difficult political controversies, only to move on to more contentious ones. He abhorred bureaucracies, but he created new ones to handle politics. And he treated institutions imperiously, only to come to agreements that significantly fettered his actions.

Cavallo mastered the politics of self-binding precisely because they are so only in the short term. In fact, Cavallo mastered politics. He fashioned a highly effective political machinery to interact continuously with the political system. At times, this machinery ran faster than Congress, and many criticized Cavallo for this. The mere existence of this machinery, however, suggests a mind that appreciates the importance of politics over technical questions.

Since he left his Cambridge alma mater, Cavallo has changed his mind several times, often contradicting his own writing. But it is precisely because he was willing to change his mind that Cavallo also qualifies as a technopol. A technocrat would find it hard to break away from his or her own dogmatism. For Cavallo, changing technical "details" was easy, in fact necessary, if doing so served a political purpose or was merited by circumstances. If anything, the only obstacle to compromising, Cavallo would argue, was his personality.

Cavallo combined what he learned from studying economics with what he learned from practicing politics. In many ways, he made politics conform to modern economics. First, he applied the scientific approach of modern economics to the role of the opposition. Politicians, like researchers, should be judged on the validity and consistency of their methods and on whether they deliver on their promises. For Cavallo, the *decretismo* of the Plan Austral and the disregard of Congress under Alfonsín undermined the validity of this presumably democratic experiment. Cavallo also applied lessons from neoclassical economics to politics. His triangular campaign, for instance, reveals a political mind that appreciates the Ricardian principle of comparative-advantage specialization. And his insistence on *seguridad jurídica* is based on the rational-choice insight that signals of continuity and predictability are necessary for sustained credibility. But Cavallo also made neoclassical economics conform to political necessity. Liberalization, privatization, and deficit reduction are sound economic goals, but only if obtained through consensus. Seeking compromises may very well have been the most onerous thing Cavallo had to do as minister, but it was also what made him such a unique *técnico* in Argentina. Thus, Cavallo's more "scientific" style of opposition, "economics-conforming" type of politics, and "politically viable" version of economics are further justification for his technopol label.

But however flexible his intellect, the core of Cavallo's thinking has remained fundamentally unaltered. The solution to economic predicament is not a structural but an institutional revolution. Reforming the public sector is pointless without reforming the private one. And rather than resist international forces, Argentina must accommodate them.

Although sympathetic to neoliberalism, Cavallo is not a full believer in the invisible hand or the invisible state. Clearly, the state has no business running businesses. But the notion of a passive, uninvolved state is inadequate for Argentina, a country of ferocious rent seekers. The state must be active in safeguarding institutions, especially in the face of undue stress or volatility, and in providing incentives for the proper functioning of markets.

Cavallo has always argued that Argentina needed a shock of confidence, which would "only be attained with a dose of transparency, and to the extent that people understand the language of their leaders and the information that is conveyed to them."[83] In Argentina, it has always been easy to identify credibility deficits—the volatility of the exchange rate markets is a good indicator. Before Cavallo, the Argentine currency was in a decades-old nosedive. Almost twenty-five stabilization attempts were made by seven different ministers of the economy. None, however, delivered stability for more than one year. The hyperinflation of early 1989 could not prevent the hyperinflation of early 1990 and the quasi-hyperinflation of 1991. Cavallo put an end to

83. Cavallo, *Economía en tiempos de crisis,* 197.

this cycle of instability. And he upheld this stability despite trade imbalances, external shocks, and the skepticism of even international gurus. This was not simply the result of power concentration, but of resorting to Congress. True to his word, Cavallo came to accept political negotiations as necessary transaction costs of credible economic governance.

The Cavallo case thus provides concrete lessons on how credibility is gained. Talk alone is not enough. Transparent institutions and rules (e.g., simplified tariff structure, better-monitored capital markets, weekly disclosure of Central Bank reserves) are no doubt important. But legislative endorsement of public policy can be more credibility-enhancing than technical perfection. Agreements that tie the hands of policy makers can also be more credibility-enhancing than arbitrary decrees. Policy is more credible when it originates from bureaucracies whose standards of competence are perceived to be high and unbiased. Improving tax collection and fighting tax evasion are more critical contributors to credibility than perhaps lowering taxes.

The Cavallo case offers lessons on the conditions for "successful techno-politics," that is, success at "reshaping" politics on behalf of the reform process. Two variables seem to be especially important: personality and linked independence. An amenable personality that is predisposed to get along with the political sector is important because it softens the transaction cost of dealing with the political sector. Cavallo did not score high on this count (although at times his abrasiveness was politically beneficial).

On the other hand, Cavallo scored very high in the area of linked independence, that is, a relation in which the reformer is not beholden to, but simultaneously commands the respect of, the social sectors targeted for reforms. Part of linked independence must exist in the technopol's own résumé before assuming office (that is, the technopol must possess a neutral professional background that is still well respected by the sectors targeted for reforms). But linked independence can also be built while in office (through institutional grounding, cohesive team building, transparent hard-posturing).

Cavallo exhibited linked independence vis-à-vis the two societal groups whose consent was most crucial for economic reform in Argentina: the industrialist private sector and the Peronist Party. By coming from an academic setting rather than a specific business firm, Cavallo (unlike Rapanelli in Argentina but like Aspe in Mexico) avoided the image among business leaders of being beholden to a specific business firm. This allowed Cavallo to eschew accusations of favoritism that the private sector often levies against economic reformers. It also spared Cavallo a situation in which a private firm could believe it "owned" the minister. And while in office, Cavallo excelled at nurturing this business loyalty—being uniformly tough but transparent, and yielding only when necessary.

Likewise, Cavallo's Peronist-friendly background (his 1987–89 participation in Congress as a Peronist affiliate) and his overtures to Peronism while in office (e.g., exempting labor markets from liberalization, allowing Congress to participate in decision making, helping the party win elections, consenting to state participation in the privatized pension system) allowed Cavallo to placate the fear of technocrats and aversion to reforms of many Peronists. This accorded Cavallo an enormous degree of freedom throughout his tenure.[84] Cavallo thus managed to obtain a marriage between *técnicos* and politicians, unusual not just in Argentine politics but in reform processes worldwide. Without linked independence, Cavallo would not have survived the reform mistrust of both the Peronist and the business sectors.

Argentina's economic calamities are far from over. Moreover, the decay of Argentina's once radiant social programs may have accelerated with the rise of unemployment and the sluggish pace of reforms at the provincial level. But the Plan Cavallo, unlike any other stabilization and adjustment programs attempted in Argentina, has given Argentina more than five years of stability and four years of growth (not to mention that it has renewed the middle class's ability to vacation abroad). Most stabilization packages collapse, not in the beginning, but halfway into the reform process. In Argentina, economic hardline policies never paid off politically, as Economy Ministers Krieger Vassena in 1969, Rodrigo in 1975, Martínez de Hoz in 1980, and Sourrouille in 1987 discovered. Cavallo is the first Argentine minister of the economy to have passed this post-stabilization test.

It remains to be seen whether Cavallo will pass the test of effective state building. Successful state building requires creating institutions that will outlast the "founding fathers." For now, it is unclear whether it is the new institutions that Cavallo created or Cavallo himself that Argentines have come to trust. In some way, this Cavallomania was a tribute to Cavallo's successes. But it also reveals that much remains to be done to depersonalize economic institutions in Argentina. The ultimate test of a successful technopol is whether he or she becomes discardable, and it is not yet possible to judge Cavallo accordingly.

But while the future of Cavallo's exchange rate regime remains uncertain, it is already certain that Cavallo has made returning to the past very hard. This,

---

84. See Chapter 3 in this volume for a description of how Aspe, by respecting some of the Mexican ruling party's sacred principles (e.g., team playing, presidential authority, adherence to the "unwritten rules" of party politics), also obtained some freedom of action within the party.

in and of itself, is the first goal of any state builder and one that Cavallo has clearly met.

Bresser Pereira argued: "The generic dilemma facing governments that embark on the path of reform is that broad consultation with diverse political forces may lead to inertia, while reforms imposed from above may be impossible to implement in the face of political resistance and economic incredulity."[85] Cavallo's record so far suggests that more than understanding this dilemma, he may have come close to resolving it. In this sense, Cavallo, perhaps involuntarily, has made an impressive contribution to democracy. He has defied the long-held notion that democracies, especially young and fragile ones, are unable to survive, let alone resolve, severe economic predicaments. For Cavallo, the *seguridad jurídica* provided by democratic institutions makes them adequate, perhaps even better suited, for delivering economic stability. This does not necessarily earn Cavallo the label "democratic technopol," but it makes his a case in which democracy was made to work for economic reform.

Unlike most successful economic reformers in Latin America, Cavallo worked without the "benefit" of an authoritarian executive. And yet, unlike his predecessors, he expended enormous resources to engage the most important, and at times the most hostile, institutions in the process of state reform. In doing so, Cavallo made democratic institutions not just the licensers but also the protagonists of one of Latin America's most impressive economic transformations.

---

85. Luiz Carlos Bresser Pereira, "Economic Reforms and Economic Growth: Efficiency and Politics in Latin America," in *Economic Reforms in New Democracies: A Social-Democratic Approach*, ed. Luiz Carlos Bresser Pereira, José María Maravall, and Adam Przeworski (Cambridge: Cambridge University Press, 1993), 9.

3

"Making Possible What Is Necessary"
Pedro Aspe, the Salinas Team, and the
Next Mexican "Miracle"

Stephanie R. Golob

Though analysts tend to characterize the 1980s as the "lost decade" for Latin American economies, Mexico spent that same time in a process of economic reconstruction and rebirth, emerging into the early 1990s as a leader in the hemispheric movement toward a new model of development. Having undertaken a faster, more consistent, and more intense adjustment than most of its neighbors, Mexico made great strides over the past decade toward dismantling its bloated state sector and encouraging recovery through the efficient operation of free and open markets. Outstanding among the structural and policy changes of the administrations of Miguel de la Madrid (1982–88) and

Carlos Salinas de Gortari (1988–94) were the first international debt-relief agreement under the so-called Brady Plan; the stabilization of inflation through a social pact; the privatization of nearly all viable state enterprises and the reprivatization of the banking system; and the liberalization of trade, investment, and agricultural policies, fortified by accession to the General Agreement on Tariffs and Trade (GATT) and the realization of a North American Free Trade Agreement (NAFTA) with the United States and Canada.

Such ambitious reforms raised expectations abroad and at home of the birth of a second Mexican "miracle," promising to match the achievements of the first so-called miracle of the 1950s and 1960s, when the government and private sector worked together to keep inflation low and growth high under the banner of "stabilizing development." Indeed, the apparent coming of this second "miracle" seemed all the more miraculous given the depths to which the Mexican economy had sunk in the early 1980s. In 1982, with oil prices plummeting and real interest rates skyrocketing in response to a world recession, Mexico's attempt in the previous decade to finance a new "shared development" model of state enterprises and protected industry through oil earnings and foreign debt had finally collapsed.[1] Unable to pay even the service on the debt, then totaling $85 billion, Mexico entered into agreements with the International Monetary Fund to adopt programs of structural adjustment in exchange for further emergency loans; however, these same policies resulted not in recovery, but in a severe recession that lasted for most of the 1980s. Businesses failed due to import competition and the reduction of subsidies, unemployment also increased, and the real minimum wage deteriorated by nearly 40 percent[2] — all of this compounded by inflation that reached triple digits by mid-decade. Because Mexico maintained its commitment to the harsh medicine despite unrelenting external pressures — most notably the drop in oil prices in 1986 and the 1987 stock market crash — as well as growing unrest at home, it appeared that the cure was far worse than the disease.

However, by the early 1990s the sustained and highly coordinated reform project began to produce significant indications not only of short-term recovery in growth rates and per capita income,[3] but of deeper structural

1. For a concise overview of the crisis conditions of 1982, see Organization for Economic Cooperation and Development, *Mexico, 1991–1992,* OECD Economic Surveys (Paris: OECD, 1992), 180–81; more extensive treatment can be found in Pablo González Casanova and Hector Aguilar Camín, comps., *México ante la crisis: El contexto internacional y la crisis económica* (Mexico City: Siglo Veintiuno Editores, 1985), vol. 1.

2. Between 1982 and 1988. See OECD, *Mexico, 1991–1992,* 136.

3. After nearly a decade of contraction, in the early 1990s the Mexican economy started

transformation in the economy. Through strict fiscal discipline, the public-sector deficit was lowered to 5.6 percent of gross domestic product (GDP) by 1989 and, by late 1992, had converted into a surplus of 3.4 percent of GDP.[4] Proceeds from privatization (*desincorporación*) went toward reducing the internal debt rather than increasing the budget, and the debt-relief agreement signed in February 1990 promised to decrease net resource transfers by $4 billion per year, on average, between 1990 and 1994.[5] Single-digit inflation and liberalization of direct foreign investment regulations further signaled Mexico's commitment to a new direction. As a result, international and domestic private-sector confidence in the Mexican economy, elusive despite the "good behavior" of the 1980s, rebounded,[6] as reflected in record levels of foreign investment[7] and a reputation on Wall Street that made Mexico the envy of other so-called "emerging markets." And while this reputation arguably encouraged policy makers toward overconfidence, risky strategies, and serious miscalculations, culminating in the dramatic peso crisis of December 1994,[8] Mexico's relatively rapid return to international markets in 1995 demonstrated how far the reform process had taken the Mexican economy since its "basket-case" days of the early 1980s. Even though the crisis may have brought back memories of 1982, the process by which the Mexican economy was opened, stabilized, and revived beyond expectations in the intervening years remains a striking "before-and-after" story for students of policy reform.

To appreciate fully the significance of the post-1982 transformation of Mexican economic policy, however, one must also take into consideration the transformation of the Mexican economic policy-making elite and of the ideas

recording growth rates between 3 and 4 percent; likewise, per capita income, which declined on average between 1982 and 1988, rose a respectable 2.1 percent in 1991. See Secretaría de Hacienda y Crédito Público, *El nuevo perfil de la economía mexicana* (August 1992), 53.

4. Secretaría de Hacienda y Crédito Público, Minister's Advisory Staff. This figure includes the proceeds from privatization.

5. Secretaría de Hacienda y Crédito Público, Minister's Advisory Staff. For an overview of the components of the agreement, see *Latin American Weekly Report,* 15 February 1990, 4.

6. The psychological aspect of Mexico's recovery and its prospects for continued upward mobility in years to come are highlighted in "Free Market Mexico: The Rhythm of the Future," *The Economist,* 14 December 1991, 19–21.

7. According to Banco de México figures, between 1990 and 1992 total foreign investment quadrupled from $4.6 billion to nearly $19 billion.

8. For a schematic chronology of the decisions leading to the crisis, see "The Development of a Crisis (More Than a Year Ago There Were Signs That Mexico Was Ready for a Fall)," *Washington Post*, 13 February 1995, A16. These issues are analyzed at greater length in a latter section of this chapter.

held by this elite regarding development, the state, the private sector, and markets at home and abroad. Specifically, the shift toward a greater trust in markets paralleled the rise within the Mexican economic policy bureaucracy of a group of young foreign-educated professional economists who worked in tandem and used their technical expertise as well as their positions of responsibility to lead Mexico in a new direction.[9] Lauded in 1991 by the *Economist* as "probably the most economically literate group that has ever governed any country anywhere,"[10] the team assembled by President Salinas (himself the recipient of three advanced degrees in political economy and government from Harvard)[11] began its ascent in the bureaucracy at a time when the previous development strategy and the ideology on which it was based were perceived to have failed and new ideas and expertise became valuable political assets. As economists at the service of the Mexican state, this group was following in a long tradition that spanned both the prerevolutionary *científicos* associated with the modernization project of the dictator Porfirio Díaz and the "nationalist" economists of the 1970s, who championed import substitution and a greater state role in development as the legacy of the Mexican Revolution.[12] Similarly, the career paths of former presidents José López Portillo (finance minister under Echeverría), Miguel de la Madrid (minister of programming

9. Larry Rohter, "The Northern Connection," *New York Times*, 3 June 1990, sec. 3, p. 6. Outstanding among this group are the following: Salinas's finance minister, Pedro Aspe Armella (b. 1950, Ph.D. Massachusetts Institute of Technology, 1978); minister of commerce, Jaime Serra Puche (b. 1951; Ph.D. Yale, 1979); minister of programming and budget (before this ministry's dissolution and merger with Finance in 1992), Ernesto Zedillo Ponce de León (b. 1951, Ph.D. Yale, 1978); and chief negotiator of the North American Free Trade Agreement for the Commerce Ministry, Herminio Blanco Mendoza (b. 1950, Ph.D. University of Chicago, 1978). In addition, José Córdoba (b. 1950), perhaps the closest economic adviser to President Salinas, has graduate training from the Sorbonne and Stanford. For more detailed biographical and career path information, see listings in Presidencia de la República, *Diccionario biográfico del gobierno mexicano,* 3d ed. (Mexico City: Presidencia de la República, 1989).

10. *The Economist*, 14 December 1991, 19.

11. Salinas earned three advanced degrees from Harvard: a master's in administration from the John F. Kennedy School of Government (1973) and a master's (1976) and Ph.D. (1978) in political economy and government (a joint program of the Kennedy School, the Government Department, and the Economics Department). *Diccionario biográfico*, 323

12. Economists were only one of a number of academically trained groups that took advantage of the resources available through state service to influence society, just as the state took advantage of their "scientific" credentials to legitimate policies and, in some cases, its authority as well. This observation forms the central thesis of Roderic A. Camp, *Intellectuals and the State in Twentieth-Century Mexico* (Austin: University of Texas Press, 1985). For a more detailed look at economists in the bureaucracy during the 1970s, see idem, *The Role of Economists in Policy-Making: A Comparative Case Study of Mexico and the United States* (Tucson: University of Arizona Press, 1977).

and budget under López Portillo), and Salinas himself (minister of programming and budget under de la Madrid) reflected a shift over the course of the 1960s and 1970s in the "balance of power" within the Mexican state from those with political experience (through work with the labor, popular, and rural sectors of the ruling Partido Revolucionario Institucional [Institutional Revolutionary Party], or PRI) to those with technical abilities and administrative careers within the key economics ministries. From that point of view, members of the "new generation" were the right economists in the right place at the right time.

At the same time, there were some significant differences in training, career paths, and ideas about state and market that set this new generation and its project apart and that identify its leading members as Mexican-style technopols. To begin with, their world-class training as professional economists connected them to each other and to economists and policy makers in other countries through a common technical language and a shared curriculum of market-oriented approaches. Next, their education abroad also exposed them to new ideas about Mexico's role in the world and the importance of insertion, as opposed to isolation, as a means of advancing the national interest. This cosmopolitan outlook was accompanied by a new attitude toward the role of the state in development, according to which the state should seek a "partnership" with the private sector while preserving a "rectorship" role for a new, streamlined, yet still influential, version of itself. Finally, while their technocratic image, language, and style may have communicated a lack of political ambition, in reality they also owed their ascent to their political savvy in building a network around a winning contender for the presidency and to their skilled practice of two key political activities within the bureaucracy: team building and team playing. This generation of Mexican technopols applied themselves relatively effectively and collectively toward learning the unwritten rules of the Mexican presidentialist game, thus advancing both their ideas and their careers.

It is within this collective context that we can best understand the rise of one such individual, former finance minister Pedro Aspe Armella, an MIT-educated economist and once-and-future academic known equally for mastery of theoretical concepts and practical economic policy-making skills. Very much a technopol in this sense, Aspe approached policy making in a most professorial way, relying on coordinated teams of his best former students to study problems and design policy, maintaining high standards for intellectual rigor and effort among his staff, and using a logical, if not didactic, lecturing style that transformed him into the "teacher to the nation" for the Salinas reform project. At the same time, Aspe also demonstrated that he was a "quick study" as he made the transition from theory to practice, addressing such diverse political activities as renegotiating the external debt with the international financial community and negotiating an anti-inflationary social pact with representatives of business, labor, and agriculture. More important, as a Mexican technopol, Aspe also owed his success to his ability to decipher the rules of the top-down game of presidentialist politics, as well as to his position within a generation that has worked together to advance their ideas through that game. This combination of traits made Pedro Aspe a Mexican technopol par excellence, acting on ideas that have transformed his nation's economy while transforming himself into an influential and at times surprisingly effective political actor in a system that has traditionally rewarded those who have played by its rules.

This chapter begins, as the technopol story in Mexico does, from a generational perspective, portraying the speed and depth of the reform project as a result of a collective effort rather than simply the product of any one individual. This pattern also reflects how, within the Mexican institutional framework, individual political actors continue to be defined and constrained by their membership in groups such as generations, policy teams, and what are known as *camarillas,* or personal-political cliques, mainly because it is through the competition within the state between elite groups and the ideas held by those groups that the single-party-dominant system has renewed itself and thereby perpetuated its control. In the remainder of the chapter I focus on Pedro Aspe, both as a microcosm through which to observe these collective experiences and as an individual whose own personal background, intellectual orientation, abilities, personality, and ambitions contributed to the consolidation of the reform program and to his own political ascent. On one level, I am concerned with tracing continuity and change in the ideas held by Aspe across the transition from academia to public service; on another, I am interested in how and why Aspe was offered a chance to take those ideas and put them into practice, specifically asking who benefited from associating with Aspe's expertise and scientific credentials.

I then present a series of minicases of Pedro Aspe in action, focusing on the correspondence of Aspe's ideas to his actions as a policy maker, and on the impact of technocratic styles and approaches to building support for those policies. Such scrutiny reveals that Aspe took economic ideas seriously, but believed that being an economist-policy maker meant both a normative commitment to identifying what was "necessary" for recovery and a pragmatic commitment to making those goals "possible" through effective policy design and implementation. Though his scholarly detachment and patrician image undermined his public perception, Aspe used those same traits to his best political advantage within the norms of Mexican presidentialism, forging a role within the Salinas team as the guarantor of Mexico's new model with domestic capitalists and foreign investors. At the same time, as evident in the final minicase, Aspe's role in the peso meltdown of 1994–95 suggests that too much success can also backfire for technopols. Indeed, many of the same qualities that contributed to Aspe's "success" as a technopol—particularly his fervent personal commitment to the reform project and his equally fervent respect for the code of presidentialism—when taken to an extreme also jeopardized the very project he sought to consolidate.

As a final note, I address the connection between economic and political transformation hypothesized in this project's working definition of "technopols," and ask how it relates to the "historic" project advanced by Aspe and the new generation in the Mexican bureaucracy. The answer, I argue, is far more pessimistic than in the other countries under study, where technopols have negotiated the balancing act between the top-down nature of economic policy making and the bottom-up pressures of civil societies empowered in democratizing contexts. By contrast, in Mexico the "pol" in "technopol" has referred not so much to the acquisition of political skills associated with democratic processes (such as coalition building or sensitivity to electoral contests) as to the "insider" skills of *camarilla* building and bureaucratic politics associated with the one-party system. Technopols in Mexico have also depended upon the centralized and hierarchical presidentialist system to enable them to accelerate the reform process while remaining relatively insulated from political or social turmoil. They have acted on a shared belief in what has been called Salinastroika—the idea that, while both economic and political reform were important goals, economic reform must be consolidated prior to opening the floodgates of political dissent. The gamble seemed a sure one: Mexico's technopols were confident that they could justify delaying political opening by playing up the results—real and expected—of economic reforms as the public's reward for its patience; however, the outcome, as represented by the Chiapas uprising and the post-peso crisis unrest, suggests the risks of their strategy in a context of great pent-up demand for political openness. Thus, Mexico's technopols may have been the advocates of economic change, but their top-down approach relied heavily upon the forces of political continuity.

New Ideas, New Generation: The Collective Story of the Mexican Reform Project

Most analysts of the recent Mexican reforms readily cite the ideological cohesion and the common professional training of the Salinas economic team as important factors explaining the success and speed of the program.[13] The seeds of this convergence were planted in the early 1980s at the start of the administration of Salinas's predecessor, Miguel de la Madrid (1982–88), when a new generation of young professional economists started moving into more visible positions of responsibility in the economics ministries.[14] Key members of this generation had first entered the state in the late 1970s as economic advisers to David Ibarra, minister of finance under President López Portillo, most notably Jaime Serra Puche (Ph.D. Yale; later commerce minister under Salinas), Herminio Blanco (Ph.D. University of Chicago; Salinas's chief negotiator for the North American Free Trade Agreement), and, as coordinator of the advisory group, Pedro Aspe Armella.[15] Under more normal circumstances, given that Ibarra lost out in his bid to become the presidential candidate of the ruling Institutional Revolutionary Party in 1982, this group may have returned to academia or remained in marginal positions within Finance or the Central Bank. However, in the context of the 1982 crisis, it made sense for López Portillo's designated successor, his minister of programming and budget, Miguel de la Madrid, to recruit his political rival's team of economic advisers, flush as it was with economists skilled in and committed to the same free market reforms demanded by the major international financial institutions. This experience—being recruited at the start of a new administration facing a deepening international and domestic economic crisis—gave the new generation its first point of reference as a political entity.

13. For an in-depth analysis of the Salinas team, its ideological project, and its rise to political power, see Miguel Ángel Centeno, *Democracy Within Reason: Technocratic Revolution in Mexico* (University Park: Pennsylvania State University Press, 1994).

14. This recruiting process is analyzed and documented in Roderic A. Camp, *Political Recruitment Across Two Centuries: Mexico, 1884–1991* (Austin: University of Texas Press, 1994), 237–67. The importance of one economic ministry—Programming and Budget (Secretaría de Programación y Presupuesto, or SPP)—in the consolidation of the reform generation is emphasized in Centeno, *Democracy Within Reason*, 88–94.

15. As of 1 December 1994, with the beginning of the *sexenio* of President Ernesto Zedillo, a later arrival to the Salinas *camarilla*, Serra became minister of finance, and Blanco moved up to the top job at Commerce. After the peso crisis later that month, Serra resigned and was replaced by Guillermo Ortiz, who had been the undersecretary at Finance under Aspe, responsible for the privatization of the banks.

Still, while the circumstances of their recruitment gave this group a common project, a common historical memory provided a deeper bond. These young economists, all born in the late 1940s and early 1950s, belong to a defining generation, just as did those who fought in the revolution and those who implemented the radical agenda it inspired under President Lázaro Cárdenas in the 1930s. Raised during the low-inflation, high-growth years of "stabilizing development," they watched as the social peace of their youth unraveled as a result of rapid economic and social modernization in the 1960s. They were cutting their teeth on economic theory as undergraduates in the early 1970s when President Luis Echeverría replaced "stabilizing development" with "shared development," a program that gave the state a more active role in the economy as an owner of industrial enterprises and as a "safety net" for failed private firms, a role financed increasingly by external debt; they then witnessed the collapse of this high-spending, high-borrowing scheme in the mid-1970s. As they pondered the theoretical arguments in favor of fiscal responsibility from the distance of U.S. campuses, a new president, José López Portillo, jubilantly proclaimed the discovery of vast oil reserves, considered to be Mexico's ticket to "First World" prosperity as well as the means to avoid the pain of adjustment. Returning to Mexico in the late 1970s, these newly minted Ph.D.'s found themselves in dissent from optimistic "mainstream" government economists; all the same, being proved right by the debacle of the early 1980s was cold comfort. Thus, on a very personal level, the members of this generation felt collectively committed to rebuilding the Mexican economy.

Another common bond within this generation was forged through their training in world-class economics departments in top United States universities. Unlike economists recruited in previous generations, whose training had often been at the National Autonomous University (Universidad Nacional Autónoma de México, or UNAM) or in postgraduate programs in Europe or elsewhere in Latin America, this group sought U.S. doctorates as the "universal" measure of professional legitimacy. While steeped in theoretical approaches emphasizing market efficiency and well-trained in state-of-the-art macroeconomic analysis, they also absorbed new attitudes toward the external world more generally and about the connection between national development and insertion in the world economy specifically. Participation in academic life at Harvard, MIT, Stanford, Yale, and the University of Chicago connected them to an international community of scholars and practitioners and encouraged the confidence with which they would approach dealings with foreign interlocutors in the future. Moreover, once back in Mexico, members of this generation shared both a common technical language and a cosmopolitan outlook that allowed for greater coordination of policy toward international opening. In addition to advancing these "horizontal" linkages, returning Ph.D.'s also expanded their political and professional networks by forging "vertical" links through university teaching: top students were identified, groomed for advanced work, and later recruited into the state as loyal team members. Building upon a traditional recruitment pattern,[16] this new generation positioned itself advantageously in the economic policy bureaucracy, establishing what amounted to a vast think tank through which to manage the transformation of the economy.

This new generation also distinguished itself from previous generations in the scope and nature of its members' political activity. As more recent works on the Mexican elite have contended, the career paths of this new generation departed from those of more narrowly defined *técnicos* in their active pursuit, and achievement, of political advancement;[17] however, it should be recalled that they did not take the route of the *políticos* either, leaving them detached from traditional power bases. This reflected not only their subjective orientations but also the objective shift occurring in the Mexican political system in the 1960s and 1970s, which saw those taking the traditional *político* career path fall behind those advancing through the federal bureaucracy. When the new generation of economic policy makers was recruited into the state in the late 1970s, the primary means of career advancement within that bureaucracy was the "insiders' " political game organized around membership in a *camarilla,* a group loyal to an up-and-coming political patron.[18] Thus, without

16. Past generations were recruited mainly from the National School of Economics of the UNAM. In fact, Salinas's father, Raúl Salinas Lozano, was one such mentor who recruited his former UNAM students and built a "team" in the bureaucracy back in the 1940s and 1950s. See Roderic A. Camp, "The National School of Economics and Public Life in Mexico," *Latin American Research Review* 10, no, 3 (1975): 137–51. According to Camp, with the generation of Salinas de Gortari (whose recruitment style followed his father's model), the universities, most notably the historically less influential private institutions, have now become even more crucial as loci for political recruitment in Mexico. See Camp, *Political Recruitment,* 252–57.

17. This statement reflects the consensus in recent studies of Mexico's political elites that the oft-cited "técnico-político" dichotomy must be replaced by more complex typologies that recognize the political and ideological characteristics of highly trained bureaucrats. See, for example, Roderic A. Camp, "The Political Technocrat in Mexico and the Survival of the Political System," *Latin American Research Review* 20, no. 1 (1985): 97–118; Miguel Angel Centeno and Sylvia Maxfield, "The Marriage of Finance and Order: Changes in the Mexican Political Elite," *Journal of Latin American Studies* 24 (February 1992): 57–85, esp. table 1, p. 62; Juan D. Lindau, "Schisms in the Mexican Political Elite and the Technocrat/Politician Typology," *Mexican Studies 8/Estudios Mexicanos* (Summer 1992): 217–35.

18. This concept has been developed by Roderic A. Camp, *Mexico's Leaders: Their Education*

populist vocation and without incentives to "pay their dues" in grassroots organizing, these young economists could look forward to climbing the ladder in ways congruent with skills they had already begun developing in academia, such as team building and the identification of mentors, and with the help of the informal networks of *cuates* (close pals) and their roommates from Cambridge, Palo Alto, and Chicago.

After 1985, such a *camarilla* had coalesced around Carlos Salinas de Gortari, connecting like-minded economic reformers in Finance, Programming and Budget, and the Central Bank to one another and to a leader willing and able to wage the traditional subterranean power struggle within the PRI for the presidency.[19] Also notable at this time is that, for the generation in question, participation in party activities, traditionally focused on groups (labor, peasants) and electoral contests, was inconsequential compared with the importance of personal and professional contacts made through the PRI think tank, IEPES (Instituto de Estudios Políticos, Económicos y Sociales [Institute of Economic, Political, and Social Studies]), this reflecting the expertise of the newcomers and underlining the importance of *camarilla* politics for their career building within the Mexican state.[20] Indeed, by entering IEPES during the 1982 campaign, the former Ibarra team and several other promising economists, such as future president Ernesto Zedillo Ponce de León (Ph.D. Yale, minister of programming and budget and then minister of education under Salinas), came to work for de la Madrid and to connect with the politically savvy and ambitious Salinas, who served as the institute's director general at that time.[21] In *camarilla* politics, ideas and political interests are often difficult to distinguish as motivating factors; it follows, then, that while ideas helped forge the connection between generation members,

---

and Recruitment (Tucson: University of Arizona Press, 1980); as applied to the Salinas *sexenio*, see idem, "*Camarillas* in Mexican Politics: The Case of the Salinas Cabinet," *Mexican Studies/Estudios Mexicanos* 6 (Winter 1990): 85–108; Centeno, *Democracy Within Reason*, 146–149.

19. A useful chart documenting the formation of the Salinas *camarilla* can be found in Camp, *Political Recruitment*, 253.

20. See Centeno and Maxfield, "Marriage of Finance and Order," 63.

21. Various members of the Salinas *camarilla* were also connected through Leopoldo Solís, a top economist and former UNAM professor who directed economic and social planning in the Office of the Presidency (predecessor of SPP) in the early 1970s. As a mentor to many young economists entering the state, he served as a point of contact between Serra and Zedillo, who shared connections to Yale with Solís, and Aspe, who studied under a Solís's "charge," Francisco Gil Díaz, and whose other ITAM mentors, Miguel Mancera and Gustavo Petricioli, had studied with Solís at Yale. Salinas himself, as well as Camacho, knew Solís from their UNAM days. See Camp, *Political Recruitment*, 251–55. I wish to thank Rod Camp for bringing this set of connections to my attention.

their decision to cast their luck with Salinas was in all likelihood based as much on his relationship with de la Madrid and his chances to reach the highest office as on any intellectual affinity that may have existed between Harvard graduate Salinas and themselves.[22] To advance their project and their careers, individual members of the new generation needed to play the collective *camarilla* politics game, making their rise to power necessarily a joint venture.

Another institutional element crucial for our understanding of the collective nature of the Mexican technopol story is the historic practice of ritual battle within the economic policy-making elite between two opposing camps of development ideas. One of the hallmarks of the postrevolutionary Mexican political system has been the ability of leaders of the dominant party to incorporate competing groups, thus channeling what might otherwise have been open dissent into managed "participation." Over time, a considerable degree of intellectual pluralism has thus been promoted within the state, but it has functioned primarily as a strategy of legitimation: the more intellectual currents the state could lay claim to, the greater its policy options, and the more likely it could legitimate unexpected changes of policy.[23] In the field of economic policy in particular, two competing camps have coexisted within the Mexican federal bureaucracy in the postrevolutionary period: one more internationalist and classically liberal (housed in the Finance Ministry and Central Bank) and the other favoring greater state participation and leadership in development (centered in Programming and Budget and ministries that controlled natural resources). At key moments—for example, the 1930s and the late 1970s—the internal debate between these two views has been billed as a "struggle for the nation" over the direction of development policy;[24] at other times, these two main factions have coexisted within the state, with one

22. Though Salinas's ideas about poverty programs can be traced back to his doctoral dissertation, it is more difficult to substantiate continuity in his support of free-market reforms. As an ambitious bureaucrat, Salinas carefully moderated his positions to maximize his own political advancement; for example, in 1985-86, his decision to avoid giving "bad news" to the president helped him to prevail over a rival of equivalent training and economic knowledge, Finance Minister Jesús Silva Herzog, and secure de la Madrid's support for the PRI candidacy. This example is discussed in Centeno, *Democracy Within Reason*, 162–63.

23. The strategy also purposefully allowed all groups to "take turns" and share power over time. The idea of a circulating postrevolutionary elite is treated extensively in Peter H. Smith, *Labyrinths of Power: Political Recruitment in Twentieth-Century Mexico* (Princeton: Princeton University Press, 1979).

24. For an account of the debate in the 1970s written by a "nationalist" participant, see Rolando Cordera and Carlos Tello, *La disputa por la nación: Perspectivas y opciones del desarrollo* (Mexico City: Siglo Veintiuno Editores, 1981).

normally dominant and the other waiting in the wings.[25] From this perspective, the new generation joined the ongoing debate in the late 1970s, then, benefiting from the massive policy failure in 1982 and the collapse of the "nationalist" model, took advantage of the turn of the historical policy cycle to establish their economic project. Again, coordinated action was required both to seize the opportunity and to prove through results that their model had long-term value beyond the immediate crisis.

Though they stood collectively against the policies of the 1970s, in the 1980s the new generation acted on a synthesis of ideas about economic policy and development that was, in reality, far less "liberal" than the image projected. They agreed on the goal of a more dynamic, open economy and on the importance of fiscal discipline, low inflation, and a greater role for the private sector as the engine of development; at the same time, they fell short of true Adam Smith liberalism by favoring a strong "rectorship" role for the state in the economy. In this conception of "liberalized state-led" development, an active state reserves the right to intervene judiciously to compensate for market failure or to step in when markets favor efficiency over another national goal, such as poverty alleviation. In that sense, this new generation of policy makers rejected the static debate between "neoorthodox" and "heterodox" viewpoints[26] and advocated a third option for development that recognized both the necessity of adjustment and the advantages of using the centralized powers of the Mexican state—and the privileged positions of policy makers within it—to that end.

From the above analysis of the collective aspects of the Mexican reform story, we can extrapolate a rough blueprint for the "Mexican technopol" phenomenon. First, it has been generational, linking those economists born in the late 1940s and early 1950s who studied abroad together and entered the state at the same time. Second, unlike their *técnico* predecessors, this

25. Sylvia Maxfield looks at coalitions formed between the two camps within the state and their societal counterparts—in her terms, the Cardenistas and the bankers. See Maxfield, *Governing Capital: International Finance and Mexican Politics* (Ithaca: Cornell University Press, 1990), 78–134.

26. "Neoorthodoxy," the successor to monetarism in the Latin American development debate, emphasizes efficiency, outward orientation, and minimizing government intervention in the functioning of markets; "heterodoxy," by contrast, inherited from its predecessor, structuralism, the core assumption that the state has a primary responsibility to intervene on behalf of less powerful groups, even at the cost of economic efficiency. For an excellent tracing of these intellectual currents, see Miles Kahler, "Orthodoxy and Its Alternatives: Explaining Approaches to Stabilization and Adjustment," in *Economic Crisis and Policy Choice: The Politics of Adjustment in the Third World,* ed. Joan M. Nelson (Princeton: Princeton University Press, 1990), 33–61.

generation of economists sought political advancement and reached high levels in the bureaucracy. Third, they have acted in teams and have organized their political networks in informal ways that are congruent with their advancement in a *camarilla*-based presidentialist system. Fourth, cosmopolitan attitudes prevail, making Mexican technopols more likely to be skilled and confident negotiating partners with banks, foreign governments, and international institutions. Finally, they concur on the need to reform both the public and private sectors and on the preferability of a leaner, more efficient state with a delineated mission to one that has been allowed to wither away. Overall, what differentiates this new generation of economists-turned-policy makers is the combination of specialized training and political sense used to advance both their ideas and their ambitions for power simultaneously.

Pedro Aspe Armella: A Mexican Technopol

I turn now to the case of former finance minister Pedro Aspe Armella, whose achievements and career make him at once prototypical of his generation and exceptional within it. In the course of his rapid rise from a part-time economic adviser in the Finance Ministry to the president's economic cabinet, Aspe designed and implemented solutions to some of the most difficult problems facing Mexico during the 1980s, tackling inflation, tax reform, external debt, public-sector deficits, and the privatization of state enterprises. He also recruited some of the best and the brightest Mexican economics students to assist him in these efforts, building himself a core support group that expanded beyond the Finance Ministry and giving the reform project a greater measure of policy cohesion. All of this time, in true technopol fashion, Aspe acted upon his ideas within the constraints set by the Mexican political system, learning the basics of *camarilla* politics, group-based negotiation, and, above all, presidentialism. Playing strictly by the rules of etiquette and deference, Aspe managed to deflect or redirect much of the attention lavished upon him abroad and maintain his political legitimacy as a technical expert and a team player.

Portrait of the Technopol as a Young Man: Background and Training

By the traditional standards of postrevolutionary Mexican politics, Pedro Aspe Armella came from the wrong side of the tracks: the side of relative wealth and privilege. He was born into an upper-middle-class family whose forebears in the state of Michoacán had been relatively prosperous land-owners dispossessed by the revolution. His father was a successful business-man, and the family lived quite comfortably in the capital's better neighbor-hoods. Thanks to their financial resources, Aspe's education-minded parents were able to send him to the Colegio Patria, a private Jesuit school known for its high standards as well as its notable graduates, many of whom have gone on to prominent positions in business, government, and academia.[27] In addi-tion to his family's economic and social status, its ties to the Catholic Church—another traditional "villain" of the revolution—also boded poorly for Aspe's future political aspirations.

Further weakening his political profile, Aspe went on from the select Colegio Patria to pursue his *licenciatura*[28] at the Mexican Autonomous Insti-tute of Technology (Instituto Tecnológico Autónomo de México, or ITAM), a private university founded in the 1940s by leaders of the private sector, rather than the National Autonomous University of Mexico (UNAM), arbiter of the "national consciousness," or the prestigious and publicly supported Colegio de México, which stressed public service or academic, rather than commer-cial, priorities for its graduates.[29] ITAM was established, in part, to offer more market-oriented approaches and to counter the growing influence within the state of the import-substitution model taught at UNAM and advocated at the time by Raúl Prebisch and his colleagues at the United Nations Economic Commission for Latin America (ECLA).[30] Particularly in the 1970s when Aspe attended ITAM, the student body was considered elitist and their course work in economics deemed "out of touch" with Mexican reality by their counterparts at UNAM, many of whom were headed toward positions in the

27. Carlos Rico, interview by author, Mexico City, 13 May 1992. Rico, a Colegio Patria graduate from the same generation as Aspe, attends periodic reunions of his fellow alumni, whom he identifies as the high-achieving sons of the middle- to upper-middle-class intellectually and commercially oriented parents (many of them Spanish Republicans who had fled the civil war and the Franco regime).

28. In Mexico, the *licenciatura* is the first degree earned at university.

29. For a concise comparison of UNAM, ITAM, and the Colegio de México in the context of their socializing roles, influence over particular professions, and recruitment by class, see Camp, *Intellectuals and the State*, 170–76. Among earlier ITAM graduates are Gustavo Petricioli, finance minister under Miguel de la Madrid (1986–88) and ambassador to the United States under Carlos Salinas (1988–92), and Miguel Mancera, director general of the Central Bank (Banco de México) since 1982.

30. Often referred to as "developmentalism" or "structuralism," these ideas had a great impact throughout Latin America, most notably in the 1950s. See Albert O. Hirschman, "Ideologies of Economic Development in Latin America," in *A Bias for Hope: Essays on Development in Latin America* (New Haven: Yale University Press, 1971), 270–311.

government of Luis Echeverría, champion of "shared development." Furthermore, Aspe did not pursue postgraduate studies in Mexico, but rather chose to pursue a doctorate in an elite private university in the United States, the Massachusetts Institute of Technology.

As it turned out, by the time Pedro Aspe was recruited into the de la Madrid administration in the early 1980s, many of these same qualities had become assets of sorts for the young economist-turned-public servant. To those in the state seeking to bolster the system's political legitimacy through economic performance, Aspe's professional expertise became both practically necessary and politically attractive, given the progressive loss of confidence in the system as the economic crisis deepened. Even Aspe's privileged background eventually became an asset: hailing from a business-oriented family and having grown up with some of the country's leading young entrepreneurs, Aspe was well positioned to negotiate credibly and effectively with the private sector. Still, there were certain personal and intellectual qualities that Aspe developed during his years at ITAM and MIT that are far more important in explaining his distinguished career in economic policy making. Far from having been ripped untimely from the womb of university life, Pedro Aspe had long advocated, practiced, and valued academic research that engaged in solving real-world problems.

Pedro Aspe's intellectual development can be divided into three distinct and formative moments. The first moment was his time as an undergraduate at ITAM (1969–74), when he found his calling to the economics profession and was first introduced to the "engaged" academic life. Aspe actually started out at ITAM as an accounting major, but was virtually recruited by two notable members of the economics faculty, Antonio Bassols and future ITAM rector Javier Beristain, who recognized his potential in introductory classes. Apart from Bassols and Beristain, the one professor who had the most lasting intellectual and professional impact on Aspe at ITAM was his first mentor, Francisco Gil Díaz. Only seven years Aspe's senior and recently returned from the United States, where he had earned his doctorate at the University of Chicago, Gil had already been involved in several year-long projects for the Central Bank and the Finance Ministry. This experience, and Gil's dedication to a very practical intellectual passion—the study of tax policy[31]—made a great impression on Aspe as he realized that economists could make a difference in the

---

31. See, for example, Gil's doctoral dissertation, "Three Essays on the Taxation of Capital" (University of Chicago, 1973). For a useful summary of his professional and academic trajectories, see *Diccionario biográfico,* 144.

policy world. Following in the venerable Mexican academic tradition of strong patron-client ties, Gil, himself an ITAMista, served as a mentor for a small group of top students, including Aspe; indeed, it was Gil's encouragement that led Aspe, along with classmates Jesús Reyes Heroles and Juan Díaz Canedo, to pursue doctorates at the Massachusetts Institute of Technology. There, during the second formative moment of his intellectual development, Aspe would find in a second mentor an even more vivid example of how economists can apply their knowledge and specialized training to address society's biggest problems.

In the 1970s, as it still is today, the Economics Department at MIT was known for a focus on public policy and a belief in the benefits of market liberalization tempered by attention to market failure and consideration of limited government intervention to restore equilibrium. The MIT approach appealed to Aspe, who, while doubting the economic wisdom of the statist Mexican development model of the 1970s, was also skeptical about solutions that rejected state intervention under any circumstances. At MIT, Aspe's critical sense was sharpened by a variety of outstanding faculty with whom he studied, among them Professors Richard Eckaus and Nobel laureate Franco Modigliani, both of whom served on his dissertation committee. However, it was the third member of that committee, his primary adviser and mentor, Rudiger Dornbusch, who shaped Aspe not only as an economist but also as a policy maker, a negotiator, a teacher, and an international actor. With a penchant for confronting the most intractable problems of economic policy, Dornbusch wrote extensively on ways to tackle the structural imbalances of Latin America's closed economies as well as methods to address specific problems, such as hyperinflation and external debt.[32] Dornbusch's unapologetic combination of theoretical and empirical concerns, as well as his personal and intellectual encouragement as a mentor, convinced Aspe to view his doctoral studies as the first step toward a career dedicated to tackling the obstacles to Mexican development, and to view economic theory as a powerful tool in pursuit of that goal.

Dornbusch also advocated studying actual cases of policy design and implementation comparatively across national settings. This was made all the

---

32. See, for example, Dornbusch, "Capital Mobility and Portfolio Balance," in *The Political Economy of Monetary Reform,* ed. R. Aliber (London: Macmillan, 1976); "External Debt, Budget Deficits, and Disequilibrium Real Exchange Rates," in *International Debt and the Developing Countries*, ed. Gordon Smith and J. Cuddington (Washington, D.C.: World Bank, 1985); "México: Estabilización, deuda y crecimiento," *El Trimestre Económico 55* (October–December, 1988): 879–937; and "Credibility and Stabilization," *Quarterly Journal of Economics* 106 (August 1991): 837–50.

easier by the presence of students, scholars, and practitioners from around the world who gravitated to MIT and Harvard to partake in the ongoing dialogue on development policy. In seminars and in the hallways of the National Bureau of Economic Research (virtually a clubhouse for MIT and Harvard economists and their top graduate students), this intergenerational international community offered Aspe a living, breathing resource that was important for his intellectual development and, later in life, for opening doors in international financial institutions, private banks, and foreign governments. Dornbusch's students also had opportunities to discuss actual policies with the economist-policy makers who had designed and implemented them. Aspe learned a great deal from one such visiting scholar, Michael Bruno of Israel's Hebrew University, whose advice about stabilization policy would later assist Aspe in navigating Mexico's inflation crisis of the late 1980s.[33] Aspe also connected with a talented cohort of graduate students, one of whom was a young Argentine at Harvard named Domingo Cavallo.[34] Aspe even cited Cavallo's 1977 Ph.D. dissertation in the second essay of his own 1978 dissertation, "Essays on the International Transmission Mechanism: The Mexican Case," pointedly taking issue with Cavallo's assertion that stagflation would necessarily result from monetary stabilization programs. Moreover, Aspe and Cavallo also forged a bond in Cambridge with Alejandro Foxley, then a visiting scholar at MIT, who added another national example and a more fully developed political sensibility to the mix and, in the future, became a resource to both men as they sought to enact some of the ideas they discussed in their youth.[35]

While enjoying his new cosmopolitan connections, Aspe spent the majority of his time and energy during graduate school focusing on his own country and its problems. Following an undergraduate interest in the labor effects of rural-urban migration,[36] and possibly influenced by his discussions with Foxley, Aspe went beyond the usual ration of courses in international finance to study income distribution. Considered a "soft" subject by his fellow foreign students, income distribution, as far as Aspe was concerned, represented Mexico's toughest development dilemma, just as the trade-off between equity

---

33. Pedro Aspe, interview by author, Washington, D.C., 18 September 1992.
34. Ibid.
35. For a more detailed account of the Aspe-Cavallo-Foxley connection, see Matt Moffett, "Seeds of Reform: Key Finance Ministers in Latin America Are Old Harvard-MIT Pals," *Wall Street Journal*, 1 August 1994, A1, A6.
36. Pedro Aspe and Ignacio Trigueros, "Migración, expectativas y probabilidades de empleo: Un caso práctico" (*licenciatura* thesis, Instituto Tecnológico Autónomo de México, 1974).

and efficiency in market systems represented the hardest lesson of economics.[37] These courses reinforced Aspe's growing skepticism about pure market solutions, while presenting him with the rationale for selective state intervention into markets to promote justice. In another departure from the standard curriculum, Aspe studied Mexican history at Harvard with John Womack, a leading expert on the economic roots and consequences of the Mexican Revolution.[38] For an upper-middle-class Mexican raised in relative privilege and preparing to be an economist, this course was both a revelation and a wake-up call: he saw that historic patterns and institutions, not current misguided policy alone, presented the greatest obstacles to equitably distributed economic development in Mexico. Looking at his country through these new lenses, Aspe was at once filled with pride and remorse: how could this nation of institution builders, with such tremendous intellectual resources and creativity, allow so many to live in poverty, and how could his own generation allow this to continue?[39] Aspe, like others of his generation, returned to Mexico believing that the right tools and the right level of personal commitment on their part could make the difference in writing the next page of Mexican economic history; for Aspe in particular, this meant combining "cosmopolitan" training with a "nationalist" sense of history to identify and then remove the underlying structural impediments to development.

From 1978 to 1982, the third crucial moment of his intellectual journey, Aspe returned to ITAM to construct the kind of "engaged" life he had admired in his mentors. Just as Francisco Gil Díaz had done in 1973, Aspe became the chairman of the Department of Economics shortly upon his return from the United States. According to his account of the decision, Aspe saw in the ITAM position a chance to affect fundamental change in Mexico in the longer term by training the next generation of economists, specifically at a time when López Portillo's profligate policies contradicted what he had learned at MIT about "sound" economic policy.[40] The ITAM position also promised to give Aspe two distinct career advantages: his own "power base" independent of the state, and an identity and position apart from his mentor and sponsor, Gil Díaz (who had left ITAM that same year to become director general of incomes policy at the Finance Ministry). With both intellectual and

37. For one interesting treatment of this issue, see Arthur M. Okun, *Equality and Efficiency: The Big Tradeoff* (Washington, D.C.: Brookings Institution, 1975).

38. Womack is best known for his outstanding narrative history, *Zapata and the Mexican Revolution* (New York: Vintage Books, 1968).

39. Pedro Aspe, interview by author, Washington, D.C., 18 September 1992.

40. Ibid.

professional commitment, in his four years at ITAM Aspe realized his vision of an acclaimed economics department designed to prepare top students for public service and the construction of a new development model.

As chairman, Aspe's first job was to reshape the ITAM economics program to reflect his priorities for training the next generation of economists. He overhauled the curriculum, which he viewed as too narrowly focused on theory and methods without attention to contextual variables such as history and culture. Specifically, he added a requirement in economic history and one in income distribution, the latter a radical addition at a market-oriented institution. Most crucially, Aspe left his stamp on the department as a professor, throwing himself into the task of educating the next generation with a gusto often depicted as "relentless" by those he taught. Famous for causing near panic with his "weed-out" classes and examinations from which students would seek "liberation," Aspe was first and foremost a dedicated teacher, a real *maestro* in the Mexican sense of a professional educator who earns students' respect and devotion through tough, almost parental insistence on high standards. Aspe was truly in his element in the classroom; there he was able to impart personally and directly not only his knowledge and technical expertise but also his conviction that the study of economics was of vital national interest. His brand of high-impact education, though roundly criticized as authoritarian by some, inspired respect and loyalty in those who would later follow him into the state as his "team."

His administrative and teaching accomplishments reflect only two of the four jobs that Aspe performed simultaneously while at ITAM. In his third capacity as a university professor and academic economist, Aspe followed Dornbusch's example by addressing intransigent policy problems and communicating ideas across borders. A fine example is found in the project on income distribution that Aspe coordinated with Princeton political scientist Paul Sigmund in the early 1980s.[41] Bringing together scholars from Mexico and the United States, including Mexican government officials, such as Gil Díaz and Salinas (then the director general of economic and social policy at Programming and Budget under Minister de la Madrid), this project focused directly on the distributive bottlenecks that neither the growth of "stabilizing development" nor the activist state of "shared development" had relieved. Consistent with Aspe's views on the subject, the project sought to counter the

41. Pedro Aspe and Paul Sigmund, eds., *The Political Economy of Income Distribution in Mexico,* The Political Economy of Income Distribution in Developing Countries Series, ed. Henry Bienen (New York: Holmes & Meier Publishers, 1984).

ideological objections of more orthodox free market economists and the reluctance of risk-averse policy makers by demonstrating both the dangers of inaction and the need to forge solutions that were, above all, viable politically as well as economically.

At closer range, his five coauthored essays—nearly one-third of all contributions to the volume—collectively address two themes that foreshadow Aspe's later work in government and give us some clues to the ideas Aspe took into government with him. First, in all five pieces, but notably in the four substantive studies, Aspe advances a broader definition of development that questions "neoliberal" economists' supreme normative goal of efficient markets. While criticism of the "irresponsible" economic policies of the 1970s is also a running theme, Aspe's work focuses on the persistence of historical, structural causes of skewed income distribution as evidence of even greater obstacles to long-term, sustainable development. Departing from the stereotype of a "free-marketeer," Aspe's analysis reflects his belief that liberalizing markets alone would not necessarily liberate Mexico from its most intractable developmental dilemma. This leads naturally into the second dominant message of Aspe's work, a rejection of a strictly "laissez-faire" vision of the state's role in the economy. Given that markets are designed to clear, not to distribute gains according to a particular normative standard, the state may serve as the mechanism to accomplish that distributional goal. From Aspe's perspective, while the state should not attempt to preempt the market, it is best suited to provide a "safety net" according to normative goals. Moreover, in essay after essay, Aspe and his coauthors conclude that the government's "political will" would make the difference in the end, implying that the state is destined to play an integral role in any attempt to address the underlying causes of income inequality in Mexico.

These themes are particularly well stated in the essay by Aspe and Beristain entitled "The Evolution of Income Distribution Policies During the Post-Revolutionary Period in Mexico."[42] Through a review of the historical origins of Mexico's income-inequality problem, Aspe and Beristain suggest that greater distributive justice should be treated in policy making as an end in itself, rather than merely as a way to achieve other goals, such as stability or growth. Herein we get a direct glimpse of Aspe's normative and intellectual rationale for economic reform, which is viewed as a necessary means to the goal of social justice. As he writes with Beristain: "[G]rowth must have a meaning, an orientation, and a goal. . . . We do not share the belief that

42. Ibid., 15–29.

efficiency is enough: an efficient but unjust system cannot endure. Neither do we believe that justice can be achieved through stagnation, because stagnation leads to the spread of poverty. We reject the possibility of dealing with efficiency and justice as interchangeable goods; both are to be desired. We propose the search for efficiency as a necessary but not sufficient condition for justice."[43]

Equally telling is the attitude toward the state reflected in their argument. Rather than suggest the need for "more" or "less" state intervention to correct the inequalities of income that have plagued Mexican society, Aspe and Beristain focus on the requirement of "strong government . . . to receive from society the redistributive assignment as well as the power and resources to carry it out."[44] The state, according to this point of view, is not inherently good or bad, but rather is a necessary and powerful tool. Intervention with distributional ends, they add, is also consistent with the tradition of the "revolutionary" Mexican state, whose legitimacy has rested upon its ability to provide social justice. Rather, what must be assessed as "better" or "worse," according to Aspe and Beristain, is the type of policy chosen by the state to meet national distributional needs and how that policy is implemented. For example, policies that focus on investing in human capital through education and on reducing subsidies that make labor expensive relative to other inputs (such as energy) are to be judged superior to policies that attempt to stimulate aggregate demand, which may create employment in the short run but are macroeconomically unsustainable. In other words, it is not the state per se that will make the difference, but the individuals within it, their ideas and priorities, and their political will to make use of the institutional apparatus and to choose sound, long-term solutions.

By the time he was preparing these views for publication, Aspe had already made his first step toward contributing his own ideas and expertise within the state. In 1978, at approximately the same time that he took over the Economics Department at ITAM, Aspe was invited to join some of the most promising newly minted Ph.D.'s in the economic advisory staff of Finance Minister David Ibarra, an experience mentioned earlier as a key factor in the collective "technopol" story. For Aspe individually, this—the fourth of four jobs he performed simultaneously while at ITAM—proved to be the one that changed his life most profoundly, launching his political career and linking him more concretely to his generation and its project. Assisted by his own

43. Ibid., 17.
44. Ibid.

talents for economic analysis and quiet self-promotion, Pedro Aspe was able to parlay his membership in Ibarra's group into a leading position among the architects of a new development model during the de la Madrid *sexenio*. Although his influence on policy was minimal at first, Aspe went on to prove to his students and to those who followed his rise to power that change could be effected within the system by the entry of individuals sharing new ideas.

From *Maestro* to Minister: Ideas and Interests in the Mexican Bureaucratic Game

Pedro Aspe's rise through the bureaucratic ranks reads almost like a fairy tale for aspiring economists-turned-policy makers. Aspe entered the new administration of Miguel de la Madrid buried in the backwater of the Programming and Budget Ministry, heading up the much-maligned National Institute of Statistics, Geography, and Information (Instituto Nacional de Estadística, Geografía e Informática, or INEGI). However, after only three years, Aspe transformed that backwater into a showpiece, and was rewarded with a direct promotion to a position closer to the policy-making action. Gaining a reputation as a miracle worker during his two short years as undersecretary for planning and budget control, Aspe was then catapulted to instant stardom, taking over the helm from Salinas when the latter began his presidential campaign. Aspe then used his one year at the head of Programming and Budget to slay the dragon of inflation and stabilize the economy in time for his boss's election, securing for himself the top position at Finance, a berth within a like-minded economic cabinet, and the power to do what he had always dreamed of: transforming ideas into actions.

As most fairy tales do, this version of the Pedro Aspe story oversimplifies the mechanism by which dreams come true, making it appear that Aspe's rise through the ranks was the result of a meritocratic process based on ideas rather than a political process based on power. In reality, the political rules that have historically governed advancement through the bureaucracy in Mexico blur the lines between ideas and interests: those who aspire to the nation's highest office routinely use ideas as the means of building personal and institutional bases of support, often adopting new ideas at politically strategic moments and with political goals in mind. In that context, we may then view Aspe as the tool of two veterans of the succession game: Miguel de la Madrid and Carlos Salinas. In this scenario, de la Madrid was a transition figure, a pragmatist who had held off on radical state reform for as long as he could, but who had also recognized Aspe as a valuable player long before publicly sharing the young economist's ideas on liberalization. Salinas then played the role of political entrepreneur, starting with his efforts in IEPES during the 1982 campaign and accelerating around 1985 — the time of de la Madrid's first major import-liberalization measures — when his main goal was to coordinate a team of young talented economists to design and implement the new reform program that would reflect well on his boss and, by extension, increase his own political capital. Salinas promoted Aspe ostensibly because his talents as an economist and his ability to speak authoritatively on the theoretical underpinnings of the reforms would serve to legitimate and promote the program and its political champions, de la Madrid and Salinas. Aspe was given the opportunity to put his ideas into action; however, by this interpretation, that opportunity was extended for political purposes and could easily have been revoked at any moment without regard to the objective quality of Aspe's work.

At the same time, I would argue that Aspe was hardly a passive participant in his own political elevation. In fact, his rapid rise through the ranks testifies to his ability to play the *camarilla* game to his best advantage and toward the promotion of his ideas within policy-making circles. While Aspe may have had little experience in politics when he returned from MIT, he was not a total innocent in the ways of influence within the Mexican bureaucracy. He had been groomed by Gil Díaz, who had recognized early on the potential political value of creating within the state a network of like-minded young economists that could collectively push policy in the "right" direction. Gil's strategy was not only prescient, anticipating the 1982 crisis and the consequent explosion of demand for skilled market-oriented economists, it was also congruent with the overriding importance given historically in Mexico to personal connections and patron-client relationships within both the bureaucratic elite and the official party leadership. One might logically ask why it was Aspe, and not his young talented mentor, who eventually rose to the pinnacle of power within the economic policy bureaucracy. Though part of the answer may lie in a comparison of the quality of their ideas or technical skills, Aspe's prodigious ability to absorb the subtleties of the political game, reflected in his efforts as a team builder and a team player, marked him as a rising star. Aspe set out to learn the way up the ladder and proved himself an excellent student in the process.

Aspe's experience as a professor and mentor in the university setting made the team-building aspect of political life the easiest for him to master. Following Gil's example, as chairman of the Economics Department at ITAM Aspe sought out those he judged to be the brightest and most motivated students, whom he sponsored for graduate study in the United States. However, in addition to recruiting top technical talent, Aspe also recognized the importance of building a philosophical and ideological consensus on the need to use those techniques to foster both equity and efficiency. These efforts yielded a core "team" of ITAMistas dedicated not only to public service but also to Aspe himself and to a "shared vision" of development.[45] Though the Aspe team's "vision" was not the dogmatic veneration of markets often attributed to "neoliberals," it did bear a close resemblance to a secular faith: in addition to believing in a moral imperative for reform, young initiates were encouraged by Aspe to approach their work as a "calling" as much as a career.[46] While remaining very much the *maestro* in some respects, particularly in his insistence on high standards, Aspe evolved into a veritable leader for these young professionals, who, in turn, aspired to advance the "cause" through optimal performance and loyalty.[47] The construction of this team of "true believers" was arguably Aspe's most profitable investment as a policy maker; indeed, as he wrote later with his team in mind, "[to advance economic modernization] it is indispensable to count on top-notch people who are also of one mind regarding the necessity of stabilization and structural change."[48]

Within the Mexican political context this team-building process was also a shrewd and profitable investment for Aspe as one aiming for higher office within the bureaucracy.[49] First, the proven effectiveness of his team raised

45. In separate interviews, when discussing what made Aspe's team so effective, Aspe, his former students, current staff members, and a variety of observers all gave a similar description of this "shared vision" and Aspe's role in defining that vision.

46. Pedro Aspe, interview by author, Washington , D.C., 18 September 1992.

47. Carlos Sales Sarrapy, interview by author, Mexico City, 6 August 1992. Sales (Lic. ITAM, Ph.D. Harvard), one of Aspe's young economic advisers, spoke of a "meritocracy" among those who work closely with Aspe: no matter what the personal relationship or the quality of their work in the past, they expect to be removed if they do not meet Aspe's high expectations. In reality, as Sales notes, most devote themselves to the work out of their own commitment to it rather than a fear of Aspe's wrath; still, this account reveals the way Aspe is both *maestro* and leader, setting standards and building consensus.

48. Pedro Aspe, *El camino mexicano de la transformación económica* (Mexico City: Fondo de Cultura Económica, 1993), 56; author's translation.

49. Pedro Aspe was not the only one of his generation to build an academically based team. Most notably, Jaime Serra Puche, Salinas's trade minister, built his own from students at the Colegio de México. However, Serra was not as successful as Aspe in raising the profile of his home institution: in the past decade the ITAM program has overtaken even the National University as the recognized home of the ideas dominant within the state. Moreover, in the Salinas *sexenio,* Aspe's team had more long-term political potential simply because Serra—one of whose parents is a Spanish Republican exile and thus not Mexican-born—was, until recently, ineligible for the presidency according to the constitution.

Aspe's profile within the bureaucracy and made him valuable to Salinas as he built his own reputation as a reformer. Second, Aspe continued to sponsor and recruit ITAMistas long after he stopped teaching, giving him a steady supply of newly minted Ph.D.'s for his policy-making team. Indeed, by the latter part of the Salinas *sexenio,* Aspe's "team" came to comprise several "generations" and branched out well beyond Finance, providing its leader greater visibility and influence throughout the bureaucracy. Known as *gente de Aspe,* or Aspe's people, they appeared in entities as diverse as the Ministry of Agriculture (Luis Téllez),[50] the Ministry of Social Development (Carlos Hurtado), and the Ministry of Education (Pascual García de Alba); one was a PRI deputy and leading member of the Finance Committee of the Chamber of Deputies (Miguel Angel Aceves), while another, ITAMista Diódoro Carrasco, surprised analysts when he was elected governor of the rural and primarily indigenous state of Oaxaca using the Aspe-inspired slogan "Efficiency and Equity!" Between these younger allies, his ITAM classmates (such as Carlos Camacho Gaos and former head of deregulation and current ITAM rector Arturo Fernández), ITAM professors (Gil Díaz and Beristain, the latter then the minister of finance in the government of the Federal District), and well-placed ITAMistas of previous generations (Central Bank director Miguel Mancera and former finance minister and former ambassador to the United States Gustavo Petricioli), one might say that in under a decade Aspe had built a political and intellectual empire within the Mexican policy elite.

Aspe's team building did not stop with the consolidation of his own team; a closer look at the dynamics of *camarilla* politics in the early and mid-1980s shows that Salinas's efforts to position himself advantageously were met with parallel efforts by Aspe. It is difficult to say who was recruiting whom at that moment. While Salinas appreciated the value of Aspe's technical talents, Aspe was equally astute in recognizing in Salinas the qualities necessary for a successful bid for Mexican politics' grand prize, most notably drive, ambition, and understanding of the unwritten rules of the subterranean ritual. Since Aspe was looking for a way to promote his ideas as well as his own position, it stands to reason that he might seek out a "champion" like Salinas, who spoke the same technical language and possessed the high-level political experience Aspe lacked. Viewed that way, Aspe recruited Salinas to lead the political battle for free market reforms as much as Salinas recruited Aspe to

50. As of 1 December 1994, Luis Téllez, who had been head of the Zedillo presidential campaign, became the new president's "chief of staff," a position held in the Salinas administration by José Córdoba; see note 51 below.

formulate, implement, and legitimate (scientifically) that project. In the end, an alliance was forged that served both men well: Aspe was never considered a close friend (or *cuate*) of Salinas, but several of Aspe's strengths—expertise as an economist, international connections, leadership abilities, and so forth—earned him Salinas's respect and led Salinas to trust him with significant areas of economic policy. His appointment as minister of finance in 1988 stands as the ultimate proof that Aspe had successfully navigated *camarilla* politics, culminating in the Salinas presidency, while his tenure for the entire *sexenio* reflects the durability of the symbiosis between Aspe and the president.

Aspe further demonstrated his willingness and ability to learn the basics of Mexican *presidencialismo* through a second politically motivated activity: team playing. There is an adage often used to describe the contradictory requirements for advancement within the Mexican political elite: roughly translated, it reads, Playing politics is like being photographed: he who moves does not come out well (La política es como la fotografía: el que se mueve no sale bien). The taboo on overt self-promotion connoted by the adage intensifies once an individual attains a position within the president's cabinet, historically the subset from which incumbents have chosen their de facto successors. For example, it was arguably a violation of these rules by de la Madrid's charismatic finance minister, Jesús Silva Herzog, that doomed his "bid" for the presidency. Such a logic may seem counterintuitive to those accustomed to political systems with open campaigning on the part of prospective candidates for party nomination; what must be recalled is that, although the PRI may be in the process of adapting itself to the more competitive post-1988 electoral context, its own internal rules for the nomination of presidential candidates remain centered on the personal choice of the incumbent and the perpetuation of the ritual of a covert race, both of which reflect the continuity of *presidencialismo* in Mexico.

By the time Pedro Aspe had reached cabinet rank, he had witnessed close-hand two of these ritual battles, and he had also learned to strike a balance for himself between eye-catching performance and understated behavior with his superiors. Unlike Cavallo, who used confrontation with Menem to his advantage, Aspe took great care to discuss his accomplishments in terms of "the president's program" and observed the rules of etiquette surrounding the presentation of innovative ideas so that credit could be deflected upward. On one level, to paraphrase Henry Kissinger, this projected image of "team playing" had the added advantage of being true: Aspe made his contribution in tandem with his talented and like-minded colleagues in Salinas's powerhouse economic cabinet. Headed up until the spring of 1994 by the president's closest adviser, José Córdoba,[51] the economic cabinet accomplished two important goals for the Salinas administration: coordination of the activities of the individual ministers,[52] and more direct presidential control over all areas of economic policy by constraining the autonomy of the ministers on a weekly basis. On another level, Aspe also actively and deliberately cultivated a public image of team playing in order to deflect the attention lavished on him from abroad. Quite telling indeed was how decisively a member of Aspe's public relations office put an end to a discussion of Aspe's role in the design of tax policy with the comment "Salinas is the conductor; we are the orchestra."[53] Respecting the rules of the game, Aspe proved himself adept in the ways of presidentialist politics, managing to move up without moving too much.

By arguing that he developed and demonstrated significant political skills in the course of his rise to the top of the economic policy-making bureaucracy, I call into question the widespread notion that Pedro Aspe's role in government did not go farther than his specialized knowledge as an economist could have taken him. To be fair, part of that image is well-deserved: lacking not only electoral experience and popular vocation but also key political contacts within traditional sectors of his party, Aspe became identified with a limited base of antipopulist interests such as the private sector, foreign capital, and international financial institutions. Indeed, unlike the other Latin American technopols profiled in this volume, Aspe had a strictly bureaucratic career;

51. Córdoba, whose official title was "chief of the office of coordination" at Presidencia, has gained fame variously as the "éminence grise" of the economic team and Salinas's alter ego; the two met in the early 1980s, shortly after Córdoba, born and raised in France, the son of Spanish Republican exiles, was brought to Mexico by his roommate at Stanford, Guillermo Ortíz (Ph.D., 1977), a future finance minister under Zedillo. Though not a Mexican citizen until 1985, Córdoba had advised Salinas since the latter was director general of IEPES in 1982, and held several positions in Programming and Budget under Salinas, including chief of Salinas's economic advisory staff. Even with the new constitutional changes, Córdoba remained ineligible for the highest office; however, he created a niche for himself at the top of President Salinas's economic team, arguably as its most powerful and influential member. His sudden move in late March 1994 from Presidencia to Washington, D.C. to represent Mexico at the Inter-American Development Bank appeared to be a political exile of sorts, associated with strategic calculations made by Salinas in naming Ernesto Zedillo, known to be close to Córdoba, to replace the assassinated Luis Donaldo Colosio as the PRI's presidential candidate for the August 1994 elections.

52. For his own assessment of the importance of cabinet meetings and team cohesion for policy reform, see José Córdoba, "Mexico," in *The Political Economy of Policy Reform*, ed. John Williamson (Washington, D.C.: Institute for International Economics, 1994), 282–84.

53. Juan Antonio Chirino, interview by author, Mexico City, 30 July 1992, translation by author. Chirino was personal secretary to the director of social communication at the Ministry of Finance.

thus, his need to develop the political skills of a legislator or a party leader was limited as much by personality as by position in the executive branch of a hierarchical, presidentialist one-party-dominant system. This is not to say that Aspe remained completely insulated from other aspects of Mexican political life: as I demonstrate in the next section, Aspe did develop hands-on political skills that permitted him to move from theory to practice as an economic policy maker. Whatever his ambitions or shortcomings as a potential "politician," Aspe was aware that implementing ideas within a political context requires expertise in how to act, not just how to think.

Aspe in Action: Making Possible What Is Necessary

When asked to discuss his key formative experiences, Pedro Aspe cites a conversation he had late one night with a favorite professor, ITAM Economics Department founder Miguel Palacios Macer, during which the venerable Palacios commented that politics should not be viewed as "the art of the possible," but rather "the art of making possible what is necessary" ("La política no es el arte de lo posible, es el arte de hacer posible lo necesario").[54] What Palacios meant, and what stayed with Aspe over the years, was that public service should be a moral commitment, first, to defining "what is necessary" and, second, to making it possible. Three themes, traceable to his background and training, formed the center of Aspe's own normative vision: attacking the roots of the income-distribution problem; debunking the myths about the outside world and Mexico's relationship to it; and going beyond rigid models to find solutions that work in the real world. In this section, I address how Aspe the policy maker attempted to make possible these changes, which he considered necessary. To that end, I present four "mini-cases," which together illustrate the evolution of Aspe's political style and the advancement of his career, as well as the concomitant advancement of the economic liberalization project. In contrast to these cases of policy "success," in a fifth and final minicase I address the 1994–95 peso meltdown, specifically noting Aspe's individual contribution to the crisis. Though not quite the dramatic personal "rise-and-fall" story evident in the case of Evelyn Matthei,

54. Pedro Aspe, interview by author, Washington, D.C., 18 September 1992; author's translation. See also Federico Reyes Heroles and René Delgado, "Pedro Aspe Armella: La privatización del sector privado," *Este país*, no. 11 (January 1992), 23.

the collapse of the "second Mexican miracle" presents a cautionary tale of its own for technopols who risk becoming victims of their own success.

Leader of El Pacto: Greatest Challenge, Greatest Success

In mid-1985, following a standout performance in his first administrative position—transforming the statistics bureau—Aspe was recruited by Salinas to serve as his undersecretary for planning and budget control. A mere two years later, a total of five years since he entered government, Aspe completed his ascent, taking over the reins of Programming and Budget when Salinas became the PRI's presidential candidate. Unfortunately, the fulfillment of his dream was accompanied by his worst nightmare: following the stock market crash of October 1987, an unexpected run on the peso sent inflation spinning out of control.[55] The timing could not have been worse, given his lack of experience and the vulnerability of the Salinas candidacy to the crisis. Within weeks, however, Aspe put together a proposal for ending the crisis, and within two months his solution—a heterodox "social pact" of wage and price controls—had been negotiated successfully with representatives of labor, agriculture, and the private sector, bringing inflation down from triple-digit levels to an average of 1.2 percent per month by mid 1988.[56] The Economic Solidarity Pact (Pacto de Solidaridad Económica, or PSE), or El Pacto, as it was popularly called, was both an economic and a political success; it was renegotiated four additional times as such before 1989, then repackaged politically first as the Pact for Economic Stability and Growth (Pacto para la Estabilidad y el Crecimiento Económico, or PECE) and then, in line with the Zedillo campaign's main theme, as the Pact for Well-Being, Stability, and Growth.[57]

Aspe's training in cross-national comparison, his international contacts, and his own ability to learn contributed to the innovative and ultimately successful design of El Pacto. The ideas behind the Mexican pact were not

55. For a concise overview of the 1987 crisis and its underlying causes in the 1986 policy of an "overdevalued" exchange rate, see Nora Lustig, *Mexico: The Remaking of an Economy* (Washington, D.C.: Brookings Institution, 1992), 50.

56. Ibid., 51. For an analysis of the pact and its prospects in the post-1988 context, see Lawrence Whitehead, "Political Change and Economic Stabilization: The 'Economic Solidarity Pact,'" in *Mexico's Alternative Political Futures*, Monograph Series no. 30, ed. Wayne A. Cornelius, Judith Gentleman, and Peter H. Smith (La Jolla: Center for U.S.-Mexican Studies, University of California at San Diego, 1989), 181–213.

57. Anthony DePalma, "Mexicans Sign New Accord on Economy," *New York Times*, 25 September 1994, 17.

new; indeed, Aspe had been studying the stabilization strategies of other countries since his MIT days, building a "file" of these experiences gleaned from conferences, articles, and personal contacts.[58] As early as 1985, when he became undersecretary at SPP, Aspe had begun to design a stabilization program for Mexico, calling on friends such as MIT economists Dornbusch, Modigliani, and Stanley Fischer and sending students to Israel to study with Michael Bruno. Though studying the Brazilian (Plan Cruzado) and Argentine (Plan Austral) experiences of 1985–86 helped him identify pitfalls to avoid, Aspe drew his plan for Mexico mainly from two successful cases: Israel and Spain. His willingness to consider an incomes policy—rejected as too interventionist by most mainstream economists but proven successful in Israel when paired with fiscal discipline—reveals Aspe's pragmatism and his refusal to be limited by ideological blind spots. From the Spanish Pacto de la Moncloa, based on the concept of *concertación* and participation of societal groups, he learned that (to quote Dornbusch) "effective stabilization is, above all, not a technical issue but a political one."[59] After nearly a decade of austerity, Aspe reasoned, Mexican society would embrace a mechanism that committed all groups—including the private sector—equally and publicly to sharing the sacrifice.

Next, Aspe had to adapt to a new, more practical and political responsibility: negotiating the pact with the business, labor, and agricultural sectors. As useful as foreign models had been, for this job Aspe looked to Mexican institutions for the guidelines for successful policy, finding that the long tradition of corporatist relations between groups and the state could serve as a framework in which to begin the negotiation process. He also found that the overwhelming power and autonomy of the Mexican executive, particularly relative to labor, offered him far more bargaining leverage than his counterparts in other countries, most notably Argentina. The negotiation process, which lasted for two months (and was to be repeated every time the pact came up for renewal), was an eye-opening experience for Aspe, who had never had this kind of close political contact with domestic groups before, let alone served as the chief negotiator for the state in a landmark agreement with them. Aspe adapted to his new role by approaching negotiation much as he would a classroom experience: at the table, Aspe the student listened to labor

58. This section draws primarily on the interviews held with Pedro Aspe, Washington, D.C., 18 and 19 September 1992.

59. Rudiger Dornbusch, "Comments, Chapters 7–10," in *IMF Conditionality*, ed. John Williamson (Washington, D.C.: Institute for International Economics, 1983), 229.

leaders' demands, and then Aspe the teacher used his powers of explication and reasoning to formulate informative and effective responses. Aspe continued this dialogue with pact participants throughout his tenure as finance minister, meeting with them every Thursday morning at 8:30 at the Labor Ministry.

Over time, the pact has faced its share of criticism, mostly from those who claim that the private sector has not sacrificed nearly as much as labor and agriculture. Similarly, meeting regularly with selected labor leaders does not necessarily imply that as finance minister Aspe was actively building a labor coalition in support of his policies. Rather, Aspe demonstrated through these meetings a willingness and an ability to communicate with a variety of societal groups because, in this instance, it was what he had to do to make possible what was necessary—that is, to control inflation and to ensure entry of his patron to office without the weight of an economic crisis. By opting for *concertación*, Aspe clearly recognized the importance of dialogue between social groups and the government to ensure the consolidation of economic reforms; however, it should be recalled that this dialogue was held very much within the confines of corporatist channels, which historically have stressed inclusion and limited more direct and critical forms of participation.

Perhaps the most controversial aspect of the pact over time has been its connection to the exchange rate mechanism. During the Salinas *sexenio*, wage and price increases, as well as the "band" defining the maximum devaluation of the peso, were renegotiated with each renewal of the pact. This system, which pegged the peso to the dollar without fixing a one-to-one parity as Cavallo did in Argentina, allowed the peso to devalue on a daily basis while offering a guarantee against a rapid, all-out devaluation. While it was credible for most of Salinas's time in office, by early 1994 this system was clearly becoming an artificial prop. Given the intense political uncertainty surrounding such unexpected and destabilizing events as the rebellion in Chiapas and the assassination of PRI presidential candidate Luis Donaldo Colosio in early 1994, the prop was an understandable intervention of the state to avoid an economic crisis; at the same time, the government's inability to show weakness in the face of foreign investor anxieties following the August elections and the assassination of a key PRI reform figure may have led Salinas and Aspe to miss an opportunity in September 1994 to use the pact mechanism to increase the slippage band to more credible levels. Also contributing to this missed opportunity was Aspe's own deep personal commitment to controlling inflation, reinforced by his desire to protect his greatest accomplishment from becoming a casualty of a political quagmire.

The 1989 Debt Agreement: At Home Abroad, Abroad at Home

In his inaugural address of 1 December 1988, President Salinas charged his new finance minister with meeting the administration's immediate economic goal: the renegotiation of the external debt.[60] Renegotiating the debt was crucial to Salinas's "open-economy" project because it would build confidence in the Mexican economy for those important economic actors still waiting on the sidelines: domestic investors and flight capital, foreign investors, and, ultimately, the creditor banks. Such an international agreement would also "lock in" the new president's reforms and guarantee the permanence of the free market project. Moreover, as the first Latin American country to hammer out a debt-reduction scheme, Mexico could burnish its global reputation as a site for investment, standing out from its competitors in the region and positioning itself to compete with Eastern Europe and Southeast Asia.

Aspe turned out to be an ideal chief negotiator for these international talks despite his lack of formal experience in economic diplomacy. First, he arrived with a top-notch support team characterized not only by impressive analytical skills and rapport with their interlocutors from the International Monetary Fund (IMF) and creditor banks but also by cohesion around his leadership. Aspe himself was remarkably comfortable with his own upper-level counterparts, thanks to his MIT-Harvard contacts and his experience accompanying Finance Minister Petricioli to the IMF during the renegotiation of Mexico's external debt in 1986. At that time, Aspe impressed Fund officers as a first-rate professional economist and laid the groundwork to be viewed later as the guarantor of Mexican commitment. In 1989, however, the international lending community was still hesitant to trust Mexico again, but Aspe counted on his powers of persuasion, his command of accurate data, his first-rate team, his training, and his intense work style to win them over.

Aspe drew upon these advantages to bring the negotiations to a swift and arguably beneficial conclusion for Mexico. Reversing the order originally planned, Aspe decided to negotiate first with the IMF—counting on his understanding of that institution, its preconditions for funding, and its staff—prior to entering into negotiations with the creditor banks. He reasoned that gaining the "seal of approval" from the IMF would give Mexico a stronger case with the banks. After the IMF, Aspe went on to pursue agreements with the World Bank, the Inter-American Development Bank, and the so-called

---

60. Carlos Salinas de Gortari, "Discurso de toma de posesión," reprinted in *Comercio exterior* 38 (December 1988): 1140.

Paris Club in the spring of 1989, prior to approaching the private banks in July. Second, in his discussions with both IMF staff and bank representatives, Aspe maintained and even enhanced his reputation as the leader of an exemplary Mexican team. He also came prepared to work all day and all night and surprised even his staff with the extremes to which he would go to make sure that each round of negotiation led to progress. He continued this pattern of behavior when the team moved on to face the creditor banks, impressing many of their ranks as well with his straightforward, energetic approach.

Third, while Aspe's negotiating style incorporated few of the niceties associated with traditional diplomacy, it did rest soundly upon respect for his foreign interlocutors and the institutions they represented. Historically, particularly in economic areas and for domestic political reasons, Mexican negotiators had bristled at "playing Washington's game," in some cases working out deals that were never meant to be implemented at home.[61] Since international confidence building was so crucial to the success of Salinas's economic reforms, his finance minister was not constrained by those concepts of nationalism; rather, Aspe was free to act on his own "cosmopolitan nationalist" vision. Accordingly, Aspe saw no contradiction between Mexican sovereignty and respect for IMF guidelines and the rules set down by creditor banks, believing instead that the measure of his patriotism was the vigor with which he pursued an agreement that was of maximum benefit to Mexico's long-run economic prospects. While critics have challenged whether the debt deal completed in July 1989 went far enough in objective terms,[62] the greater impact on the future of the Mexican economy may well have been made by Aspe's bargaining style and the new attitude toward the external world it reflected.

Once the preliminary agreement with the banks was signed in July, the debt agreement went to the Mexican Congress in August for debate and approval; this called for Aspe to hone yet another important political skill, namely, explicating policies to Congress. Even before the 1988 elections and the resulting increase in opposition representation within the legislature, periodic consultations with congressional committees had already become mandatory for the ministers of finance and of programming and budget under President López Portillo in the late-1970s. By the early 1990s, Aspe was required to

61. For a study of the contrast between these tendencies and the growing lobbying activities by leaders of Sinaloa's export agriculture sector, see David Mares, *Penetrating the International Market* (New York: Columbia University Press, 1987).

62. See, for example, Jorge Castañeda, "Salinas' International Relations Gamble," *Journal of International Affairs* 43 (Winter 1990): 411.

appear before Congress once per year in November or December to present the amendments to the Income Laws (addressing the tax code and the sources of government income) for the year; in addition, the finance minister might be summoned at any time to explain particular policies that come under congressional consideration. He might also be called in to explain the reports on the state of the economy that he was required to submit to Congress three times per year.

Aspe's personal experience with this process started when he became undersecretary at SPP in 1985. He recalls his initiation clearly, counting twenty-six appearances before Congress in only two years in the position.[63] This reaction does not necessarily reflect an objection to being required to defend his policies, or even the whole reform project, before the legislature; if anything, Aspe the *maestro* was prepared to turn any joint session of Congress into an economics lesson. As he has subsequently expressed, his experience with the pact and the success of Mexican-style *concertación* also convinced him that effective communication with the public was essential to the success of reforms.[64] At the same time, it was a challenge for Aspe to accustom himself to the level of discourse employed by opposition deputies, who used their questions to attack Salinas, the PRI, the whole government, or even Aspe himself. After having mastered the political rules of the game of the executive bureaucracy, where he was taught not to engage in open conflict, Aspe had to shift gears entirely to deal with Congress. As a result, he developed there a professorial persona that, though often overly didactic, allowed him to maintain distance and effectively perform the role of official explicator of economic policy.

A good example of Aspe in action before Congress can be found in the transcript of his appearance before the Chamber of Deputies on 15 November 1989, during which he specifically discussed the debt agreement.[65] During the "dialogue" that followed his presentation, Aspe the *maestro* demonstrated his signature command of detail and analytical reasoning. He answered various charges of "lack of truthful information" surrounding the debt agreement with a detailed account of the progress of negotiations and the schedule of

63. Pedro Aspe, interview by author, Washington, D.C., 19 September 1992.

64. Pedro Aspe, "The Recent Experience of the Mexican Policymakers," in *Sea Changes in Latin America,* by Pedro Aspe, Domingo Cavallo, and Andrés Bianchi (Washington, D.C.: Group of Thirty, 1992), 3.

65. "Comparecencia de Pedro Aspe, Secretario de Hacienda y Crédito Público, ante la LIV Legislatura de la H. Cámara de Diputados, Noviembre [15] de 1989" (Secretaría de Hacienda y Crédito Público, Unidad de Comunicación Social, November 1989).

congressional consultations that had been followed.[66] He was not given such an easy time by one deputy from the Democratic Revolutionary Party (Partido Revolucionario Democrático, or PRD), the main center-left opposition party, which had grown out of the candidacy of Cuauhtémoc Cárdenas in the 1988 elections. This deputy referred to the governing group as "neoconservative and antidemocratic," and after citing numerous examples of exaggerated claims made for the government's economic reforms, including the debt agreement, he concluded by accusing the Salinas team of putting the needs of international capital ahead of those of the Mexican people.[67] True to form, Aspe assumed the role of chastising professor and backed up his rejoinders with corroborating data cited from memory. He also went as far as to imply that the deputy's misinformation on the debt agreement was due to the fact that he had "obviously" not attended the meetings held in Congress over the summer, during which the agreement was discussed in detail.[68] Ever the professor, Aspe used his knowledge to refute criticism, but also risked appearing impatient with those who lacked his specialized knowledge and disrespectful of what were, in essence, differences in ideological perspective rather than intellectual rigor.

Finally, when a National Action Party (Partido Acción Nacional, or PAN) deputy repeated the concern with government secrecy surrounding the debt agreement, Aspe momentarily lost his composure, exclaiming: "I have here one report on the debt from June and another from September . . . [that were] submitted to you, the Chamber of Deputies. . . . We have done enough to explain [the analysis of the agreement] to you! [It] is in the reports, you know it, we have discussed it, and I don't know where this surprise and insistence that we have not told you have come from. Fine. Let's move on."[69] Aside from revealing the more authoritarian aspect of his professorial persona, Aspe's outburst also reflected his inexperience handling Congress, particularly as it was composed after 1988. However, his inexperience was further compounded by the way his political activities were constrained in a top-down manner by the president himself. Within the division of labor established by Salinas, Aspe was not responsible for building coalitions within Congress, but rather with addresses, like this one, in which he was cast as the administration's official teacher. Clearly, Aspe was not able to stay completely

66. Ibid., 43, 47–48.
67. Ibid., 55, 59.
68. Ibid., 60.
69. Ibid., 68, translation by author.

"scientific" in his answers, but his style helped Salinas to confront his opposition from a "high ground" of superior technical knowledge. Over the course of the *sexenio*, Aspe became gradually more skilled in the ways of communicating before Congress, though his professorial demeanor continued to draw criticism and to generate an unpopular image. Still, unlike Cavallo, who had to build support for his policies through legislative and party mechanisms, Aspe's primary political duties did not lie in the legislature. If anything, given his leadership roles in the pact and in the project of privatization, Aspe was more actively engaged with societal groups, not opposition parties or congressional representatives.

Privatization: For Richer and For Poorer?

The original project of privatization of state-owned enterprises (SOEs), known as *desincorporación*, was initiated during the de la Madrid era; however, it was not until Pedro Aspe took over at Finance that the process accelerated and started having a significant impact on the structure of state-private-sector relations and on the budget. And while the stabilization pact may go down in history as his most important individual contribution to Mexico's recovery, Aspe's approach to privatization most directly reflects the ideas he carried with him from his academic days as well as his academic style as a policy maker. On one level, privatization, like the pact, reflected a learning experience for Aspe and his team. First, they identified and sought corrections to the mistakes made during the first phase, most notably the lack of transparency of the sale process and the persistence of government participation for too long a period after sale.[70] Next, Aspe studied various foreign models, even traveling to France to discuss the details with high-ranking officials. Aspe returned concerned that the French system of bidder pre-classification was vulnerable to arbitrary or biased rankings. Instead, pre-classification was made the first of a two-stage process, the second of which became an open bidding process.[71] Finally, in order to fine-tune the system, Aspe suggested starting off with small companies under the new procedure, thus giving the team adequate experience prior to embarking on the sale of a larger entity that could prove excessively costly if mishandled.[72] The project was thus constructed to make learning, and the inevitable mistakes involved, normal and manageable rather than signs of failure.

70. Aspe, "Recent Experience," 5.
71. Reyes Heroles and Delgado, "Pedro Aspe," 15.
72. Pedro Aspe, interview by author, Washington, D.C., 19 September 1992.

The goals, rationale, and design of the privatization program also reflected Aspe's personal commitment to solving the equity-versus-efficiency dilemma. Congruent with what he wrote in his 1984 income-distribution volume, Aspe viewed privatization as a way to reallocate government resources so that they are both more efficiently and equitably distributed. Aspe himself cites the example of Aeroméxico, the chronically insolvent national airline, which lost billions of dollars for the government of a country in which only a small percentage of the population could afford air travel.[73] Reflecting his concerns for both justice and sound public accounting, he devised a strategy to use proceeds from privatization to pay off the public debt, thus creating a permanent reallocation toward social spending through the National Solidarity Program (Programa Nacional de Solidaridad, or PRONASOL), Salinas's community-based antipoverty program.[74] Indeed, according to Aspe, whereas only 27 percent of the budget in 1982 was dedicated to health, education, housing, and basic infrastructure, ten years later they commanded almost two-thirds.[75] Though in a top-down manner and concerned with the aggregate level, Aspe designed the privatization program to promote both equality and efficiency, his long-standing normative goal.

The privatization program was also shaped by Aspe's ideas about the proper role of the state in the economy, specifically his support of a competent state that is more effective in fulfilling its social justice mission. In his annual address to Congress in 1989, Aspe presented a useful summary of this point of consensus within Salinas's economic team:

> As the president of the Republic has stated: "The crisis has shown us that a larger State is not necessarily a more capable State; a State that owns more is not necessarily a State that is more just. The truth is, in Mexico, more State has meant less capacity to respond to the social needs of our fellow countrymen and, in the end, greater weakness of the State itself. All the time the activity of the public sector was increasing, attention to the problems of highest social priority was decreasing." Because of this, the administration has moved with resolve in a new direction: a public sector concentrated in strategic areas

73. Ibid.

74. Salinas announced the establishment of PRONASOL in his inaugural address (1 December 1988). See Salinas, "Discurso de toma de posesión," 1141.

75. Pedro Aspe, address to the Washington Exchange, 21 September 1992, in *The State of Latin American Finance* (Washington, D.C.: Washington Exchange, 1992), 3.

and, consequently, with greater capacity for action and more effective to satisfy the demands of our society.[76]

Aspe also believed that the private sector must take the lead in the areas of the economy no longer dominated by the state. However, a risk-averse and dependent private sector reliant on cheap energy and public bailouts had developed in the statist economy. In order for privatization to work, the private sector had to be independent enough to finance its purchases of the former SOEs; moreover, all private companies, including those formerly owned by the state, had to adjust to liberalized trade policies and the reduction and elimination of subsidies. By forcing adjustment through these policies, Aspe hoped to "privatize the private sector,"[77] thereby creating a responsible and nondependent partner for the new development project.

While many businesses failed in these more unforgiving market conditions, the state has found its autonomous partner in a small group of very powerful firms and export-oriented industrial groups.[78] This segment of the private sector, far from needing to convince the government of its commitment to free markets, was the target of official efforts to regain the confidence eroded by the arbitrary, antibusiness acts of Presidents Echeverría and López Portillo. The reprivatization of the banks, in particular, sweetened the deal for a select number of extremely wealthy financiers, many of whom had felt betrayed by the bank nationalization of 1982 and still could threaten the government with capital flight. This brings out the paradox of Aspe's privatization program and perhaps its greatest weakness: while the very poor were arguably the targeted recipients of new resources as a consequence of the sale of state enterprises, in practice the very rich benefited disproportionately, and private oligopolies replaced public monopolies, leading many to question whether the ostensibly free market-oriented policies of the Salinas government actually encouraged the concentration of economic power rather than its dispersion.

There is a further irony: Pedro Aspe, who had advocated privatization in part for poverty alleviation and income redistribution, became popularly identified with these powerful business interests.[79] One especially strong

76. "Comparecencia," 8, translation by author.

77. This is a phrase that has become associated with Aspe, since he uses it in nearly all of the interviews and speeches he gives. See, for example, Reyes Heroles and Delgado, "Pedro Aspe," 14; Aspe, "Recent Experience," 5; interview by author, Washington, D.C., 18 September 1992.

78. For a discussion of the bifurcation of the Mexican private sector into those for and those against state intervention in markets, see Maxfield, *Governing Capital*, 97–116.

79. These perceptions were heightened in early 1996, when Aspe left the ITAM teaching post

contingent, the Group of Ten (Grupo de los Diez) from Monterrey, started meeting with President Miguel de la Madrid on a bimonthly basis in 1985 and also met regularly with Salinas and the members of his economic cabinet, including Aspe. In fact, these entrepreneurs routinely prepared draft proposals on the reforms they advocated expressly for submission to key government agencies, including important departments of the Ministry of Finance.[80] It made perfect sense for Aspe, so successful in the role of guarantor of government policies abroad, to assume that same role for Mexican bankers and big business; it was also consistent with his ideas regarding the importance of the private sector as the engine of the country's economic recovery and the long-term hope for dynamic, internationally oriented growth. At the same time, the fact that the Salinas *sexenio* produced an unprecedented number of millionaires and even billionaires calls into question the wisdom of trusting the combination of "trickle-down" theory with the perpetuation of structural incentives within the Mexican economy toward concentration of wealth to produce income distribution.

Tax Reform: Enter the "Fiscal Terrorists"

One part of the process of adjustment designed and implemented by Aspe and his colleagues at Finance haunted even those firms, oligopolistic and otherwise, that survived trade liberalization and the end of subsidies: tax reform. Most closely associated with Francisco Gil Díaz, who became Aspe's undersecretary for income, the reform was based on the same principle as privatization: the state should no longer subsidize the private sector at the expense of the rest of society. Tax rates were simplified and even lowered by up to a half; however, as of 1989, Finance would audit a full 10 percent of all returns and would impose jail sentences for tax evasion. In fact, Aspe, Gil, and their tax team, dubbed the "Fiscal Terrorists," prosecuted and sentenced 278 cases between 1988 and 1992, compared with two cases in the preceding sixty-seven years.[81]

---

that had awaited him upon his departure from office in December 1994 and took a position with the investment banking division of the Monterrey conglomerate Pulsar. Aspe had, in fact, waited a full year before entering the private sector, thus abiding by rules governing conflict of interest, but not necessarily defusing criticism of his choice of employer.

80. Lourdes Melgar, "The Monterrey Industrial Elite: Ideological Contradictions, Political Alliances, and Economic Practices" (paper presented at the Seventeenth International Congress of the Latin American Studies Association, Los Angeles, 24–27 September 1992), 15, 19.

81. Aspe, address to the Washington Exchange, 4.

The tax reform offers another example of Aspe acting on his ideas and learning from his experiences. Like El Pacto, the tax reform showed Aspe rejecting "neoliberal" dogmas (in this case, the "supply-side" argument for private-sector tax relief); moreover, once again all sectors—the private sector and private citizens alike—were publicly charged to bear their respective burdens. The tax reform also largely derived from Aspe's ideas about the active but not unduly interventionist role of the state in promoting development. Although, in practice, Gil became the target of most of the political heat for the tax reform, Aspe took public opportunities to laud his undersecretary's initiatives, demonstrating his own commitment to this instrument as a way of generating not only revenue but also respect for the state as the arbiter of economic fairness.

While the tax reform proved a relatively significant economic success on paper—between 1988 and 1992, non-oil tax revenues increased by 31.3 percent, compared with a 14.6 percent increase in GDP during the same period[82]—its political consequences were quite troublesome for Aspe. By emphasizing enforcement, he in effect turned Gil's office into the Tax Police, with all the negative connotations involved; moreover, without a solid public relations campaign, in practice, tax reform pitted Gil and Aspe—two out-of-touch "neoliberals"—against all sectors of Mexican society.[83] Without a popular power base of his own and without populist appeal, Aspe's "success" in this area only compounded an increasingly unappealing public image that associated him with economic pain and, ironically, with arbitrary state power.[84] Objectively, tax reform is a political "hard sell", but it might have been marketed as an anticorruption policy or by emphasizing the democratic aspects of a system that holds all citizens responsible, regardless of wealth and power. Instead, it appeared that Aspe went about this project much in the

---

82. Source: Secretaría de Hacienda y Crédito Público, minister's advisory staff.

83. See Sallie Hughes, " 'Fiscal Terrorism': Despite Reputation Abroad, Aspe Lacks Critical Support," *El Financiero International*, 30 August–5 September 1993, 16.

84. The anger against Aspe and Gil peaked in April of 1992, when a group called the National Contributor's Congress (Congreso Nacional de Contribuyentes) was formed from private-sector leaders and private citizens to push for inclusion of a "Declaration of Contributors' Rights" to the chapter of the Mexican constitution dealing with individual rights. See Carlos Acosta y Fernando Ortega, "Ausencia de Miscelánea para ablandarle a Aspe la reputación de 'duro,' " *Proceso* 837 (16 November 1992): 28–31. Besides the private sector—which resented both the increased rates and the number of times their cost calculations had been thrown off by Hacienda tax policy changes—intellectuals were a second vocal and organized group that objected to the rigidity of the Aspe-Gil position. See, for example, Gerardo Ochoa Sandy, "El Secretario Pedro Aspe sólo ilusionó a los intelectuales: No hay marcha atrás en la exención por derechos del autor," *Proceso* 852 (1 March 1993): 46–47.

same way he cleaned out the statistics bureau, INEGI, where he was admired by many as "El Bulldozer"; in this case, however, comparisons drawn between him and a brutal, relentless machine were not in the least affectionate.

The Peso Crisis of 1994–95: A Cautionary Tale for Technopols

Up to this point, I have focused on policies through which Pedro Aspe earned the reputation as a key architect of the Salinas team's economic "miracle" of the early 1990s, hoping to identify the characteristics that enabled Mexico's technopols to transform their economy. Perhaps equally revealing and important for my purposes is an examination of the role of Pedro Aspe individually and his generation of technopols collectively in the peso crisis of 1994–95. Such an examination reveals other, less "positive" characteristics that predisposed these young leaders to indulge in risky strategies, unrealistic expectations, and political miscalculations, eventually costing their reputations dearly and their country more dearly still. Since it is beyond the scope of a "minicase" to discuss the full spectrum of causal elements that gave rise to the crisis,[85] I instead focus specifically on three ways in which the Mexican "dream team" under Salinas created the nightmare unleashed in December 1994.

The fatal flaw of the Mexican technopols was their overconfidence, manifested in two specific and equally damaging spheres. First, they became overconfident in their ability to maintain a very risky economic strategy: propping up the peso using international reserves, and relying on short-term foreign capital inflows. Even before the crisis, a vivid symbol of this overconfidence and the vulnerability of the Mexican strategy to foreign investment was the ballooning current-account deficit.[86] As early as 1992, Aspe himself sought to dispel growing concerns abroad regarding the external imbalance, arguing to a London audience that importing capital was a necessary and

85. For an analysis of the causes of the crisis, see Laurence Summers, "Ten Lessons to Learn," *The Economist,* 23 December 1995–5 January 1996, 46–48; see also Tod Robberson, "How a Miracle Went Wrong: Political Setbacks, Economic Miscalculations, and Bad Luck Led to Crash," *Washington Post,* 8 January 1995, A24, and various articles highly critical of the Zedillo economic team in *Proceso* 950 (16 January 1995).

86. Mexico's current-account deficit has increased rapidly since 1990, when, at $7.1 billion, it gained the dubious distinction as Latin America's largest. See Chris Aspin, "The Year in Review: Government Tries for Golden Ring," *El Financiero International* (28 December 1992), 11. Banco de México figures estimate that in 1992 the current-account deficit amounted to 15.1 percent of GDP. See the chart reproduced in Secretaría de Hacienda y Crédito Público, *El nuevo perfil de la economía mexicana* (August 1992), 55. By the time of the December 1994 peso crisis, the current-account deficit was measured at $28 billion.

relatively safe means of financing private-sector modernization given that public finances were in surplus.[87] He cited historical examples (late-nineteenth-century United States) and contemporary models (the so-called Asian dragons), without admitting the increased risks of "betting" on the superfluid global markets of the 1990s, or the importance of high domestic savings rates and lower proportions of portfolio versus direct investment for Asian successes.[88] Perhaps more of a miscalculation than the "hot-money" strategy itself was the technopols' belief that Mexico's status as a preferred emerging market and their own reputation abroad as "miracle workers" would be enough to keep such "hot money," by definition extremely sensitive to even minor government slipups, from fleeing en masse.[89] This false sense of security was arguably encouraged by U.S. investment firms and government agencies, which muted their growing concerns in 1994 in order to protect Mexico's reputation and their own exposure;[90] however, as Mexico's techno-pols began to believe their good press, they overestimated their ability to manage market forces that were out of their control.

Part of this error was ostensibly collective, reflecting what Miguel Ángel Centeno has criticized as this generation's self-righteousness regarding their qualifications to run the economy and, by extension, to determine the "right path."[91] The error was also partially due to the miscalculations of individuals, such as newly minted finance minister Jaime Serra Puche, whose closed-door strategy as the crisis broke alienated those investors accustomed to "accessibility and straight talk" associated with Pedro Aspe.[92] Though

87. "Desestiman Salinas y Aspe los riesgos del déficit externo; durará 'algún tiempo más,' " *El Financiero,* 21 July 1992, 3.

88. For an evaluation of the Asian experience, as well as the general risks and rewards of capital inflows for developing economies, see "Coping with Capital Inflow Surges: The APEC Experience," *IMF Survey* (20 February 1995): 49–53. On globalized markets, see Thomas L. Friedman, "Ante Up: International Investors Bet Everything on Anything," *New York Times,* 17 April 1994, sec. 4, p. 1, and David E. Sanger, "Do Fickle Markets Now Make Policy?" *New York Times,* 19 March 1995, sec. 4, p. 3.

89. See Peter Passell, "Mexico's Lesson: Don't Depend on the Kindness of Foreign Investors," *New York Times,* 12 January 1995, D2.

90. See, for example, Henry Kaufman, "Why Alarm Bells Didn't Ring Over Mexico," *Wall Street Journal,* 26 January 1995, A14; David E. Sanger with Anthony DePalma, "On Both Sides of the Border, Peso Ills Were Long Ignored," *New York Times,* 24 January 1995, A1, A9; and R. Jeffrey Smith and Clay Chandler, "Peso Crisis Caught U.S. by Surprise," *Washington Post,* 13 February 1995, A1, A16.

91. Centeno, *Democracy Within Reason,* 215–22.

92. "The Egg on Zedillo's Face," *The Economist,* 7 January 1995, 31. Aspe was also defended by his former professor at the ITAM, Antonio Bassols. See Sonia Morales, "Bassols, maestro de Aspe en el ITAM, lo defiende: La culpa fue de Serra Puche," *Proceso* 950 (16 January 1995): 15.

hypothetically Aspe might have been more successful than Serra in reassuring global markets, it has recently been suggested that the roots of the crisis can be traced to Aspe's role as the guarantor of the Mexican project abroad.[93] In that role, Aspe adopted a policy of "no surprises" and, by emphasizing direct communication, established a credibility with investors unmatched except by the president himself; at the same time, he also created a set of expectations—specifically regarding the exchange rate—that left little room for maneuver even as the events of 1994 shook markets and the peso became seriously overvalued. Having transformed himself into a symbol of constancy, Aspe lobbied against devaluation throughout that year, reportedly rejecting a final opportunity on the eve of the Zedillo presidency and implying that he would resign if Salinas went ahead against his admonitions. His rigid insistence that Mexico would never devalue, however, was but one of several overoptimistic positions that set him at odds publicly with his MIT mentor, Rudiger Dornbusch,[94] and privately with top officials in his ministry, such as future finance minister Guillermo Ortiz, but that remained credible to the majority of his international interlocutors until it was too late. In retrospect, devaluation may have been inevitable, but had Aspe not concentrated Mexico's credibility so entirely in himself, and had he not indulged his own pride and personal identification with particular policies, the crisis of confidence may not have grown to such epic proportions with his departure.

A third aspect of the crisis can be traced to the dependence of this generation of leaders on the presidentialist system and their participation in intraelite competition through *camarillas*. Under normal circumstances, given the "no-reelection rule" in Mexico, the final year of the *sexenio* is one of vulnerability for the outgoing president's project; in 1994, violent events added unprecedented levels of political uncertainty to this transition moment. In such a political year, and with Salinas lobbying to lead the newly created World Trade Organization upon his "retirement," advertising the bad news about the economy was viewed from inside the president's circle as not only damaging to their patron's image but perhaps even dangerous for their country's stability. Instead, the policy team closed ranks: for example, Pedro Aspe, as a

93. For a detailed account of the devaluation decision and Pedro Aspe's role, see David Wessel, Paul B. Carroll, and Thomas T. Vogel Jr., "Peso Surprise: How Mexico's Crisis Ambushed Top Minds in Officialdom, Finance," *Wall Street Journal,* 6 July 1995, A1, A4. The discussion below draws upon this account.

94. See Rudiger Dornbusch and Alejandro Werner, "Mexico: Stabilization, Reform, and No Growth," *Brookings Papers on Economic Activity* (Spring 1994): 253–98.

player in the presidentialist system, worked assiduously to salvage his boss's final year and his eventual legacy. Moreover, in the context of growing demands for political opening from opposition parties, civic groups, and the Zapatista movement, the Salinas team gambled on *triunfalismo,* foreign money and cheap imports to consumers to salvage the legitimacy of the Salinastroika model and their "right" to run the country in the next *sexenio.* Though pumping the economy in an election year is commonly used to aid incumbents in more open political systems, in Mexico's presidentialist system information was controlled and resources marshaled in ways that demonstrated that the Salinas team was not prepared to risk losing power and the advantages the system had afforded them.

On another level, the December 1994 "peso meltdown" itself reflected the gradual disintegration from internal competition of what had been a cohesive and coordinated policy team. For example, although Aspe and Zedillo had been allies as members of the Salinas *camarilla* and later as cabinet ministers, by 1993 their competition had intensified: Salinas eliminated SPP, giving Aspe a "superministry" and moving Zedillo to Education. While Aspe had been one of the three top "precandidates" favored by Salinas, Zedillo "advanced" by luck, by becoming Colosio's campaign manager, a position that eventually made him, and not Aspe, eligible to replace the slain candidate. As president, Zedillo was unlikely to shift gears on economic policy, and retaining Aspe in the cabinet could have guaranteed market confidence during the transition; however, Aspe's personal international prestige might equally have threatened Zedillo as he contemplated consolidating presidential authority. Likewise, though remaining at the pinnacle of economic policy making surely had its attraction for Aspe, joining the Zedillo team could do little for his chances for political ascent, which, according to traditional *camarilla* practices, had become minimal with his loss of the PRI nomination in 1993. In the end, Aspe was not in Zedillo's cabinet, and the Finanace job went to Jaime Serra Puche, himself an ambitious technopol with his own well-developed policy team, international status through NAFTA, and presidential aspirations. In the context of the devaluation, one might have expected this appointment to bring continuity and the likelihood of turning to what had calmed markets during the Salinas *sexenio,* meaning the kid-glove treatment of investors perfected in Finance under Aspe. However, egos and *camarilla* politics interfered with "rational" and "efficient" measures, and the outgoing team was neglected as a source of policy experience and models for crisis management, demonstrating how ideas and politics can be at odds even for technopols.

Most dramatically, rather than rely on Aspe's methods—or his phone list of important investors—Serra saved his pride, but at the price of a major financial crisis and, ultimately, his own political career.

In sum, the peso crisis serves as a cautionary tale to technopols in Mexico and in other countries seeking to restructure their economies in line with global market forces. First, while their ability to speak the language of international investors can help build confidence abroad, technopols are therefore more vulnerable to becoming victims of their own success, either through overexposure in international markets or through overconfidence. Second, most technopols may share a common educational, social, ideological, and even personality profile, but these are merely the raw materials of their leadership, necessary but not sufficient for their "successful" action in more complex situations. Their training as professional economists is just as likely to be "used" politically to justify questionable policies as it is to design sound policy. Third, technopols' personal investment in policy can also limit their flexibility unnecessarily. Finally, technopols may work in teams, but as these teams begin to produce more second-generation technopols, these ambitious scions will begin to compete against one another. Technopols may be differentiated from technocrats by their political ambitions, but these ambitions may not always be channeled in the direction of a unified reform project.

Conclusions

This chapter presents Finance Minister Pedro Aspe Armella as both an example of and exemplary within a new generation of economic policy makers leading Mexico toward a model of market-oriented development. First, I focused on the independent role of generational change in explaining the direction, speed, and depth of the Mexican reform project. Within that context, I identified two new ideas that this group carried into the state and advanced by consensus: a cosmopolitan nationalist approach to interactions with the world outside Mexico, and a belief in the need for a competent state to ensure the consolidation and implementation of market reforms. I also argued that these young economists stuck together in political ways as well, establishing their own power bases within the bureaucracy by forming teams with their students and, more crucially, attaching themselves to a successful presidential *camarilla* headed by Carlos Salinas de Gortari.

Having told the collective story, I then turned to the case of Pedro Aspe, one of the more prominent individuals of this new generation. Following his intellectual and professional development through three crucial stages, I observed several themes that connected his life in academia with his later career in the state, most notably an understanding of economics as a practical, not just theoretical, vocation; a concern with the trade-off between equity and efficiency in market economies; a philosophy that permitted looking to the state, as well as the market, for workable policy solutions; and an intense commitment to reform. In Aspe's own words, he was drawn toward policy making for the chance to define what was necessary, and then to make it possible. Next, I identified the personal and political skills involved in Aspe's own rapid rise to the economic cabinet, highlighting his abilities as a team builder and a team player in the Mexican presidentialist system.

To illustrate the process by which Aspe acquired these skills, and to evaluate his ability "to make possible what is necessary," I presented five "minicases" that depict him in action and outline his solutions to various policy problems. These cases, first and foremost, help us to evaluate Aspe as a "technopol" and to demonstrate how certain qualities he shared with this group—such as rapport with international interlocutors and an ability to bridge economic theory and policy—contributed to his performance in office. These cases also reveal a distinct, professorial "Aspe style," which earned him the admiration of negotiating partners and the loyalty of generations of students-turned-team members but limited his broad political appeal and alienated opponents. In a final minicase, the 1994–95 peso crisis, I demonstrated how Aspe and his colleagues in the Salinas reform team became victims of their own success by overestimating their skills and their reputations while underestimating the power of markets and the warnings of dissenting voices around them. If the rise of Pedro Aspe reads as a technopol's manual of "how to succeed," the peso crisis offers a more cautionary tale for both technopols and those who place their faith in the hands of these talented but still imperfect leaders.

Finally, the question remains whether the transformative power of Aspe and his technopolitical cohort has gone much beyond the economic realm. Indeed, the inclusion of Mexico in a project on the connection between freeing markets and freeing politics invites comparison of the top-down and partial nature of recent political change in Mexico with the more open processes in the other countries under study. The Mexican reform project owed a great deal of its scope, success, and speed to the unusual concentration of authority in the executive. Rather than "spill over" into greater power for civil society, the market-oriented reforms championed by the Salinas team were more closely associated with the consolidation of presidentialism, the strengthening of a streamlined state, and the deliberate delay of political reform under the rules of Salinastroika. The group of young economists I have identified as "technopols" rose through the system before 1988 through "insider" politics and were not required to develop the skills of conciliation, lobbying, and negotiation associated with more openly competitive systems; moreover, their policies faced less direct interference and oversight from legislative actors and (with the exception of the private sector) societal groups.

Thus, unlike the other technopols profiled in this volume, Pedro Aspe operated within a relatively closed system that did not require him to build popular support for his policies and limited his practice of "politics" to networking through *camarillas*, preaching to the converted in the private sector, serving as the "teacher to the nation" in testimony before Congress, and leading state-sponsored *concertación* using traditional corporatist arrangements. However, while Aspe did produce numerous policy successes with the help of concentrated executive authority, he arguably did so on borrowed time, since Salinastroika proved unsustainable both economically and politically by early 1994. Up to that point, macroeconomic indicators and foreign investment figures gave the impression that Mexico had succeeded where Mikhail Gorbachev had failed, producing economic results while maintaining political stability. Still, as the technopols were toasting their post-NAFTA entry into the "First World," their twenty-first-century economy was confronting a political rebellion in the southern state of Chiapas, a part of Mexico still living with the feudal arrangements of the sixteenth century. Further cracks in the much-vaunted "stability"—political assassinations, opposition party mobilization, and civic-group agitation—underscored the risks inherent in having postponed political reform. Instead of using democratic opening as a means of consolidating economic reform, as did other technopols profiled in this volume, Mexico's technopols learned the hard way that top-down reform goes quickly at first, but is more vulnerable in the end. Zedillo and his team will clearly have to go further than their technopolitical predecessors toward developing the political institutions, alliances, and skills necessary to continue economic reform while coping with politics defined more broadly and democratically.

In sum, the case of Pedro Aspe and the Salinas team does not necessarily help us answer one question raised by this project regarding the qualities that a technopol must cultivate to succeed in a democratizing context, nor does it demonstrate, except by counterexample, that there is a consistent elective affinity between economic liberalization and democratic process. What it does show is that technopols used Mexico's semiauthoritarian institutions to their best advantage to advance their ideas and careers in the state, but ultimately their project was jeopardized by their inability, or unwillingness, to subject the project to the rigors of democratic process. Herein lies the great challenge for the future of the technopol phenomenon in Mexico: we can only speculate whether the same group of people whose radical ideas raised the possibility of another Mexican "miracle" in the economy can make possible what is necessary in the political sphere and bring about the next miracle in politics: democratization.

4

Fernando Henrique Cardoso

Social and Institutional Rebuilding in Brazil

João Resende-Santos

In this chapter I trace some of the major themes and ideas in the political thought and policy choices of Fernando Henrique Cardoso. In so doing, I hope to examine the relationship between the actions and policy choices of the political leader and the ideas of the intellectual who had once described himself as belonging to the "radical tradition" of Latin American thought. I make an

This chapter benefited a great deal from the assistance and comments of many individuals. I especially wish to thank the other members of the Technopols Project. I am grateful to Fernando Henrique Cardoso and his staff for their time, assistance, and patience. Special thanks to André

effort to bridge the past and the present, to outline the foundations of Cardoso's current thinking on democracy in Brazil, institutional reforms, social rebuilding, economic reforms, and the country's relations with the outside world.[1]

Cardoso defies neat categorization. His ideas are as nuanced as they are eclectic and fluid. His is an integrated political philosophy, but one that stresses change and the need to refine continuously ideas and political agendas as circumstances change. Whether as a young sociologist in the turbulent 1960s or as party leader in the 1990s Cardoso has always rejected dogmatic thinking, especially as displayed in the political projects of both the left and the right in Latin America. He has always maintained that ideas must change as circumstances change. Today many people, particularly those on the left, cannot reconcile the ideas and policy choices of Cardoso the political leader with what they believe to have been the ideas and political commitments of Cardoso the dependency theorist. To many, Cardoso has embraced the so-called neoliberal gospel at the expense of the progressive social philosophy and reformist idealism that, in their view, defined the young scholar. On both the left and the right, some even question whether he ever was a progressive reformer or was ever committed to a more egalitarian and just society. During the 1994 elections, the left accused him of opportunism, and even his long-time mentor, the Marxist Florestán Fernandes, denounced him for abandoning his past. Antonio Carlos Magalhães, perhaps the most powerful political figure on the right and leader of the party Cardoso allied with in the 1994 elections, said of Brazil's new president that "behind the brilliant Marxist sociologist was always an elitist and a man of the Right."[2] How does this confusion over who Cardoso is, and what he stands for, affect our definition of a technopol? Likewise, what are the implications for our assessment of the relationship between ideas and policy choices?

This chapter is divided into four main sections. In the first section I briefly outline Cardoso's scholarship and social democratic thinking. In the second

Elias Rodini, Edésia Gomes, and Professor José Augusto Guilhon Alburquerque. This chapter was written with the support of the Inter-American Dialogue, the Center for International Affairs at Harvard University, and the National Science Foundation.

1. Cardoso's prolific and nuanced writings and political thought cannot be assessed fully within the scope of this chapter. The discussion is based on a variety of books and articles by Cardoso, including unpublished materials from his own collection, essays from *Ensaios de Opinião* and *Movimento,* two publications that Cardoso cofounded during the military regime but that were only intermittently published, and Cardoso's long-running weekly articles in *A Folha de São Paulo.* I provide my own translations.

2. Quote cited in José Luiz Fiori, "Cardoso Among the Technopols," *NACLA Report on the Americas* 28, no. 6 (1995): 22.

section I examine the first phase of Cardoso's political career. Nothing in his early life and scholarship suggests Cardoso had political ambitions, but it was this very scholarship, and its incisive critique of the country's socioeconomic and political order, that propelled him into politics. This section shows how Cardoso the scholar attempted to reconcile his ideas and commitments with the exigencies and peculiarities of Brazilian politics. Of all the technopols, Cardoso's ideological profile, political trajectory, and policy agenda most closely correspond to those of Alexandro Foxley. The discussion also focuses briefly on Cardoso's Brazilian Social Democracy Party (Partido da Social Democracia Brasileira, or PSDB). The third section sketches the political program of Cardoso and the PSDB as it pertains to social welfare, institutional change, and economic reforms. Cardoso's meteoric rise to positions of strategic decision making is the focus of the fourth section. I argue that any assessment of the relationship between Cardoso's ideas and his policy choices is incomplete without placing Cardoso in the larger political and institutional context in which he operates.

The study of the role of ideas in politics has a long history. During the 1980s this literature flourished, particularly in the field of political economy. A good deal of attention focused on the role of "epistemic communities" or individual policy makers in the economic reforms and structural adjustments then taking place in various parts of the world.[3] Tracing the impact of an individual's ideas on policy outcomes is never an exact science. The relationship between ideas and policy choices, I suggest, is particularly difficult to trace in a setting such as Brazil. For ideas to have a discernible imprint on policy preferences, they must first either be "nested" in specific governmental institutions or relevant organizations outside of the public sector or be personified and "carried" by a stable and viable group of individuals or political coalition.[4] Cardoso, however, acts in a political and institutional context that has been historically inhospitable to ideas and idea-based coalitions. It is, in addition, a context where the levels of institutional instability are high, where regressive, institutionally distorting practices are long-standing and

3. See, for example, Peter A. Hall, ed., *The Political Power of Ideas: Keynesianism Across Nations* (Princeton: Princeton University Press, 1989); Kathryn Sikkink, *Ideas and Institutions: Developmentalism in Brazil and Argentina* (Ithaca: Cornell University Press, 1991); Judith Goldstein, "Impact of Ideas on Trade Policy: The Origins of U.S. Agricultural and Manufacturing Policies," *International Organization* 43, no. 1 (1989); idem, "Ideas, Institutions, and American Trade Policy," *International Organization* 42, no. 1 (1988); Peter M. Haas, ed., *Knowledge, Power, and International Policy Coordination*, a special issue of *International Organization* 46, no. 1 (1992).

4. This point is frequently made in the institutionalism and epistemic-communities literatures.

widespread, as Frances Hagopian and others have noted.[5] Political institutions that are traditionally considered the carriers of ideas, such as parties, are weak and personalistic in Brazil.

A defining feature of Cardoso's political thinking is his notion of a "middle-range utopia" and the subsequent political strategy it entails. It is a reformist vision committed to a more egalitarian and democratic society. Perhaps much of the confusion and frustration with Cardoso the political leader stems from the *perception* that he was at one point a radical idealist or revolutionary. But Cardoso is, and has always been, much more of a pragmatist than a revolutionary. His is a moderate, gradualist agenda that stresses what is politically viable, rather than one committed to absolutes. Admittedly, this political pragmatism and concern with programmatic ideas are more pronounced in his thinking since he entered politics. Cardoso's social democratic thinking has deep roots, however. The very same ideas and issues that preoccupied the young scholar some thirty years ago continue to concern the political leader of today. The case of Cardoso provides fruitful research avenues on the role of ideas in politics, for here is a world-renowned scholar, a theoretician with a vast and enduring body of writing inserted into the highest levels of decision making.

Intellectual and Political Beginnings

Cardoso was born into an upper-middle-class military family on 18 June 1931 in Rio de Janeiro. Although he is a Carioca by birth, São Paulo became home to his academic and political careers (even though he still claims to be Carioca at heart).[6] He earned his bachelor's (1952) and doctorate (1961) degrees at the University of São Paulo (USP), the flagship university of Brazilian higher education. Married at twenty-one, he began his teaching career at USP in 1953 and remained there until the military coup d'état of March 1964. Along with many other intellectuals, Cardoso fell victim to the regime's political cleansing offensive. He was expelled from USP soon after the coup, and in 1969, soon after he returned to Brazil from exile and was promoted to full professor, he was forced into retirement under Institutional Act-5.

---

5. Frances Hagopian, "After Regime Change: Authoritarian Legacies, Political Representation, and the Democratic Future of South America," *World Politics* 45, no. 3 (1993).
   6. A Carioca is a native of Rio de Janeiro.

Cardoso began his university education as a philosophy student, but switched to sociology his third year. During his years at the university, Cardoso was introduced to an eclectic collection of literature and schools of thought ranging from Weber, Mannheim, and Durkheim to Marx. Weberian ideas and Durkheimian structuralism would remain essential features of Cardoso's intellectual eclecticism. At first he and his fellow classmates were completely lost, says Cardoso, "because we arrived expecting to debate and discuss, to change the world; [we came with] a bit of socialism, a bit of politics, and what we found was a rigorous discipline, an attempt to make of all this a piece of Europe."[7] Most of his university years were devoted to study rather than politics. Cardoso explains that he and his fellow students (a core group that included José Arthur Giannotti, Francisco Weffort, Paul Singer, Bento Prado Junior, Roberto Schwarz—most of whom would become long-standing collaborators) were not very concerned with politics or getting involved in the radical political movements of the time, even though the national political scene in the 1950s was stormy.[8]

From his fourth year on, the intellectual influence of his mentor, Florestán Fernandes, a Marxist sociologist at USP, was "absolute," as Cardoso himself describes it. Fernandes wanted to model the Sociology Department at USP after that of the University of Chicago, which (in addition to the renowned Economics Department) was an important influence in the field during the 1940s and 1950s. With funding from UNESCO, Fernandes coordinated a study on race relations in Brazil. Cardoso's part in the project was a 1960 study of race and social mobility in the city of Florianópolis, which he coauthored with Octávio Ianni.[9] Cardoso's first book, *Capitalismo e escravidão no Brasíl meridional*, also dealt with the question of race in Brazil. In this work, which addressed the dynamics of capitalist production under a system of domination, he first examined the expansive nature of capitalism and its effects on peripheral economies. These first scholarly works showed an early interest in and a commitment to exploring questions of democracy and social justice. Additionally, this scholarship displayed a political economy perspective that always considered the social and political implications of a peculiar type of economic development pattern or industrial organization.

7. Interview, *A Folha de São Paulo*, 17 May 1992, 6.

8. Francisco Weffort would become one of the principal founders of the Partido dos Trabalhadores (PT), one of the main rivals to Cardoso's own future party. The newly elected Cardoso appointed Weffort as his minister of culture in 1994.

9. Cardoso, Fernando Henrique, and Octávio Ianni, *Cor e mobilidade social em Florianópolis* (São Paulo: Cia. Editora Nacional, 1960).

In 1964, Cardoso published his *livre-docente* thesis, *Empresário industrial e desenvolvimento econômico no Brasíl*. "In that book," explains Cardoso, "there were already the fundamentals of the theory of dependency."[10] The book posited that capitalist development in Latin America was unlikely to follow the classic European pattern, where the national bourgeoisie, or industrial-entrepreneurial class, had led development and exercised political hegemony. Nor was capitalist development likely to have the same social and political consequences, tending to be more centralizing and illiberal in the periphery of the capitalist system. He doubted the capacity of the national industrial class to engage in large-scale modern production, because of the capital and technological limitations it faced. This pessimism regarding the capacity of the industrial class to lead development in the periphery would become a hallmark in Cardoso's scholarship. Peripheral development, Cardoso argued, would entail a large and dominant role for the state and foreign capital. Completed on the eve of the military coup, the book anticipated Guillermo O'Donnell's classic argument about the breakdown of populist developmentalist governments and the rise of bureaucratic-authoritarianism.[11] Although Cardoso's main thesis regarding late development was not original, in this 1964 work he was already considering the socio-political implications of the internationalization of capitalist development.[12]

Forced to flee Brazil in 1964, Cardoso spent the next several years in Santiago, Chile, where the Economic Commission for Latin America (ECLA) had its headquarters. Santiago was a city of intense intellectual activity during the 1960s; scholars from all over the region (as well as from outside it) and a variety of intellectual traditions and disciplines came together there. Here Cardoso, as he often puts it, "discovered" Latin America; that is, his scholarship began to take a more international perspective.[13] Cardoso became the

10. Interview, *A Folha de São Paulo,* 17 May 1992, 7.

11. Guillermo O'Donnell, *Modernization and Bureaucratic-Authoritarianism: Studies in South American Politics* (Berkeley: Institute of International Studies, University of California, 1973).

12. See ibid. The claim that the periphery cannot repeat the classic development pattern that many modernization and neoclassical theorists believed possible, of course, had already been posited in the literature. Modernization theorists like Karl Deutsch and Alexander Gerschenkron had already argued that political and economic development in the Third World would not reflect the classic pattern. See Karl Deutsch, "Social Development and Political Development," *American Political Science Review* 55, no. 3 (1961), and Alexander Gerschenkron, *Economic Backwardness in Historical Perspective: A Book of Essays* (Cambridge: Harvard University Press, 1962).

13. Joseph A. Kahl, *Three Latin American Sociologists: Gino Germani, Pablo Gonzalez, and Fernando Henrique Cardoso* (New Brunswick, N.J.: Transaction Books, 1988).

deputy director of the newly established Latin American Institute for Economic and Social Planning (ILPES), a research annex of ECLA.

Evolving International Links

In addition to doing research at ILPES, Cardoso also taught at the Facultad Latinoamericana de Ciencias Sociales (FLACSO) and the University of Chile. He left Chile in 1967 for France, where he joined the faculty of the University of Paris-Nanterre (1967–68). Cardoso was in France during the height of student activism, and one of his students, Daniel Cohn-Bendit, became one of the principal leaders of the French student movement. During the 1970s and 1980s Cardoso was a guest professor at the International Institute of Labor Studies, Stanford, Berkeley, and Cambridge, in addition to being a member of the Social Science Research Council's (SSRC) Joint Committee on Latin American Studies, the Argentine Centro de Estudios de Estado y Sociedad (CEDES), and the Corporación de Investigaciones Económicas para América Latina (CIEPLAN), the prominent Santiago-based economic policy think tank whose key member was its founder, Alejandro Foxley. Cardoso also served as the president of the International Sociological Association (1977–82) and, in 1982, began his long association with the Inter-American Dialogue. Meanwhile, he continued to be active in numerous other research institutes and professional associations all over the world. While his academic productivity decreased considerably after he entered politics full-time, he retained links to an international pool of ideas.

Back in Brazil in late 1968, Cardoso and some of his colleagues founded the Centro Brasileiro de Análise e Planejamento (CEBRAP) in April 1969. He served as its president and senior researcher between 1969 and 1982. The Center brought together academics and intellectuals who had been persecuted by the military regime. CEBRAP remains a leading research institute in a wide array of socioeconomic and public policy areas; its highly respected journal, *Novos Estudos,* remains an important forum for scholarship and public policy analysis.

Dependency and Development

While some of Cardoso's core ideas on the problem of economic development in peripheral economies had begun to germinate long before his arrival in Santiago, it was during his stay in Chile that they matured and evolved. Cardoso disagreed with many of the ideas floating around ECLA. His own thinking on dependency broke with ECLA's structuralism in important ways, though he and the dependency school in general borrowed a great deal from it, as expounded by Raúl Prebisch.[14] In Cardoso's view, ECLA's structuralist prescriptions were too optimistic about the capacity of the national bourgeoisie and the state to lead development. Cardoso wanted to refocus the entire debate concerning Latin America's economic development, not just to add a sociological perspective but also to argue against rigid Marxist and nationalist interpretations. He wanted to show that there were more possibilities for Latin American development than socialism or underdevelopment with authoritarianism. "I wanted to open the [intellectual mindset] against the Communist-populist vision and against the Cepalino vision."[15] Cardoso's rejection of statism and the revolutionary fervor of the left came early, and was as severe as his criticism of the traditional, conservative socioeconomic order. Just as Foxley had done in authoritarian Chile, as Kinney-Giraldo explains in this volume, Cardoso rejected both the leftist thesis that the choice was between revolution and underdevelopment and the rightist claim that development necessitated postponing freer politics. For Cardoso, democracy and equity were simultaneously possible. While in Santiago, Cardoso teamed up with Chilean economic historian Enzo Faletto to produce *Dependencia y desarrollo en América Latina*, which became the classic statement on dependency analysis.

As a school of thought, dependency was characterized more by divergence than convergence, as Jorge Domínguez has observed.[16] Cardoso's associated-dependent development thesis (which regarded development and dependency as simultaneously possible) rejected the stagnationist versions of dependency

14. For a good discussion on the influence of structuralism and Marxism on dependency analysis, see Joseph Love, "The Origins of Dependency Analysis," *Journal of Latin American Studies* 22, no. 1 (1990).

15. Interview, *A Folha de São Paulo*, 17 May 1992, 7.

16. Jorge I. Domínguez, "Consensus and Divergence: The State of the Literature on Inter-American Relations," *Latin American Research Review* 13, no. 1 (1978). For discussions on dependency theory, see also Ronald H. Chilcote, "A Critical Synthesis of the Dependency Literature," *Latin American Perspectives* 1 (Spring 1974); Gabriel Palma, "Dependency: A Formal Theory of Underdevelopment or a Methodology for the Analysis of Concrete Situations?" *World Development*, no. 6 (1978); Robert Packenham, *The Dependency Movement: Scholarship and Politics in Development Studies* (Cambridge: Harvard University Press 1992); Vincent A. Mahler, *Dependency Approaches to International Political Economy: A Cross-National Study* (New York: Columbia, 1980); Tony Smith, "The Underdevelopment of Development Literature: The Case of Dependency Theory," *World Politics* 31 (January 1979): 247–88; Albert O. Hirschman, *A Bias for Hope: Essays on Development and Latin America* (New Haven: Yale University Press, 1971); Dudley Seers, ed., *Dependency Theory: A Critical Reassessment* (London: Pinter, 1981); Peter B. Evans, *Dependent Development: The Alliance of Multinational, State, and Local Capital in Brazil* (Princeton: Princeton University Press, 1979).

analysis, the so-called development-of-underdevelopment strand exemplified in the writings of André Gunder Frank.[17] He accepted the general claim that the dynamic elements of international capitalism lie outside the periphery and its control, but argued that dependent development itself did not lack dynamism in many parts of the periphery, that a new international division of labor was emerging as international capitalism itself changed. Above all, he argued that situations of dependency were neither stable nor permanent. Everyone except Cardoso seems to have forgotten this original statement. When Cardoso today speaks of the need for Brazil's closer integration into the global economy, he is not contradicting himself. Above all, Cardoso showed that dependency was about *position* and *function* within the international economy, about *how* the periphery participated in the global economy, and not about the fact of integration itself. His innovation was to emphasize that possibilities for locally generated change—and not just self-perpetuation—existed. He argued (and would later act upon the belief) that historical options and political possibilities always existed within the periphery because human collective action could shape the future.

Despite features of dynamism, Cardoso stressed that this dependent development entailed both structural limitations (that is, it lacked a local "essential dynamic component" because of continued reliance on the center economies for capital and technology) and high socioeconomic and political costs.[18] It was both politically and economically concentrating. It generated institutional distortions as well as the marginalization of the lower classes. Cardoso's dependent development thesis, then, was a social as well as an institutional analysis. Domestically and internationally, it was a question of who benefits, who rules, who decides. It was fundamentally a question of power and of domination, internationally and locally. Politically, dependent development produced institutional deformities and exclusionary politics. But just as Cardoso rejected the orthodox assertion that dependency produces underdevelopment, he typically rejected the claim that it necessarily produces authoritarianism (though in his 1964 book he suggests this).[19] While he

17. André Gunder Frank, *Capitalism and Underdevelopment in Latin America* (New York: Monthly Review Press, 1967).

18. Fernando Henrique Cardoso and Enzo Faletto, *Dependency and Development in Latin America* (Berkeley and Los Angeles: University of California Press, 1979), xx. See also Fernando Henrique Cardoso, *As idéias e seu lugar: ensaios sobre as teorias do desenvolvimento* (Petrópolis: Editora Siciliano, 1993); Chilcote, "Critical Synthesis"; and John Myer, "A Crown of Thorns: Cardoso and Counter-Revolution," *Latin American Perspectives* 2, no. 1 (1975).

19. See Fernando Henrique Cardoso, "On the Characterization of Authoritarian Regimes in

shared O'Donnell's view that an "elective affinity" exists between peripheral industrialization and authoritarianism, this is not a necessary outcome in his view.[20] Of the institutional distortions none weighed more heavily than the expansive, antidemocratic, bureaucratic-producer state. The state itself became an obstacle to democracy, equity, and true development.

Dependent Development and Democracy

For many of his critics, the question is why Cardoso became such a defender of liberal democracy and capitalist development. Critics on both the left and right contend that his actions and ideas today have no foundations in his thinking, and that he has, in fact, abandoned those previous ideas.

In his scorching indictment of dependency analysis and of Cardoso in particular, Robert Packenham writes that "[i]n the middle and late seventies some of the Marxists or neo-Marxists who had earlier denounced bourgeois institutions and processes began to tolerate and even support them—not only theoretically but also in their political actions." He adds that "[n]o one exemplified the change in Marxist thinking in a more vivid and significant way than Cardoso."[21] Throughout the 1960s and 1970s Cardoso, it is further alleged, regarded elections, parties, and other political institutions as formal expressions of class domination, but since the late 1970s he became actively involved in these very same formal institutions.

Even though he borrows some Marxist language, Cardoso's works are generally characterized by an absence of orthodox and elaborate Marxist analytical categories.[22] He has never regarded himself as a Marxist thinker, and, in fact, Latin American Marxists have often chastised him for attempting to disguise bourgeois ideas in Marxist language.[23] Packenham himself recognizes that Cardoso's thinking has always had liberal elements. Packenham is correct in stating that Cardoso was a critic of so-called bourgeois institutions and formal democracy, but he fails to mention that Cardoso is still today a critic of formal institutions and has been an outspoken advocate of fundamental institutional restructuring in Brazil.

Latin America," in *The New Authoritarianism in Latin America,* ed. David Collier (Princeton: Princeton University Press, 1979).

20. See O'Donnell, *Modernization and Bureaucratic-Authoritarianism.*
21. Packenham, *The Dependency Movement,* 214, 216.
22. Myer, "Crown of Thorns."
23. See Chilcote, "Critical Synthesis," and Myer, "Crown of Thorns."

From early on (but especially beginning in the early 1970s) Cardoso had in mind a particular kind democracy—what he often called "substantive democracy" rather than political or formal democracy. This notion of democracy, as it has evolved into his social democratic philosophy, corresponds closely to Robert Dahl's notion of polyarchy.[24] It is a lofty and ambitious vision, though neither Cardoso nor his party have outlined the concrete steps toward its fulfillment. This vision entails the democratization not only of political participation but also of political institutions and social and economic organizations through extensive popular participation in decision making and management. In other words, substantive democracy, or this middle-range utopia he often speaks of, would be more than a collection of social policies; it would also be an active creation of public space for civil participation in different spheres of decision making that affect national well-being. It would entail a concern with procedures (i.e., political rights) as well as results in terms of distribution and social justice.

The Intellectual Leader of the Opposition and the Transition to Freer Politics

Alongside his academic activities, Cardoso became involved in national politics in Brazil. He never believed there was a necessary and inviolable separation between scholarship and politics; his scholarship inevitably brought him into collision with the political world.

Cardoso maintained, even at the height of Brazil's bureaucratic-authoritarian experience, that there were possibilities for political change.[25] There has always been—more so since the 1970s—a distinctly voluntarist trait in Cardoso's thinking, particularly with respect to political change, despite the structural-historical notions that informed much of his scholarship. Brazil's dependent industrialization was giving rise to new social forces, organizations, and class subdivisions; the modernization and pluralization of society proceeded alongside dependent development. Civil society was growing stronger. The very dynamism of peripheral industrialization opened up new

24. See Robert A. Dahl, *Polyarchy: Participation and Opposition* (New Haven: Yale University Press, 1971).

25. Cardoso returned to Brazil during the presidency of General Arturo Costa e Silva, when the hardliners in the military were in the ascendancy and repression and torture rose dramatically. Cardoso admits that early on he did not see any possibility in the near future for change in the bureaucratic-authoritarian regime. Fernando Henrique Cardoso, "Associated-Dependent Development and Democratic Theory," in *Democratizing Brazil: Problems of Transition and Consolidation*, ed. Alfred Stepan (New York: Oxford University Press, 1989).

"horizons," created "new practices," and gave rise to new groups and social actors.[26] Moreover, a distinctive feature of the Brazilian experience with military rule was the survival of political space. One of Cardoso's other major theoretical and practical innovations was to define the post-1964 Brazilian regimes as authoritarian, rather than totalitarian, which brought him into sharp disagreements with many scholars inside Brazil.[27]

The problem of dependent development was concurrently a problem of political freedom, according to Cardoso. He continued to insist that political freedom could be restored through political action. While many inside and outside Brazil fell into despair, as early as 1973 Cardoso argued that there remained an untapped potential for democratization from below because some political space and initiative still survived in civil society. Given that there was no guarantee of regime-led initiatives, in his mind the stimulus toward democratization would have to originate from below, from a revitalized and organized civil society. Many social groups, Cardoso argued in 1973, including the Roman Catholic Church, students, professionals, and workers were not yet affected by what he termed depoliticization (*despolitização*).[28] It was up to the opposition to organize and trigger the "reactivation" of civil society.

Like many of his colleagues, as already noted, Cardoso had been personally affected by the military government, which forced him to flee Brazil under threat of imminent arrest and declared him an enemy of the state. When he returned to Brazil, his international stature and his family's military and social connections provided him immunity from persecution, but some of his colleagues were jailed and tortured by the military regime.

One of the peculiarities of the Brazilian military regime was the inconsistency and incompleteness of its repression and political cleansing. Even though it had branded Cardoso and many other leftist intellectuals as dangerous to national security, the government permitted him to return without arrest and to found and operate CEBRAP as a forum to criticize the regime and its socioeconomic policies. Cardoso also cofounded various journals that provided opponents of the military regime with avenues for criticism. In 1973,

26. Ibid.; Cardoso, "A questão da democracia" in *Brasil: Do 'milagre' a 'abertura,'* ed. Paulo Krischke (São Paulo: Cortez Editora, 1982); and idem, "A questão da democracia contemporânea," *Ensaios de Opinião,* no. 5 (17 July 1977).

27. Fernando Henrique Cardoso, "O modelo político brasileiro," in *A construção da democracia* (São Paulo: Editora Siciliano, 1993), chap. 3 [originally published 1971].

28. Cardoso, "A questão da democracia."

Cardoso, Antônio Candido, and others began publishing a short-lived theoretical journal, *Argumentos*, a predecessor to *Ensaios de Opinão*, which he started with Francisco Weffort, José Augusto Guilhon de Alburquerque, and others. CEBRAP itself regrouped many of Brazil's leading intellectuals whom the regime had sought to marginalize and disempower. The regime harassed CEBRAP, frequently detaining and imprisoning Cardoso and the rest of the staff. Soon after CEBRAP published a 1976 study on economic growth and poverty in the state of São Paulo, a bomb went off at the Center. Similar to Foxley and his CIEPLAN colleagues in Chile during this same time period, Cardoso sought to use CEBRAP and his international links as platforms from which to criticize the regime and expose its sociopolitical failings. At the same time, both intentionally and inevitably, their actions made them prominent figures in the political opposition. Cardoso soon became one of the most outspoken and influential critics of the military regime. CEBRAP became not only a forum of debate and criticism of the military regime's policies but also a doorway into politics.

Cardoso became associated with the Movimento Democrático Brasileiro (Brazilian Democratic Movement, or MDB), an artificially organized opposition in congress, which was not allowed to organize itself as a formal party. The MDB served as part of the military's project to manufacture a two-party system in Brazil and to maintain the pretext of constitutional government. The MDB itself was a heterogeneous collection of mostly conservative politicians and others who had survived the military's political cleansing campaigns. Over time the opposition was able to take advantage of the democratic institutional facade retained by the military to push democratization forward.[29]

Cardoso became the opposition's intellectual leader, which gave him an opportunity to speak out on what he considered to be the social costs of Brazil's rapid industrialization. In the 1974 general elections, Cardoso and other members of CEBRAP, including Paulo Singer, put together the opposition's campaign program, a novel approach and an uncommon practice in Brazil's electoral history. Its thesis was a simple one, explains Cardoso: democratization was necessary in order to improve the socioeconomic situation. The idea of the program was to shift the campaign battleground from the regime's self-proclaimed "economic miracle" to social and political issues, such as mass poverty, income redistribution, and public welfare.[30] Cardoso

29. See Bolivar Lamounier, "*Authoritarian Brazil* Revisited: The Impact of Elections on the Abertura," in *Democratizing Brazil*.
30. See Cardoso's comments on this issue in *A Folha de São Paulo*, 17 May 1992.

especially wanted to dispel the regime-proclaimed thesis that the choice for Brazil was between development and democracy.[31]

The 1974 elections coincided with the launching of controlled liberalization under the presidency of General Ernesto Geisel. The elections proved to be a turning point; the MDB's impressive electoral gains (mainly due to the increased participation the party stimulated) altered the political landscape as well as transformed every succeeding election into a plebiscite on the regime.[32] The elections marked the beginning of the opposition's steady electoral ascendancy, especially in the more industrial and urban regions, where the electorate heavily favored it; the regime party, the Aliança Renovadora Nacional (ARENA), underwent a parallel precipitous decline.[33]

As a de facto spokesman for the opposition and one of its leading advisers, Cardoso sought to persuade the MDB to take up the banner of democracy and equality as a counterbalance to the regime's own ideological and electoral offensive. "[In our campaigns, we should] at least defend the ideas of social equality and participation of the popular strata in the decision-making process."[34] The opposition, he would urge, should not shrink from talking about redistribution and social justice, however "radical" these ideas may seem. He repeatedly stressed that democratization was the responsibility of the opposition. Early on, however, Cardoso developed some reservations about the opposition's commitment to social welfare issues and to the kind of democratic system he envisioned. As early as 1973 he was questioning the democratic commitment of the opposition, composed mostly of conservative, old-guard politicians.[35] The opposition's electoral support was likely to erode, he warned the MDB, if members elected to office continued "to behave in the worst tradition of clientelism" and to use public office for personal aggrandizement.[36]

Finally, Cardoso felt that the success or failure of democratization and of the opposition itself depended upon its remaining united. In the wake of

31. *Ensaios de Opinião*, 29 January 1973.

32. See Eli Diniz, "O ciclo autoritario: A lógica partidário-eleitoral e a erosao do regime," in *O balanço do poder: Formas de dominação e representação*, ed. Olavo Brasil de Lima Jr. (Rio de Janeiro: IUPERJ, 1990). On the liberalizing reforms of the military regime, see Thomas E. Skidmore, *The Politics of Military Rule in Brazil, 1964–1985* (New York: Oxford University Press, 1988).

33. Ibid.

34. *Movimento*, 13 March 1978, 7.

35. See, for example, *Ensaios de Opinião*, 29 January 1973.

36. *Ensaios de Opinião*, 12 March 1976.

greater liberalization during the late 1970s, factions of the MDB began pushing for the creation of new political parties.[37] Cardoso wanted the various factions to resist splintering into different parties before the return to civilian rule; he opposed the founding of a socialist party. This internal debate eventually led to the founding of the Partido dos Trabalhadores (PT), whose most prominent founder and spokesman was the pugnacious union organizer Luíz Ignácio "Lula" da Silva.[38] More important, Cardoso was skeptical that political support and favorable conditions existed for parties of the left: "I believe, however, that these currents of opinion, first of all, should not impede [the opposition's] unity and, second, should not give priority to the founding of parties that can only exist with strength in the future . . . after authoritarianism is overcome."[39]

Cardoso saw the political problem, that is, democratization, as a practical one that involved careful strategizing. The opposition's actions would have to be guided by concrete actions, by what was possible and politically feasible, not by what was utopian. Extremist ideologies and grandiose visions of a "mystified" future had to give way to the requirements of concrete problems and circumstances in the present.[40] Given that the opposition could not push for too much too fast, and given that radical or revolutionary programs were unlikely to find appeal at the time, the opposition would have to set aside its differences and work for the restoration of democratic normalcy. "But why fight for ideas so remote in the future," Cardoso asked, "when there are such grave problems here in the present over which we can and should unite?"[41] Though he opposed the founding of a socialist party by the MDB's radical faction, Cardoso collaborated with this faction in other areas. He participated in the various general strikes organized by Lula da Silva in the ABC region of São Paulo, and was a prominent supporter of Lula's release from prison.

37. As the balance of political forces shifted unfavorably for the regime, it fell back on its long-standing practice of electoral and institutional engineering to weaken the opposition. In December 1979 the regime issued the Organic Law of Parties, which permitted the formation of new parties and followed the August 1979 general amnesty that allowed the return from exile of prominent leftists and opponents of the regime. The Organic Law of Parties had the effect of splintering the opposition. The most important party of the left to emerge was the Partido dos Trabalhadores.

38. For a work in English on the Partido dos Trabalhadores, see Margaret F. Keck, *The Workers' Party and Democratization in Brazil* (New Haven: Yale University Press, 1992).

39. *Movimento*, 13 March 1978, 7.

40. Cardoso, "A questão da democracia."

41. Ibid.

Cardoso the Political Leader and Brazil's Institutional Crisis

In his first plunge into electoral politics, Cardoso was elected the MDB's substitute senator for the state of São Paulo in 1978.[42] During his campaign he put into practice many of the ideas he had been urging upon the MDB, drawing on various social movements and organizations, including students, intellectuals, artists, and factory workers. In 1982, he became a founding member of the Partido do Movimento Democrático Brasileiro (PMDB), essentially a regrouping of the MDB. He was appointed party chairman for the state of São Paulo. But according to a longtime colleague, José Augusto Guilhon, this experience proved frustrating.[43] The hard politics within the PMDB was a wake-up call for Cardoso the intellectual; this sour experience may have reinforced his pragmatic bent and recognition of the limits of ideas in Brazilian politics. Cardoso wanted to organize the party around ideas and well-defined programs, but his efforts were met with resistance from local party bosses and political entrepreneurs; soon he lost effective control over the party machinery. In 1983, he assumed the senate post vacated by André Franco Montoro, newly elected governor of São Paulo. As the opposition prepared for the upcoming presidential elections, Cardoso was one of the strongest supporters of the candidacy of Tancredo Neves, a moderate. Cardoso was also an active leader in the preelections *Diretas Já!* campaign, which called for the direct elections of the president. Though a supporter of Neves, Cardoso did, however, denounce the so-called pact between Neves and the military. In 1985 Brazil returned to civilian rule with the indirect election of Neves. That same year Cardoso was the PMDB's mayoral candidate for São Paulo, but lost to former president Jânio Quadros.

Throughout his nearly decade-long career in the Congress, the majority of the bills Cardoso sponsored dealt with social issues and institutional reforms. One hotly debated legislation was a bill he authored to tax inheritance and gifts. He also sponsored legislation to permit employee participation in the management of public companies, and persuaded Congress to establish a commission on tax evasion. As discussed at greater length below, he especially targeted institutional and electoral reforms, which he viewed as essential components of social justice and substantive democracy in Brazil.

42. Cardoso was elected under a *sublegenda,* or subslate, which allowed for more than one party candidate to run for an office, with the candidate receiving the largest number of votes winning.

43. Professor José Augusto Guilhon Alburquerque, University of São Paulo, interview by author, 13 and 15 July 1992.

Reelected to the Senate in 1986 with over six million votes, Cardoso served as the first civilian government's leader in the Senate. However, relations between Cardoso and President José Sarney, who had assumed office following the sudden death of Neves, deteriorated rapidly. Posttransition Brazil was characterized more by *continuismo* than change.[44] Cardoso has argued that there never occurred any real break in institutions, power relations, actors, or patterns of decision making in Brazil's top-down transition to civilian rule. "This transition," says Cardoso, "turned into a process in which, strictly speaking, there was no break in the preexisting structure of power."[45] Sarney was the ultimate personification of these peculiar features of the Brazilian transition. His presence, along with the role of the old conservative guard and the military's propping up the new civilian regime, only reinforced the *continuismo*. Sarney, a conservative *político* from the Northeast, had been president of the pro-military party, the deceptively named ARENA successor Partido Democrático Social (PDS), until he led a breakaway faction (the Frente Liberal, later renamed the Partido Frente Liberal, or PFL) on the eve of the elections. Cardoso broke with Sarney in May 1987 during the drafting of Brazil's new constitution.

In 1987, the Constituent Assembly (consisting of members of Congress elected in 1986 as well as those appointed by or elected under the military regime) convened to write a new constitution. One of the most hotly debated questions was the length of the presidential term. Cardoso supported a four-year term limit and a parliamentary form of government, whereas Sarney wanted an extension of his term to five years and the preservation of the presidential system. As *relator,* or rapporteur, of the Internal Rules Committee and the Commission of Systematization, Cardoso was one of the more important players in the drafting of the new constitution. The internal rules

44. There is a vast literature on the Brazilian transition. For works in English, see Guillermo O'Donnell, Philippe C. Schmitter, and Lawrence Whitehead, eds., *Transitions from Authoritarian Rule: Prospects for Democracy* (Baltimore: Johns Hopkins University Press, 1986); Alfred Stepan, *Rethinking Military Politics: Brazil and the Southern Cone* (Princeton: Princeton University Press, 1988); idem, *Democratizing Brazil*; Hagopian, "After Regime Change"; and idem, "Democracy by Undemocratic Means? Elites, Political Pacts, and Regime Transition in Brazil," *Comparative Political Studies* 23, no. 2 (1990).

45. Fernando Henrique Cardoso, "A construçao da democracia no Brasíl," in *Visões da transição, CEDEC Documentos,* 2 vols., ed. Francisco Weffort, José Alvaro Moises, and Regis de Castro Andrade (São Paulo: Centro de Estudos de Cultura Contemporanea, 1989), 4. See also Cardoso's "Regime político e mudança social: A transição para a democracia," in *A construção da democracia,* "Apresentação: Espelho convexo," in *A transição que deu certo: O exemplo da democracia espanhola,* ed. Fernando Henrique Cardoso and Adolfo Suárez (São Paulo: Trajétoria Cultural, 1989): 9–14.

governing the drafting process, which proved to be chaotic and unwieldy, became a major battleground between the forces of the left and right. Cardoso, the most important and strategically positioned representative of the left, pushed to make the process more open, public, and democratic. He was a leading advocate for a simple majority voting system in the various drafting committees and in plenary for amendments. His systematization committee, which put together the final draft, recommended a parliamentary form of government, a four-year term limit, land reform, and other progressive measures. But despite the many progressive features the final document contained in the areas of social welfare and labor rights, it turned out to represent a conservative political victory, made possible by the so-called *Centrão,* a multiparty coalition of the center and right.[46]

Just as Cardoso's relations with Sarney were failing, so were his relations with the PMDB. He had grown weary of the clientelism and undemocratic internal practices of the party. In June 1988, together with several members of the PMDB's center-left current, Cardoso broke with the PMDB and cofounded his own political party, the Partido da Social Democracia Brasileira (Brazilian Social Democracy Party, or PSDB). He became the PSDB's intellectual spokesman and leader in the Senate.

The founding of the PSDB was as much an act to redefine alternatives for Brazil's future as it was a long-in-waiting protest move. The break with Sarney and the PMDB went beyond the presidential-term-extension issue and other frequent public policy differences. The politics of corruption, clientelism, and opportunism, together with recurring efforts by the executive (with PMDB complicity) to weaken and marginalize Congress, had been longstanding sources of disenchantment for Cardoso and the social democratic faction in the party. Cardoso had also become frustrated with the PMDB's lack of discipline and constant infighting. Unable to reform the PMDB from within, he set out to create a new party, which he hoped would contribute to the larger goal of modernizing and strengthening the party system.[47]

The PSDB and the Brazilian Party System

The PSDB brought together two principal themes in Cardoso's thought: institution building and social democracy. The PSDB has been the main advocate for social democratic reforms and a leading proponent for institu-

46. See Abdo Baaklini, *The Brazilian Legislature and Political System* (Westport, Conn.: Greenwood Press, 1992).

47. PSDB, *Manifesto, Programa, Estatuto,* 3d ed. (1990), 16–17.

Table 4.1   Congressional Seats of the Largest Parties Left and Right

Party	1990 no.	1990 (%)	1994 no.	1994 (%)
Deputies:				
PSDB	37	(7.4)	62	(12.0)
PMDB	108	(21.6)	107	(20.9)
PFL	84	(16.7)	89	(17.3)
PDT	47	(9.3)	34	(6.6)
PT	35	(6.9)	49	(9.6)
Senators:				
PSDB	10	(13.6)	11	(13.6)
PMDB	26	(33.3)	22	(27.2)
PFL	13	(17.3)	18	(22.2)
PDT	5	(6.2)	6	(7.4)
PT	1	(1.2)	5	(6.2)

NOTE: The total seats in both chambers of congress increased in size between 1990 and 1994. The lower chamber enlarged from 503 seats in 1990 to 513 in 1994, and the senate from 78 to 81.

tional restructuring, including changing the form of government and reforming the electoral system. Despite its relatively thin electoral representation at the local, state, and federal levels before 1994, the PSDB was regarded as one of the main political parties, along with the PMDB (numerically still the largest party as of the 1994 elections), the conservative PFL, Leonel Brizola's Partido Democrático Trabalhista (PDT), and the PT. The political clout and respect commanded by the PSDB were attributable to the quality of its leadership and internal cohesion, and not so much to its voting strength. In the wake of the October 1990 elections, the PSDB had thirty-seven seats in the Chamber of Deputies (out of 503) and ten of eighty-one senate seats. Before 1994, the party's only gubernatorial post was in the small northeastern state of Ceará, but its successful, innovative, and corruption-free administration brought the party substantial political capital and broadened its appeal. The consecutive PSDB administrations in Ceará received national and international attention for their combination of fiscal frugality and investments in social services that dramatically reduced infant mortality rates, despite Ceará's being one of the country's poorest states. The PSDB's successful governorships proved to many Brazilians that the party was for real and that it practiced the social reforms, honest administration, and fiscal efficiency that it preached.

In the 1992 municipal elections the PSDB continued to strengthen its electoral base, but it also continued to be hobbled by a relatively weak organizational base. It was strongest in the state of São Paulo, which was also the PT's stronghold. Its electoral base, as of this writing, is still largely confined to the middle and upper middle classes, in sharp contrast to European social democratic parties. The Brazilian electorate on the whole is marked by low party identification and high volatility, with no consistent, stable, or coherent ideological tendencies or groupings.[48] The exception may be the PT's voter base and popular following.[49] The 1994 elections were a major windfall for the PSDB. It grew to sixty-two seats in the lower house and eleven seats in the senate. The PMDB and PFL remained the largest parties, though no longer able to combine for 50 percent or more of total seats. These numbers, and the shifting balances in the congress, explain much of Cardoso's decision to rely largely on a center-right coalition as finance minister and as president.

Unlike Foxley, Aspe, or Cavallo, Cardoso does not have a numerically large, organizationally strong party to rely on, though the PSDB itself is internally more cohesive and disciplined than the historical norm in Brazil. Compared to the political systems in other Latin American countries, Brazil's is a highly fragmented and brittle multiparty system that approximates Sartori's category of extreme multipartism.[50] In addition to relatively short life spans and microsizes, parties traditionally have been nonprogrammatic and uninvolved in policy formulation. Party allegiance and cohesion have been, at best, low, which makes talk of multiparty congressional majorities moot. By and large, parties (and national politics in general) are dominated by personalities and ephemeral factions, rather than well-defined philosophies or stable policy coalitions. One indicator of party weakness, for example, is the inordinate level of party switching on the eve of elections and in congress, where on

48. For an excellent discussion of the Brazilian political party system and electoral characteristics, see Scott Mainwaring, "Brazilian Party Underdevelopment in Comparative Perspective," *Political Science Quarterly* 107, no. 4 (1992).

49. On the PT, see Keck, *The Workers' Party*.

50. Giovanni Sartori, *Parties and Party Systems: A Framework for Analysis* (Cambridge: Cambridge University Press, 1976), and idem, *The Theory of Democracy Revisited* (Chatham, N.J.: Chatham House, 1987). This point is made by Leôncio Martins Rodrigues, "Eleições, fragmentaçao partidária e governabilidade," *Novos Estudos* 41 (March 1995). On Brazil's party system, see the important study by Olavo Brasíl de Lima Jr., *Democracia e instituições políticas no Brasíl dos anos 80* (São Paulo: Ed. Loyola, 1989). See also Mainwaring, "Brazilian Party Underdevelopment"; and De Geisel a Collor: O balanço da transição, ed. Bolívar Lamounier (São Paulo: IDESP, 1990).

average a third of the 584 representatives switch parties per session. This organizational and ideological fragmentation represents a major obstacle to governing and public policy making.

The PSDB is more programmatic, disciplined, and internally cohesive than other parties to its right and left. (The same can be said of the PT, which, unlike the PSDB, has managed to develop a stable, loyal mass following and militant cadre.) The PSDB's leadership is collegial and rotating, and it prides itself on its internal democratic practices. Overall, the PSDB is similar to the Socialist Party of Spain (Partido Socialista Obrero Español, or PSOE) in its policy and philosophical orientations. It consciously looks to the PSOE as a model, though it lacks the latter's working-class base.[51] There are four main tendencies in the party, as Cardoso himself describes it: a social democratic wing (where he places himself), a liberal democratic wing, a Christian Democratic wing, and a socialist wing. These tendencies have not damaged party cohesion and discipline, though the party did experience a brief but serious internal rift after Cardoso decided to align with the PFL during his 1994 run for the presidency. Many within the party opposed any such alignments or pacts with parties of the right; reportedly there were threats from organized elements within the party to break away.

Like Cardoso, the PSDB has not escaped certain identity problems. It is a center-left party, but it is not as far to the left as the PT or the PDT, nor does it see itself as programmatically or ideologically similar to them. In philosophy and policy agenda it is a party of middle-class moderates. Its rhetorical profile and focus on social welfare issues may be left in orientation, but the PSDB often displays tendencies of a party of the center, guided more by pragmatism than by uncompromising ideology. This "pragmatism" often comes at the expense of its progressive social agenda, at times more gradualist than progressive. Despite its pro-labor agenda and philosophy, it has not been able to penetrate the labor unions, in part because the PT successfully organized and captured labor.

The PSDB's relations with the powerful business community—which strategically avoids close links with any one party—are neither close nor hostile. The business community does not appear to be frightened by the PSDB's progressive agenda. Because of their moderate and centrist approach, Cardoso and the PSDB are seen as "safe" by the local and international business communities. Moreover, the party's support for a phased and managed process of trade liberalization and liberal market reforms mirrors the still dominant preferences of business. In fact, there is a good deal of overlap of

51. See Cardoso interview in *A Folha de São Paulo*, 11 March 1990.

ideas between Cardoso and segments of the business community and individual industries.[52] Nor does the PSDB support strong versions of policies traditionally associated with socialist parties, nor are its extant statist tendencies inflexible. Some members of the party are identified as pro-business, such as Mário Covas, elected governor of São Paulo in 1994. One of Cardoso's strongest supporters in the 1994 elections was the business community.

The PSDB's relations with parties of the left, particularly the PT and PDT, have never been stable or close, as indicated above. The PSDB and PT have cooperated on occasion, for example, during the *Diretas Já* campaign and the 1993 plebiscite on parliamentarism. The Brazilian left, however, is politically disunited and plagued by personal rivalries. The PSDB refused to endorse the candidacy of the PT's Lula da Silva in the 1989 presidential elections. Cardoso was one of the advocates for this PSDB position, though the party declared its nominal support for Lula in the second round of the elections. He has been critical of the PT's political rigidity and ideological orthodoxy, even though his personal relationship with Lula has been fairly amicable. The orthodox Marxist elements in the PT's philosophy and program, its defense of statist and collectivist solutions, and a nationalist foreign economic policy have been seen as inconsistent with the PSDB's beliefs. The two parties find between themselves sharp, seemingly irreconcilable differences over privatization. An equally troubling point for Cardoso is the PT's plebiscitarian orientation, advocating direct democracy, mass participation, and direct appeals to the people without the mediation of political institutions. Cardoso finds the PT's philosophy anachronistic, not just radical. "In the whole world," Cardoso explains, "the force of change-oriented utopia, of a socialist hue, has lost attraction."[53] Cardoso says that the left today has to modernize its thinking and shed ideas that no longer reflect today's circumstances:

> What is the left [today]? The left has lost its bearings. If the left identifies with what in history had materialized as the left, it is finished. Especially here in Latin America, the thinking of the left had been based too much on the idea that development was fundamental, that the state was the central agency for such development, and that

52. See, for example, the study released by the major business association Instituto de Estudos para o Desenvolvimento Industrial (IEDI), *Mudar para competir: Modernização competitiva, democracia, e justiça social* (São Paulo: IEDI, June 1992). The study identifies the need for carefully managed reforms in the economy and trade regime, but also identifies social reforms and human capital improvements as key to a modern, competitive economy.

53. *Diário do Grande ABC*, 23 September 1990, 8.

collective instruments of action had precedence over individual ones. Today, the idea that the state is fundamental for development should no longer be a maxim of the left. [The left today cannot think of] distribution without production. The modern left, in my view, is not statist; nor is it developmentalist per se; nor is it distributivist per se. It has to formulate some relation between both. It has to be more rational.[54]

Despite its growing importance in congress, the PSDB did not have any role in executive government until late 1992, though the party had fairly good working relations with the conservative administration of Fernando Collor de Mello. The Collor government had come into office with a thin congressional base. It frequently courted the PSDB to join the government's coalition and consulted with party leaders—especially Cardoso, with whom Collor developed an open dialogue—on its legislative initiatives. Collor invited Cardoso and other party leaders to join the cabinet on several occasions. In late 1991, Cardoso was reportedly offered the Foreign Ministry post (a position he had been wanting for a long time), but he declined for party reasons. Collor failed to win the PSDB's support mainly because of policy and ideological differences. Cardoso appears to have been disappointed with his party's decision not to join the Collor government. Closer relations with Collor, Cardoso thought, would demonstrate that the PSDB was capable of putting its ideas and experience to work for the country.[55]

During the 1991–92 political crisis involving congressional investigations into corruption and influence-peddling charges against President Collor, the PSDB was one of the main opposition parties demanding Collor's resignation and impeachment. On 29 September 1992, it joined in a near unanimous (441 to 38) vote for Collor's impeachment; Collor resigned on 29 December, before his Senate trial. Cardoso took a great deal of pride in the impeachment process and was impressed by the fact that Brazilian civil society had become so widely engaged in it. But Cardoso also had a sober assessment of Brazil's predicament. As the crisis was unfolding, Cardoso seemed to have understood the more immediate political problem of governance. He wistfully observed that Brazil was in a no-win situation. It would have been worse off if Collor had remained in power, but it would not necessarily be better off under Vice President Itamar Franco. Cardoso had commented that Franco's weakness was that he did not have any real political base inside or outside Congress.[56]

54. Cardoso interview, *A Folha de São Paulo,* 11 March 1990, 19.
55. Cardoso, weekly column, *A Folha de São Paulo,* 16 April 92.
56. Fernando Henrique Cardoso, interview by author, 11 July 1992.

Cardoso and the Social Democratic Agenda

For Cardoso, many of the solutions to the defects in Brazil's political and economic system were bound up in his notion of "substantive democracy." Though he never spelled out fully what this notion practically entailed, after he entered politics this developing bundle of ideas matured into a full-fledged social democratic philosophy.

Cardoso had diagnosed Brazil's crisis as a linked problem of democracy and social justice, as a problem of both liberty and equality. Social democracy makes possible the achievement of these two linked goals. Cardoso often had in mind Spain's postdemocratic transition as the model for Brazil to emulate, Spain being a country that, in his view, combines prosperity, social equity, and freedom.[57] The PSDB's social democratic philosophy places primary value on the improvement of the socioeconomic conditions of the lower classes and their inclusion in the democratic process. As interpreted by Cardoso, the fundamental task of social democracy is to address the injustices and inequalities produced by capitalism in the periphery, tasks akin to those it has performed in "center" capitalism since the turn of the century. But to this point neither Cardoso nor the party has presented any elaborate programs specifying what the goals are and how they are to be achieved. Their approach to both land reform and income redistribution, for example, has been at best gradualist in pace and modest scope.

Social democracy has only instrumental value, in Cardoso's view, in the sense that it "does not propose a finished model but a road toward the transformation of society."[58] As in his earlier works, in his writings in the 1990s Cardoso drops only scattered hints about what the end point of socioeconomic, political order is to look like. "Without a doubt, this road should lead to something better than a capitalist society."[59] Social democracy is to prepare the way for "our realistic utopia [*a nossa utopia realista*]," says Cardoso.[60]

Social Rebuilding and Democratic Consolidation

For Cardoso, social rebuilding and democratic consolidation are inextricably bound up in Brazil. Cardoso has long subscribed to the thesis that democratic stability, let alone the survival of democratic institutions, is not possible

57. Interview, *Veja*, 20 May 1992.
58. Fernando Henrique Cardoso, *Social democracia: o que é, o que propõe para o Brasil* (São Paulo: Escritório do Senador, 1990), 18.
59. Ibid.
60. Interview, *Veja*, 20 May 1992, 8.

Table 4.2   Selected Socioeconomic Indicators on Brazil, 1990

1. GDP (in US dollars)	$414.06b
GNP per capita	$2,680

2. Percentage of households under poverty line:

Brazil	40%
Argentina	13%
Mexico ¦	30%

3. Percentage of households in indigence:

Brazil	18%
Argentina	4%
Mexico	10%

4. Percentage of people below poverty line:

Brazil	45%
Argentina	16%
Mexico	37%

5. Infant mortality rates per 1,000 live births:

	1980–85	1985–90
Brazil	70.7	63.2
Chile	23.7	18.1

6. Illiteracy rates:

	1980	1985	1990 (est.)
Brazil	25.5	21.5	18.9
Argentina	6.1	5.2	4.7
Chile	8.9	7.8	6.6

7. Annual inflation rates, January-December 1992:

Brazil	1,157.8%
Argentina	17.5%
Chile	12.7%
Mexico	11.9%
Peru	57.0%
Uruguay	58.9%

SOURCES: World Bank, *World Development Report, 1990;* UN/Economic Commission for Latin America, *La equidad en el panorama social de América Latina durante los años ochenta* (Santiago, 1991); *Latin America Weekly Report,* 3 June 1993, 245.

in the context of severe socioeconomic inequities. The challenge in Brazil is to deepen democracy while at the same time reducing poverty. For Cardoso, neither is possible without the other. "We are, basically, founding democracy in Brazil," says Cardoso.[61] A true functioning democracy, as Cardoso sees it,

61. Interview, *A Folha de São Paulo,* 11 March 1990, 21.

is not possible in the context of severe social inequalities and exclusion. The challenge Brazilian democracy faces is to create the conditions for liberty to take root and to have meaning in the day-to-day lives of ordinary people. The ultimate goal, in his mind, is to rebuild a strong and competent civil society on which a true democracy can flourish. For Cardoso, democracy could not be confused with just political rights and constitutional guarantees, for conditions must be created for the full exercise of such rights. "[T]o be free is also to have employment, to have shelter, to be nourished, to be educated, and to have the capacity to be well informed, to have opinion and influence."[62] For the ordinary Brazilian, the question of democracy turned to a question of necessity. "There is no equality without liberty," and no liberty without equality.[63] In Brazil, "people do not perceive that democracy is a good thing for them. . . . People hear us talk about democracy, liberty, but they do not see an improvement in their lives. This is a grave problem."[64]

There is no consensus on the precise measurement of the country's social conditions or on the extent to which inequity has been aggravated by the decade-long economic crisis. According to the government's own 1993 report, over 20 percent of the people were living in extreme poverty or indigence, the majority of whom were in the Northeast and in rural areas.[65] A staggering thirty-two million people, 22 percent of the population, suffer from hunger. A 1990 ECLA report estimates that over 40 percent of Brazilian households are under the poverty line, with 18 percent in indigence. Brazil is one of the world's worst examples of income maldistribution: the richest 10 percent control over 50 percent of national income; fewer than 1 percent of all landowners own over 40 percent of all land.

Cardoso's thinking on social rebuilding should not be misconstrued as a throwback to the redistributive calls of the old left. His is a more measured thinking. During the 1994 presidential race, land reform and income redistribution were practically absent from his discourse. His electoral commitment to settle 280,000 families over four years could only be called modest given the enormity of the land-distribution problem and rural hunger. Much of this backtracking, of course, was due to the peculiarities of his electoral support base and his alliance with the parties of the right. The goal, in his view, is always a more just and equal society. The practical measures and

62. Cardoso, "A questão da democracia contemporânea," 3.
63. Cardoso, weekly column, A Folha de São Paulo, 28 September 1976.
64. Cardoso, weekly column, A Folha de São Paulo, 6 June 1990, 3.
65. See special report by the Instituto de Pesquisa Economica Aplicada, March 1993. See also Fome no Brasíl, a special issue of IBASE: Políticas Governamentais 9, no. 90 (April–May 1993).

concrete reforms that are required are another matter altogether. Too much, too fast, is not politically viable, in Cardoso's view. Cardoso's emphasis on gradual change and moderate politics is similar to that of Foxley in Chile. The road to Brazil's own middle-range utopia would have to be long and piecemeal. Social rebuilding would have to be a long-term process, given the country's economic problems and the enormity of the social deficit. This is really what Cardoso means by a "viable utopia," or a "middle-range utopia [utopia de alcance médio]."[66] "If alternative strategies were to deal with final ends, only values and statements of principles would be needed. But, since another development cannot be created without political action, programs and the reality principle are thus reintroduced; without them values and utopias remain mere hothouse flowers. Nevertheless, from them arises the strength of the present utopia."[67]

Markets, the State, and Economic Reforms

What is the role of the market and the state in this social democratic vision? The PSDB's legislative agenda, and Cardoso's actions as a policy maker, contain progressive, centrist, and liberal elements. Their ideas cannot be described as "neoliberal," nor do they embrace the so-called Washington consensus of the early 1990s. Cardoso's own ideas concerning the market and the state's relationship to the market predate the consensus of the 1980s and differ from it in important ways. Freer markets and freer politics have been part of his thinking, but so has social egalitarianism.

Cardoso and the PSDB do not deny that the market has an essential role. The construction of a viable utopia must, first and foremost, give primacy to the market and private initiative, but both within limits. Cardoso and the PSDB envision a regulated free market economy or a mixed economy of the Western European variant. Aside from a stress on competition and efficiency in the private and public sectors, there is some notion in the PSDB's political economy views that state intervention has to conform to general market principles. As defined by the PSDB, social democracy places equal emphasis on growth and equity, though in practice they have consistently prioritized growth. "We know that economic growth here [in Brazil] has resulted in more

66. Fernando Henrique Cardoso, "Alternativas económicas para a América Latina," in *Discursos sobre a ordem mundial*, 3d ed. (Brasília: Senado Federal, 1991).
67. Fernando Henrique Cardoso, "Towards Another Development," in *From Dependency to Development: Strategies to Overcome Underdevelopment and Inequality*, ed. Heraldo Muñoz (Boulder, Colo.: Westview Press, 1981), 301.

and more concentration and not the distribution of income. But it is here that one enters history. Alongside growth is necessary a social policy of the kind we [the PSDB] propose . . . a redistributive policy."[68] Social democracy seeks to "transform capitalist society through gradual reforms."[69]

Cardoso himself has always been less convinced than other technopols about the perfection of the market. To some extent, the language of freer markets is new to his thinking, as is the emphasis on efficiency and industrial policy. But they are not radical departures. He remains highly skeptical of the unregulated market in dependent capitalist economies. For him, the history of the market in Latin America, which has been accompanied by political and economic concentration, does not support the pure economic liberalism trumpeted by neoliberal enthusiasts. The market alone, or a market with only a skeletal state, will not solve the problems of hunger, mass poverty, illiteracy, and a myriad of other social ills that have persisted for decades. Indeed, Cardoso observes, not even "center capitalism has been able to move toward more egalitarian and socially just society without a commitment to social policy."[70]

Cardoso and the PSDB do not spell out how they intend to reconcile growth with equity or how to achieve democratic control over economic power. The party maintains that growth and prosperity, and the prerequisites for sustaining them, are key to social democracy. Indeed, much of the party's program appears to place a great deal more emphasis on production, investment, and efficiency than on redistribution. "Rapid and sustained economic growth is the necessary condition for the eradication and diminution of regional and social inequalities." Additionally, "unlike the populists of yesterday and today, we understand that the concern with a just distribution of income and wealth requires a clear definition of public policy priorities and stimulus for efficiency in production, without which no distribution measures can be sustained."[71] Cardoso observes that social democracy in Brazil "needs to resist, in the name of economic growth and of medium-term rationality, demands that, however just they may be, create situations that hinder future continuity of the desired benefits."[72]

68. Interview, *Gazeta Pinheiros*, 2 July 1989, 4.
69. Cardoso, *Social democracia*, 14.
70. Interview, *A Folha de São Paulo*, 11 March 1990.
71. PSDB, *Manifesto, Programa, Estatuto*, 21.
72. Fernando Henrique Cardoso, "Desafios da social democracia na América Latina," in *Discursos sobre a ordem mundial*, 80.

Redefining the State

Cardoso's social democratic agenda, therefore, has important implications for the role and character of the state. The state had always provided the central focus for Cardoso's writings. The pattern of industrialization in the periphery produced, and was reinforced by, an expansive state that combined repressive and entrepreneurial aspects. It was a large arbitrary state defined by patrimonialism, clientelism, and institutionalized corruption.[73] His own personal experience with the large arbitrary state made him even more disdainful of such a state. The Brazilian state, according to Cardoso, had become an obstacle to both equality and liberty. "The heart of the national crisis . . . [is] the crisis of the state."[74] Redefining and rebuilding the state, along with the country's institutional arrangement, is the only way to make the political system more accountable and participatory, to resume economic growth, and to overcome the country's enormous social deficit.

Cardoso was always more interested in the practical dimensions of the role of the state than in theoretical abstractions. Cardoso never denied that the state must have an important role in the economic and social spheres. In Cardoso's view, the state *as it exists* in Brazil in the 1990s cannot be part of the solution. But the choice for Brazil is not between an expansive welfare state or the minimal, skeletal state. The objective is a better, more transparent, and socially responsible state. "In order to redefine the role of the state and replace the liberal thesis of the 'minimal state' for the 'socially necessary state,' it is necessary to criticize the 'state as it actually is' and, from this perspective, accept some of the criticisms of liberalism [but] show, at the same time, its limitations and distortions."[75]

Cardoso has consistently defined Brazil's economic crisis as mainly a crisis of the state: a product of the fiscal collapse, inefficiency, and administrative disorganization of the public sector and the persistence of the overall statist

---

73. Brazil stands as a compelling illustration of the hypothesis put forth by Douglass North, Peter Evans, and others concerning the relationship between institutions, broadly defined, and economic growth. See Douglass C. North, *Institutions, Institutional Change, and Economic Performance* (Cambridge: Cambridge University Press, 1990), and Peter Evans, *Embedded Autonomy: States and Industrial Transformation* (Princeton: Princeton University Press, 1995). Jack Knight, *Institutions and Social Conflict* (Cambridge: Cambridge University Press, 1992), provides a good survey. For a comparative discussion of the role of the state in economic development, see the review essay by Robert Wade, "East Asia's Economic Success: Conflicting Perspectives, Partial Insights, Shaky Evidence," *World Politics* 42, no. 2 (1992).

74. Cardoso, weekly column, *A Folha de São Paulo,* 29 August 1991.

75. Cardoso, "Desafios da social democracia na América Latina," 78.

model of the economy. The Brazilian state today needs to be rebuilt and redefined because "[t]he state is bankrupt, broken."[76] As Cardoso sees it, the real tragedy is that the state has become socially irresponsible and corrupt. He remarks that Brazil resembles Nigeria more than its Latin neighbors when it comes to the scale and pervasiveness of corruption. Corruption stems from "a deformed political system that can and should be corrected."[77] The 1992 corruption scandal that brought down Brazil's first directly elected president in three decades, and the extent of the corruption network uncovered in the state, were the most glaring (known) examples. Another was the 1993 congressional corruption scandal involving the federal budget; in February 1994 eighteen members were expelled for skimming millions of dollars from the budget over the years, though many Brazilians believed the scandal was far greater and involved many more members. Institutionalized corruption constantly diverts resources from their intended uses. Though Brazil spends on social welfare as much as other countries in its income group, there are no spending priorities.

Cardoso's socially necessary state is also activist, participating in growth and competition-promoting activities similar to those envisioned by Foxley and Cavallo. The reformed state must have an aggressive industrial policy to nurture growth at home and to guide Brazil's integration into the global economy. The state is to have a pivotal role in making Brazil's economy internationally competitive, not only at the level of macro policy but also, to a more limited extent, at the level of production. Changes in the international economy, Cardoso believes, together with the impossibility of autarkic solutions, have forced a marriage between the state, science, education, and markets. Only the state can provide the needed coordination and stimulus. Cardoso and the PSDB envision a combined developmental and social welfare state. They see the state participating directly in targeted strategic industries such as aerospace, armaments, and energy, though most of these parastatals have been privatized under Cardoso.[78] Cardoso and the PSDB essentially envision a state focused on substantive social and economic goals; they are less concerned about the precise demarcation between private and public participation in production. True to its pragmatism, the party prefers to approach the relationship between the state and market on an issue-by-issue basis.

---

76. Cardoso, weekly column, *A Folha de São Paulo,* 8 February 1991.
77. Cardoso, weekly column, *A Folha de São Paulo,* 26 September 1991.
78. See PSDB, *Manifesto, Programa, Estatuto.*

What are Cardoso's views on privatization? Few other issue areas bring Cardoso and the PSDB into sharper contrast with the left than public-sector reform and economic restructuring. The social democratic philosophy, as Cardoso sees it, does not reduce to a choice between the public sector and the private sector.[79] Whereas the neoliberal gospel emanating from center economies and international financial institutions sets strict limits on the size and role of the state, Cardoso counters that for a society so stratified and unequal as Brazil's, the choice cannot be between market and state, or privatization and nationalization. The notion that "the smaller the state, the better" is misleading. The elimination of the state will not solve every problem society faces. "For a correct solution to the problems of social welfare, it is not enough to make idle references to Chile and bless it in front of the altar of privatization."[80] Although one may question Cardoso's understanding of the situation in Chile in the 1990s, he is wary of calls for a rapid and wholesale process of privatizing the Brazilian public sector (though with Cardoso as finance minister and as president the pace of privatization has been rapid). Privatization is necessary, "but one cannot make the private sector the universal salvation, because it is not. The market does not resolve the problem of misery. The problem of poverty has to be resolved along the lines of coordinated actions by the state."[81] "In Brazil, it is illusory to think about resolving [the problems of] education, public health, and social welfare [by] privatizing, [especially] with this mass of needy people. Chile can think this way, but not Brazil. I say this not because I am a statist but a realist."[82]

Cardoso and the PSDB have suggested that privatization should follow both "social necessity" and efficiency criteria that emphasize production and competition. The role and size of the state, therefore, will depend upon the number of socially necessary tasks and services it needs to perform. "Fundamental for social democracy is not that the state be small or large, but that its size and functions be commensurate with the necessities of the whole of society."[83]

To be sure, there are many potential contradictions in the philosophy and policy agenda of Cardoso and the PSDB with respect to the relationship between the market, the state, and social welfare. Cardoso's notion of the socially necessary state is vague in content and specifics; he and the PSDB

79. See Cardoso, *Social democracia*.
80. Cardoso, weekly column, *A Folha de São Paulo*, 30 January 1992.
81. Ibid.
82. Interview, *Veja*, 20 May 1992, 10.
83. Interview, *Veja*, 20 May 1992, 17.

firmly believe that it is impossible to define beforehand its size or its areas of activity. The question remains how to reconcile the developmental and social welfare state with the fit, market-conforming state? What are the parameters to ensure that the state's socially necessary activities do not distort the market or turn into runaway populism?

Institutional Reforms and Democracy in Brazil

Throughout much of the 1970s and early 1980s Cardoso had focused on the social costs of dependent development, gradually turning his attention and priorities to the country's institutional crisis. At the heart of Brazil's political and socioeconomic crisis, Cardoso had suggested, is an institutional problem. Brazil's democratic consolidation was put at risk not only by generalized disenchantment and social malaise but also by the institutional paralysis and breakdown that seemed to plague the country in the posttransition decade. Unlike the situation in Chile and Argentina, Brazil has yet to resolve fundamental questions regarding the country's institutional and constitutional arrangement. Though democracy in Brazil has not faced the same severe challenges as in Chile and Argentina, Cardoso worries about the erosion of institutional and popular support for its long-term health.

As Cardoso sees it, institutional reforms, such as restoring a balance among the branches of government, adopting a more flexible and effective form of government, and changing electoral laws, are basic to eliminating institutional distortions and to restoring public confidence in the intrinsic value of a democratic system. But they are also essential to economic growth. Both before and during his tenure as finance minister he frequently noted that the absence of institutional stability and credibility hurts economic performance.

Throughout his career in Congress Cardoso sought through speeches and legislation to strengthen the legislative branch and restore a proper balance among the branches. The authoritarian episode not only marginalized the legislature but also fortified what had been historically a strong and dominating executive. This imbalance continued into the posttransition period and was a source of tension between Cardoso and the government he represented in Congress. Cardoso's break with Sarney and the PMDB, and his opposition to the Sarney and Collor governments' repeated use of *medidas provisórias* (presidential decrees), were both part of his campaign to resist efforts from within and without Congress to weaken the legislative branch and bypass constitutional procedures. Congress itself must play a key part. It is up to

Congress to "rescue the image of the legislature," to find ways "to take the country out of the [vicious circle] of discredit, of hopelessness, and of the debilitating criticism of the institutions."[84]

For Cardoso and the PSDB, the only way to strengthen Congress, restore proper balance among the branches, and solve the myriad of defects in the political system is to change the constitutional form of government.[85] The PSDB (along with the PT, with which it collaborated) was the principal supporter of the mid-1992 legislation to move up the referendum on adoption of a parliamentary form of government to 21 April 1993. The referendum, however, was a major defeat for the proponents of parliamentarism in that about 60 percent of the voters chose the presidential system.[86]

The argument for a parliamentary form of government ties into Cardoso's overall concern with creating a more meaningful, more representative democracy by connecting the political system to its civil society base. It is part of a larger vision to devolve power from the executive to the legislature and from the state to civil society, to create a strong civil society that can act as a counterweight to the state. Making the political system more accountable and transparent, he reasons, is another key ingredient to strengthen and empower civil society. The Brazilian political system has "lost contact with the base."[87] Cardoso does not claim that parliamentarism is the panacea for all of the country's socioeconomic and political ills, but in his view, it is the most effective and stable form of constitutional government. A parliamentary system is both more effective and more flexible. Presidential forms of government, where the president and the Congress can each claim separate democratic legitimacy and checkmate each other, have proven to be ineffective and the source of instability in Brazil and much of Latin America. The problems of the presidential system in Brazil are compounded by a weak party system,

84. Cardoso, weekly columns, *A Folha de São Paulo*, 29 August 1991 and 19 September 1991.

85. On the scholarly debate between presidentialism and parliamentarism, see Larry Diamond, Seymour Martin Lipset, and Juan J. Linz, "Building and Sustaining Democratic Government in Developing Countries: Some Tentative Findings," *World Affairs* 150, no. 1 (1987); Scott Mainwaring, "Presidentialism, Multipartism, and Democracy: The Difficult Combination," *Comparative Political Studies* 26, no. 2 (1993); Alfred Stepan, "Constitutional Frameworks and Democratic Consolidation: Parliamentarism Versus Presidentialism," *World Politics* 46, no. 1 (1993); Juan J. Linz and Arturo Valenzuela, eds., *The Failure of Presidential Democracy* (Baltimore: Johns Hopkins University Press, 1994); Juan J. Linz, *Hacia una democracia moderna: La opción parlamentaria* (Santiago: Universidade Católica de Chile, 1990).

86. The plebiscite was marked by high voter abstention and null votes. There was a great deal of voter confusion and ignorance concerning the significance or relevance of the plebiscite.

87. Cardoso, weekly column, *A Folha de São Paulo*, 31 December 1984.

which makes policy coalitions difficult to forge and creates structural incentives for corruption and clientelism. Parliamentarism will not solve everything, but "[it] can help to find solutions for some of these problems, because the decision-making process in a cabinet government becomes more transparent and permits society to exert pressure directly over the political system."[88]

Cardoso and the PSDB also want to reform the electoral system, which has been another cause of the party system's weakness.[89] The Brazilian electoral system combines single-member district plurality and proportionality rules. It has produced low degrees of party loyalty and coherence, encouraged excessively individualistic behavior on the part of party members, and spawned microparties.[90] For Cardoso, there are two major concerns. First, there are too many "parties for hire" and parties that serve mainly as personal vehicles. To prevent the further fragmentation of the party system and to increase its efficiency, Cardoso advocates raising the minimum barriers to party registration. Second, the present electoral system produces gross distortions of representation: some small, thinly populated states have congressional representation equal to that of the larger, populous states.[91] Cardoso and the PSDB have proposed legislation to institute a proportional representation system similar to Germany's.[92] Cardoso's own bills advocated mixed-vote districts. Finally, working with other parties, Cardoso and the PSDB have proposed new campaign-finance regulations to eliminate the cancerous growth of corruption in campaigns. Cardoso favors public financing of electoral campaigns.

All of these reforms entail the overall revamping of the flawed 1988 constitution, in whose creation Cardoso himself participated. He favors rewriting the constitution and, as finance minister and president, pushed for voting changes in congress that would permit constitutional amendments by simple majority vote. However, both as finance minister and during the first year of

88. Cardoso, weekly column, *A Folha de São Paulo,* 17 October 1991.
89. See Mainwaring, "Brazilian Party Underdevelopment in Comparative Perspective," and idem, "Political Parties and Democratization in Brazil and the Southern Cone," *Comparative Politics* 21, no. 1 (1988).
90. Scott Mainwaring, "Politicians, Parties, and Electoral Systems: Brazil in Comparative Perspective," *Comparative Politics* 24, no. 1 (1991).
91. Regardless of population, each state is guaranteed three senators; depending on population, a state may have as few as eight deputies and as many as sixty. This means that the less populous states, such as the Amazonian states, are overrepresented compared to the more populous states, such as the southeastern states. See Mainwaring, "Politicians, Parties, and Electoral Systems."
92. Cardoso, weekly column, *A Folha de São Paulo,* 3 August 1990.

his presidency, he agreed to postpone rewriting the constitution in order to win the legislative support of parties of the right.

The Periphery, Development, and the New International Order

Cardoso, it should be recalled, understood dependency to be neither stable nor permanent. It was essentially a question of position and function. In the present world economy, Cardoso argues, the position and function of the periphery have altered dramatically. Cardoso's thinking on dependency never denied the value of participation in the international economy. What separated the center and the periphery was not industrialization per se, but the rate of growth, productivity, technical progress, and the locus of dynamism. The difference was who had control over national welfare.

For most of the periphery one can no longer speak in terms of the classic relations of dependency. With the technological and industrial changes of the past few decades, the periphery is more in danger of being left behind and excluded from participating in the global economy than of being pigeonholed as dependent suppliers of raw materials. Cardoso sees two contrasting tendencies in the world economy today: integration and marginalization. The future of Latin America, in Cardoso's view, lies in an aggressive policy of integration into the global economy.

International capitalism, according to Cardoso, has undergone a technological, organizational revolution in the past few decades.[93] In *Dependency and Development* (1979) he suggested that the global economy was already undergoing transformations that provided the periphery with more opportunities to lessen or break their dependency. These changes have created a multipolar world of new economic-political poles and a global policy agenda in which issues of pollution, democracy, and poverty gain importance and security concerns become collective. Likewise, the South itself has undergone profound changes and has become more heterogeneous. Some parts of the South, such as Brazil, India, and the East Asian states, have the potential and resources to join and compete effectively in the new global economy. The rest of the South may simply be left behind altogether. The technological transformation of the global economy potentially means the marginalization of some peripheral economies, since, in Cardoso's view, the global economy dispenses with traditional peripheral production. The periphery's abundance of natural

93. Cardoso, "Alternativas econômicas para América Latina."

resources and cheap labor—its comparative advantages—are much less important to a global market dominated by high technology and services. International capitalism turned to biogenetics, microelectronics, telecommunications, and other high-tech areas, while Latin America and other parts of the South remained stuck in an industrialization model that impeded technical progress and international competitiveness. Today one can no longer speak in terms of the classic structures of dependency described in *Dependency and Development*, says Cardoso. "One is no longer dealing with the South that was the periphery linked to the capitalist center through classic relations of dependency. Or with the phenomena, described twenty-five years ago by Enzo Faleto and myself, of the transfer of parts of the production system via multinationals and of the association of local producers with foreign capital to form the 'dependent-associated' style of development."[94] In the 1990s the challenge to the periphery is broader. The ability to prosper economically and participate in the global market on a nondependent basis entails constructing a new society. There has been a marriage of science, technology, and freedom. Technical progress and economic competitiveness—components essential to participation in the global economy—more and more depend on a well-educated, skilled, and healthy society, a society where human capital and creativity are fostered because its pillars are social justice and freedom. "There was, therefore, a *substantive* transformation in the relations of dependency between the South and the North . . . . [namely,] the loss of importance of vast areas of the planet for the world economy (even if in a condition of exploitation and dependency) and, on the other hand, the challenge that stopped being merely "economic" [and began] to involve the whole of society in other parts of the South."[95] In Cardoso's view the periphery today has no real choice. It must either integrate itself into the world economy or be left behind. "In truth it is a more cruel phenomenon: Either the South (or parts of it) enters the democratic-technological-scientific race and invests massively in R & D, and undergoes "informational" transformations, or it [risks] becoming unimportant, insignificant for the development of the globalized economy."[96]

Cardoso notes that "the world is reorganizing itself, but Brazil finds itself left at the margins."[97] Cardoso is quick to point out, however, that while

94. Ibid., 35.
95. Ibid., 36; italics in the original.
96. Ibid., 35.
97. Cardoso, weekly column, *A Folha de São Paulo*, 8 February 1991, 6.

economic isolationism is neither possible nor desirable, Brazil cannot simply throw open its markets. Cardoso and the PSDB favor a "selective" trade-liberalization process that fosters and strengthens a national industrial base. Brazil must participate in the globalized economy on the basis of an industrial-technological strategy, and it must manipulate its trade regime accordingly. They believe that there is a valid place in industrial policy for so-called market reserves (or other forms of infant-industry protection), though selectively applied.[98] According to Cardoso, the challenge for Latin America is to develop its own strategy to integrate with these global processes and to develop new centers of economic growth, such as Mercosur, the free trade bloc comprising Brazil, Argentina, Paraguay, and Uruguay that went into effect in January 1995.[99] Commenting on Brazil by means of a criticism of Domingo Cavallo's strategy in Argentina, in July 1991 Cardoso argued: "We have to get moving; we cannot cross our arms and throw open the [local] markets. If we do this, we're finished. We have to bring to the fore an active policy of technological development and identify our strategic advantages. Here in Argentina, more so than in Brazil, there is a hasty perception that it is sufficient just to lower tariffs."[100]

The Intellectual as Policy Maker: Ideas and Hard Choices

In early October 1992, Cardoso was appointed the new foreign minister by interim president Itamar Franco. In return for the party's support in congress, Franco gave the PSDB three other cabinet posts, including the Social Welfare Ministry. Several factors explain Cardoso's and the PSDB's the decision to join the government. First, Cardoso and the PSDB had been pushing for some form of *entendimento* (national reconciliation) to get the country moving again, and probably felt the opportunity was upon them, since other major parties were also joining the government, including the PMDB, the PFL, and the PT, in the wake of President Collor's impeachment. Second, with such a heavy congressional support base and the major party represented in the government, for all practical purposes parliamentarism had arrived in Brazil.

98. See PSDB, *Manifesto, Programa, Estatuto.*
99. Interview, *Página 12*, 28 July 1991.
100. Ibid., 6.

Third, Franco's positions on economic reforms and social welfare issues were closer to those of the PSDB, even though Franco often displayed populist-nationalist tendencies that alarmed Cardoso.

As foreign minister, Cardoso devoted a good deal of his time to Brazil's ongoing negotiations with its creditors and to trade disputes with the United States, particularly the dispute over intellectual property rights. Since Franco relied on a coterie of personal friends for advice, Cardoso was initially in the president's outer circle of advisers. However, Franco respected and solicited Cardoso's advice on a range of policy issues, including economic policy. By May 1993 Cardoso had become one of the key participants in the drafting of economic policy. Brazil's economic situation, however, was showing few signs of improvement, and inflation continued to spiral out of control. Since the mid-1980s, and after four presidents and a dozen or so finance ministers, sustained growth and macroeconomic stability continued to be elusive. This institutional and political instability, of course, meant that the economic as well as the social problems worsened.

Cardoso's stay in the Foreign Ministry was brief. On 20 May 1993 he was appointed finance minister, the third in Franco's eight-months-long administration. Cardoso's appointment to the Ministério da Fazenda was well received domestically and internationally. Though he lacked the technical training and experience in economics of Cavallo or Foxley, his appointment was hailed in business and financial circles. *Veja*'s cover story declared that Cardoso was "the best choice possible" and that his selection "was the best news that the country has received since the impeachment of Fernando Collor."[101] One of Cardoso's first moves was to put together a strong, disciplined economic advisory team, consisting of Edmar Bacha, Gustavo Franco, and Winston Fritsch, all respected economists and technocrats (as well as members of the PSDB). Cardoso was given carte blanche by Franco, giving him *superministro* status within the government. Despite these extensive formal powers, Cardoso's experience as finance minister contrasted with that of Cavallo and Foxley in two important respects.[102] First, he was unable to "colonize" the ministry or any other parts of the bureaucratic and decision-making apparatus with party members or his own appointments. Second, his was a brief tenure. The critical difference, however, would be the institutional context within which each operated.

101. *Veja*, 26 May 1993, 18, 20.
102. On this point, see Chapters 2 and 6 in this volume.

Cardoso as Economic Policy Decision Maker

As finance minister, Cardoso tried to implement many of the ideas and reforms he had advocated over the years, though the severe economic crisis sharply reduced his choices. The need to negotiate with Congress and to bargain with different interest groups for approval of his policies meant that he had to backtrack a great deal, to moderate his social policies, and even to abandon some policy goals altogether. The defects of Brazil's institutions—such as a bloated state, a weak party system that makes congressional majorities difficult, a constitution that stands in the way of economic reforms—haunted Cardoso throughout his short term. The political and economic circumstances were not propitious. Everyone was questioning the country's institutional and political capacity to implement and sustain economic reforms. The Franco administration was shaken by scandals and cabinet reshuffles, monthly inflation ran at 30 percent, and the mood of the country was uncharacteristically pessimistic. Moreover, policy making promised to be confusing, contentious, and inconsistent, given that the Franco cabinet was a heterogeneous collection of politicians with divergent philosophies and political ambitions. Moreover, Cardoso worried about the temperamental and impetuous Franco, whose erratic public declarations on economic policy did more harm than good. (In the midst of putting together his economic plan Cardoso was confronted with a brief but serious political crisis touched off by Franco's behavior and reported military rumblings for Franco's resignation; Cardoso was one of the key cabinet officials the military contacted regarding their displeasures with Franco and other cabinet officials.)[103] Cardoso faced an unenviable dual task: to stabilize the economy *and* to restore the credibility of the government and state.[104] The entire country and the business community were still reeling from the repeated economic "shock" treatments of the past five years; inflationary expectations and suspicions only increased with every change in the economic team. Cardoso understood his main challenge to be to reassure the country and restore calm, and immediately announced that his economic plans would not call for repeating the shock measures of the past, particularly those of the Collor government's stabilization plan. In terms of public policy, he was faced with two seemingly impossible tasks: economic recovery and constitutional reforms, since so much of the former depended on the latter.

103. On this point, see Gilberto Dimenstein and Josias de Souza, *A história real: Trama de uma sucessão,* 3d ed. (São Paulo: Editôra Atica, 1994).
104. *Visão,* 2 June 1993, 12.

Cardoso, as noted earlier, had defined Brazil's macroeconomic economic problems, and specifically inflation, as largely generated by the bloated, fiscally irresponsible state. Consequently, the bulk of his policies were directed at reforming the public sector, concentrating mainly on restoring fiscal balance in the federal budget. To combat inflation and resume growth Cardoso's June 1993 economic stabilization program emphasized fiscal restraint, deregulation, greater trade liberalization, accelerated privatization, administrative restructuring, and improved tax collection. Cardoso and his economic team devoted most of their efforts to cutting spending, though partially sparing social welfare programs, and raising taxes in order to eliminate the estimated $22 billion federal budget deficit. He also sought to refinance the estimated $49 billion in state and municipal debt to the federal government. He made it clear that the government would crack down on tax evasion, which he estimated at some $40 to $60 billion annually, and even threatened imprisonment for those who refused to pay taxes owed.

There were three main stages to his stabilization plan, whose basic objective was to combat inflation at its source, public spending and the deficit.[105] The first stage involved deep cuts in government spending and raising new and additional revenues. To achieve the latter, he raised corporate and personal income taxes, improved collection and enforced repayment of back taxes, and found new sources of revenues, such as taxing financial transactions. Since his days in the Senate Cardoso has devoted much attention to revamping the country's tax and collection system, which is complicated, since the tax system is encoded in the constitution and any changes require a constitutional amendment. By January 1994 Congress had approved the cuts and most of the taxes. It also approved the taxes on financial transactions, but refused to approve the business tax increases. Cardoso dropped the business tax in order to win the support of the parties of the right. Second, a month later Cardoso won approval from Congress to revise constitutionally mandated revenue-sharing formulas between the federal, state, and local governments. The revision permitted a 15 percent reduction in federal transfers to the states and local governments. The revenues were then to be placed in a two-year, $16 billion Fundo da Emergência Social, which was placed at the discretion of the executive and to be partially funded through tax increases. The Fundo was a major victory for Cardoso economically and politically, not only because it eliminated the need for the federal government to borrow from the public to

---

105. For a discussion of the politics involved in the making of the Plano Real, see Dimenstein and de Souza, *A história real.*

finance its social spending (and thus feed inflation) but also because it gave Cardoso enormous discretionary social spending control in an election year. The third stage of the stabilization plan, approved in March, was the introduction of the Unidade Real do Valor (Unit of Real Value, or URV), which was to act initially as an exchange- or dollar-pegged price-and-wage index for the whole economy; afterward it was to become the new, close-to-the-dollar currency, the real.

Cardoso's plan was not without its critics. Even his own friend and colleague in the PSDB, José Serra, publicly criticized aspects of the plan. What drew a lot criticism was the plan's foreign exchange regime, which, though partially floating, was kept overvalued. The principal sources of opposition to Cardoso's stabilization plan came from parties of the left, primarily the PT and PDT and labor unions, but as well from within the cabinet itself. The heads of various ministries publicly complained that the cuts were draconian, and some even threatened to resign. The PT, the major labor unions, and even the labor minister (himself a member of the PSDB) argued that because of the method of wage and salary conversion the URV would hurt labor by lowering real wages. Opponents of the URV claimed it was income regressive because, in addition to the fact that prices would remain free of controls, under its conversion rules the legal minimum wage of $100 per month would drop to around $64. Cardoso was firm in his resistance to labor demands for upward wage readjustments and an increase in the minimum wage, because of their inflationary and consumption pressures. To combat opposition to his plan, especially opposition in Congress and the cabinet, Cardoso used the media adeptly to appeal directly to the public.

The Plano Real, or Plano FHC, as it was dubbed, was an unambiguous short-term success, despite doubts about its long-term viability and the government's ability to sustain it. Much like the situation faced by Cavallo in Argentina, the long-term success of the plan and economic growth would depend greatly on similar reforms in the states and municipalities, a more urgent problem in Brazil given revenue-sharing formulas and the states' fiscal powers. The growth rate in 1993 neared 5 percent, with the manufacturing sector topping 10 percent, ending three consecutive years of recession. (Employment figures and new job creation, however, did not respond as well.) By September 1994 the plan brought down monthly inflation to 1.5 percent, and it remained low despite the efforts of producers and retailers inadvertently to sabotage the plan through their exorbitant price hikes. More important, Cardoso's Plano Real had raised the real purchasing power of the working class and poor.

Cardoso sought also to downsize the state and reduce the budget deficit through the acceleration of privatization, while combating waste and mismanagement in remaining state enterprises. Cardoso found a receptive audience among the parties of the center-right, especially the Partido Frente Liberal. The PFL has been an ardent advocate of public-sector reform and privatization. In particular, it favors the breakup of state monopolies in telecommunications, energy, and petrochemicals. It would be inaccurate to say that Cardoso was forced by the PFL and other center-right parties to adopt a rapid privatization program in return for their legislative support, since privatization had always been part of his policy agenda. It is not unlikely, however, that he had to go much faster and further than he may have wanted or anticipated. During both his tenure as finance minister and the early days of his presidency, privatization was much more hurried and indiscriminate than one would have expected from his "socially necessary" criteria. Moreover, the first year of his presidency showed that postponing the revision of the constitution would be one of the major conditions of support demanded by the parties of the right.

Another source of support for Cardoso and his stabilization plan was the business community, to which he has easy personal access. Relations between Cardoso and business were not without their problems, however. Cardoso's efforts to raise business taxes, enforce collection, clamp down on tax evasion, and even threaten imprisonment were not well received. Another source of tension was the government's highly publicized attempts to bring legal sanction against businesses that were excessively boosting their prices after the plan was introduced.

Privatization policy brought Cardoso into the sharpest conflict and ideological differences with the parties of the left. The PT was the most vocal and persistent opponent of Cardoso's legislative measures and stabilization plan. The PT has always strongly opposed privatization measures. In particular, it finds anathema any measure that seeks to privatize the huge parastatals and monopolies in strategic sectors such as petroleum and telecommunications, especially the so-called sacred cows Petrobras, Usiminas, and Telebras. There is, likewise, a great deal of resistance to privatization of these enterprises from below. The well-organized unions in these enterprises and the powerful labor confederations, most of which are politically and organizationally linked to the PT, have made it clear that they will stand in the way of privatization. Both as finance minister and president Cardoso, in turn, made it clear he would be firm when it came to strikes in the public sector. During the early months of his presidency Cardoso would face a series of general strikes, and in May 1995 he deployed troops against strikers in the petroleum sector. A major point of confrontation between the Cardoso presidency and the public-sector labor unions will be Cardoso's efforts sharply to reduce the federal payroll and put an end to lifetime job security for civil servants.

There was no scarcity of election-year reasons driving congressional opposition to Cardoso's stabilization plan. Parties of neither the left nor the right were eager to see the PSDB successful or to make a hero out of Cardoso, who by late March 1994 not only was the most talked-about noncandidate (already polling 8 percent) but was acting more and more like a presidential candidate than a finance minister. Cardoso's actions as finance minister showed that he was not entirely above putting aside principles for political expediency or engaging in some of the same practices of which he had been so critical previously. He made concessions to the right, such as forgoing his business tax increases, agreeing to delay constitutional revisions, and privatizing the telecommunications and energy sectors in order to win support for his stabilization plan. The legislative success of his plan essentially rested on a tenuous center-right coalition in the Congress. Moreover, Cardoso made use of *medidas provisórias* to launch parts his plan, such as raising certain tax brackets. This apparent divergence between ideas and practices was even more stark during his 1994 presidential campaign.

Cardoso and the 1994 Presidential Race: From Exile to the Presidency

On 30 March 1994, Cardoso announced his candidacy for the presidency. The race for the presidency presented Cardoso the finance minister with acute dilemmas. His candidacy created visible strains within his own party. These strains were in part a result of what many viewed as Cardoso's unholy alliance with elements of the right and apparent abandonment of his social democratic, progressive philosophy. But Cardoso, the former senator, understood that congress was both key to the success of his plan and a source of problems in an election year. From December 1993 to early March 1994 major components of his stabilization plan were being voted upon in Congress. Announcing his candidacy just as Congress was voting on his economic stabilization plan would have caused certain defeat or severe modification of his plan, since the major parties in Congress feared the electoral implications should the plan succeed. The PMDB, the PDT, and the PT were particularly wary of a successful stabilization plan in an election year, a plan whose major political beneficiary would be a clear presidential prospect from a competing party. On the other hand, electoral laws stipulated that any candidate for the presidency holding another public office had to resign by 2 April of the election year.

In this curious presidential race, the widely agreed top two contenders, Cardoso and the president of the Partido dos Trabalhadores, Lula da Silva, the front-runner, were considered left-of-center politicians. Yet no group seemed to be more relieved and pleased with Cardoso's last-minute decision than the business community and the upper classes. The founder of the associated-dependent development idea and critic of the national bourgeoisie found his most enthusiastic support in Brazil's powerful business community. Cardoso's support from business and the middle to upper classes, however, was at first politically costly. It played conveniently into the strategy of the PT, which began the 1994 elections by reviving its 1989 campaign strategy of labeling the opposing candidate as the candidate of the rich and powerful. The PT wanted to frame the 1994 race as one between good and evil, a strategy that succeeded as long as the only other viable candidate was the far-right Paulo Maluf. Cardoso's entry undermined the PT's strategy, given his credentials as a progressive and a democrat. Cardoso campaigned as the candidate of certainty, competence, experience, and moderation. His campaign slogan was: "O Brasíl Na Mao Certa" (Brazil in trusted hands). Like his own party, Cardoso initially had problems appealing to the masses and working class, and much of his discourse was void of the progressive, social democratic ideas expected of a candidate representing the party of social democracy.

What drew most criticism and disbelief inside and outside of Brazil was Cardoso's electoral alliance with the PFL, a party of bosses, coronéis, and civilian members and supporters of the military regime; this was the party of Sarney, with whom Cardoso had broken precisely because of its regressive ideas and practices. Sarney, in fact, quickly jumped on the Cardoso bandwagon and became one of his most vocal backers. The alliance was, for the most part, driven by political necessity. Given that the PSDB lacked the national reach and electoral support base, especially in the Northeast, where the PT was strong, the belief was that the Northeast-based PFL could deliver the necessary votes and help provide the organizational reach. This alliance with the PFL, it should be noted, was solidified while Cardoso was finance minister and became one of the PFL's conditions for legislative backing of his stabilization plan.[106] In return for the PFL's electoral support, Cardoso offered the vice presidential spot.[107]

---

106. See Dimenstein and de Souza, *A história real.*

107. Cardoso's first vice presidential candidate, the little-known junior representative Guilherme

Cardoso's electoral success was spearheaded largely by the success of the Plano Real, which many considered nothing short of a *monobra eleitoral,* an election-year gimmick designed to get him elected. Cardoso's success was also made possible by the strategic missteps of Lula and the PT. The PT strongly opposed the Plano Real, even while there were unmistakable signs that the plan was succeeding and receiving considerable working-class support. The strategy damaged the PT internally by triggering a divisive internal dispute between the party's moderate and radical factions. The badly splintered PT, with radicals in the ascendancy, tried to recover by turning the race into a rich-versus-poor campaign—this at a time when Cardoso himself was returning to a more progressive, social welfarism discourse. Cardoso's success was also due to his impeccable image of competence and honesty. His record and image as corruption-free, experienced, competent, and a defender of the public interest were significant. After the Collor experiment, the congressional budget scandal, and four years of repeated instances of corruption, private aggrandizement, and graft in the public sector, popular confidence and trust in public institutions had reached an all-time low. Cardoso was a welcome change.

Cardoso's was a meteoric rise in the public opinion polls once the Plano Real was implemented and showed early signs of success. By August, Cardoso led in every socioeconomic group, including the poorest segments. On 3 October, Cardoso won in the first round of the elections with 54 percent, while Lula—who had actively campaigned in support of Cardoso's election to the senate in 1978—received only 27 percent. For Cardoso and the PSDB, success was not limited to winning the presidency. PSDB candidates won the gubernatorial races in the three most important and powerful states in Brazil. Mário Covas, Marcelo Alencar, and Eduardo Azeredo were elected in São Paulo, Rio de Janeiro, and Minas Geraís respectively. These three states represent the commercial and industrial heartland, accounting for over 60 percent of GDP and over 70 percent of revenues. The PSDB won a total of six governorships. Cardoso, therefore, had a powerful mandate, enormous flexibility, and the crucial backing of powerful governors. (For instance, two critical areas of economic policy are the federal-state revenue-sharing formula and the renegotiation of state debts to the federal government, in all of which the three major states play the pivotal role.)

Palmeira, soon faced corruption allegations and was replaced by a senior member of the PFL, Senator Marcos Maciel. Maciel was one the many politicians within the PFL who collaborated with the military governments. Throughout the campaign Cardoso kept his PFL connection in the background as well as his vice president, who rarely appeared on the same platform with him.

Despite his considerable mandate, managing the awkward alliance with the PFL and piecing together a stable congressional majority would prove to be Cardoso's immediate challenge. The question was, how would Cardoso reconcile his social democratic agenda with the limitations imposed by his alliance with the PFL, as well as with the need to fashion a stable, winning coalition in congress (which only a grouping of the center-right could provide [see Table 4.1])? Would he have to abandon his agenda of institutional reform and social welfarism? Right before the elections Cardoso had begun to pronounce his social democratic ideas more and more. Soon after the elections he returned to these themes. "Brazil is not an underdeveloped country," Cardoso told a national audience; "it is, rather, an unjust society." He announced that his priorities would be to address Brazil's "social debt," build a competent state, and reform and simplify the tax system. Cardoso also announced that he would foster the participation of civil society in policy making and national projects by creating a supercouncil under the presidency that would include nongovernmental organizations. This idea returned to a long-standing philosophy concerning the link between true, substantive democracy and civil society. Cardoso also enhanced the idea he had earlier borrowed from Pedro Aspe and Carlos Salinas in Mexico, the social emergency fund. He announced the creation of a Communidade Solidária program, a $R 4 billion fund designed to finance housing and sanitation projects, job creation, small business activities, and combat hunger. He also suggested that the government would find ways to guarantee a monthly income for Brazil's indigent population.

Conclusion

Several major ideas and themes cut across Cardoso's academic and political life. The origins of his social democratic philosophy and his concerns with the linked problems of liberty and equality found expression early in his scholarly works. He has put these ideas to work and has been explicitly engaged in building democratic politics and institutions in Brazil. Unlike his counterpart Cavallo in Argentina, Cardoso's democratic credentials are unassailable. At the height of authoritarianism in Brazil he founded a research institute dedicated to social welfare and social justice. Like Foxley and Cavallo, he sought to give his ideas an institutional base. He helped found an important political party—a party of ideas to which he has long subscribed. It would be inaccurate to claim that every aspect of Cardoso's thinking has remained unchanged. Yet some of the major ideas and social goals of the exiled scholar have remained fixed, and have been acted upon by Cardoso the policy maker.

What have we learned from Cardoso the policy maker? Do the same ideas and commitments that drove the young scholar continue to define the political leader? Has there, in fact, been an "obvious swing to the right" in his ideas and political agenda?[108] Cardoso's infant presidency and his brief tenure as finance minister and make any solid assessment somewhat premature, though this has not stopped his critics. At the start of his presidency, and largely as a result of his efforts, the political and economic prospects for Brazil were brighter than they had been in the past decade, despite the persistence of the country's social devastation.

Cardoso and his ideas were the targets of criticisms long before his tenure as finance minister and president. Nothing in his tenure suggests Cardoso abandoned his social democratic thinking. In the context of severe economic crisis the policy choices available to any one decision maker are limited. Added to this is an overly bureaucratized, disorganized state. Cardoso's priority was to stabilize the economy and restore growth, focusing primarily on fiscal reforms, privatization, trade and financial liberalization. The distributional effects of his stabilization policies need to be studied more carefully, but his creation of the social emergency fund (which as president he asked Congress to extend for four years) and continued funding of antihunger and public housing programs suggests he remained faithful to his social welfare commitments despite the need to cut back spending. Brazil's social ills, of course, are so great that it will take sustained and extensive long-term efforts to address them. It is true, nonetheless, that aggregate spending on education and public health care were reduced and unemployment rose as a result of his efforts to fight inflation by cutting spending. There were no signs in the early days of his presidency of a massive, radical plan to address hunger and poverty.

What has distressed many people, particularly some members of his party, is Cardoso's congressional and electoral alliance with center-right parties. Is this evidence of a change in his political philosophy and program or of a practical need for cooperation and legislative support? What effect might this alliance have on policy? Whether as finance minister or as president, Cardoso's alliance options have been severely limited. Though his legislative coalition includes parties of the left, only the largest parties in the center-right provide the numbers for any successful piece of legislation. (Cardoso's

---

108. See criticism of Cardoso by Fiori, "Cardoso Among the Technopols."

electoral coalition included three of the four largest parties on the right, the PFL, the Partido Trabalhista Brasileiro [PTB], and the Partido Liberal [PL].) This reliance on the center-right undoubtedly has forced Cardoso to make some tradeoffs, but it is an alliance constructed on his own terms. This alliance nonetheless will likely display both convergence and divergence in policy content and priorities. Soon after his election Cardoso announced that the core of his legislative agenda would be tax, administrative, and social security reforms, all of which require constitutional amendments and not all of which the parties of the right support.

The distress over Cardoso's alliance with parties of the right stems in part from an expectation that only the critic of dependent capitalist development, only the "radical" scholar, could push the farthest and deepest to rid Brazil of its severe inequities and "social apartheid." Ironically, though it will take decades to make any appreciable dent in Brazil's social crisis, Cardoso is best placed to move the country in this direction. Just as Foxley was the only one in Chile with the political and ideological capital to deal with and reassure opposing economic and political interests, so too is Cardoso the only one capable of constructing a national consensus and program to overcome Brazil's social deficit. Just as his party is best able to coalesce with parties on both the left and right, so Cardoso is capable of dialogue with groups and individuals across the political and ideological spectrum, whether labor, business, landowners, or *favelados*.

Cardoso's highly integrated social democratic philosophy and political agenda intimately connect institutions, social welfare, and democracy. They have always emphasized gradual change and practical choices, recognizing political and institutional limitations and the need to incorporate congress and build viable policy coalitions. His social welfare commitment, void of populism, accords priority to fiscal responsibility and economic growth. Inasmuch as policy has to be made in the context of democratic bargaining, the dual task of restoring economic growth and eliminating inequality is formidable for any leader, given the frailties and distortions of Brazil's political institutions.

Unlike Mexico, Argentina, or Chile, Brazil has a highly brittle and unstable institutional context that stands in the way of economic and social reforms. Peter Evans, in his important study on the relationship between the state and economic development, argues that the internal structure of the Brazilian state, coupled with other institutional deformities and entrenched practices, has limited the capacity of the state to foster competitive economic growth as well as prevented its coordinated, sustained reform.[109] Policy formation, approval, and implementation are handicapped by the inordinate level of institutional instability, with respect to both branches of government as well as the rules and procedures governing their operations and functions. Whereas Aspe, Foxley, and Cavallo relied on disciplined, coherent parties and legislatures, Cardoso has endured a context of high levels of party switching, factionalism, and legislative paralysis. In fifteen months of the Franco administration there were some fifty-four cabinet-level changes. Though disciplined and programmatic, the PSDB does not have the national reach and congressional numbers to act as the main anchor or carrier of Cardoso's policy agenda. That the centerpiece of his program was to reform the public sector made his job doubly difficult because so much of the political system fed off the public sector. Brazil's institutional defects stifle the formation of reformist coalitions and the absorption of reformist ideas by institutions and groups. Outside of his own party, no one institution or executive agency has absorbed or sustained Cardoso's philosophy and policy agenda—or even similar reformist ideas.

In contrast to conditions in other major Latin American countries, in Brazil fundamental issues regarding the proper arrangement of the country's central institutions and political economy are still being debated. In part, consensus formation is made difficult both by the sheer size of the country—fifth largest in the world, with the tenth largest economy and sixth largest population—and by the complexity of political and economic interests embedded in the old political and economic order. The single greatest obstacle to the twin problems of liberty and equity in Brazil is the country's Byzantine constitution, which, paradoxically, contains many progressive (though inflationary) elements. Policy choice and flexibility are hamstrung by this overly detailed, chaotic constitution. Many badly needed economic reforms, such as privatization and overhaul of the tax system, require constitutional revisions.

Cardoso's sobering analyses and nuanced ideas were never popular with either the left or the right; Cardoso is and has always been a dissenter from the views of both. He has never embraced the revolutionary fervor and reformist idealism that many of his critics expect, but Cardoso recognizes that social democracy, like any progressive agenda, has to be more than a protest movement. Reconciling the requirements of growth and the urgent need for redistribution and social justice is not an easy task anywhere, but especially not in

109. Evans, *Embedded Autonomy.*

Brazil's institutional and socioeconomic setting. Cardoso's progressive but gradualist philosophy, for many people, will always be a reflection of some deeply conservative bias, an inherent trait of his upper-class, elite background, rather than a reflection of the pragmatism that defines so many technopols. Cardoso's *utópia realista* was always more about limitations than absolutes. "As a politician," Cardoso reflected, "your responsibility is to change reality and not just define principles. If you're committed to change, you cannot turn an ethical position into an obstacle to action."[110]

110. *New York Times,* 14 March 1988, cited in Mauricio A. Font, "A Sociologist Turns to Politics," *Hemisphere* 6, no. 1 (1994): 20.

5

The Rise and Fall (and Rise?) of a Technopol
The Evelyn Matthei Story

Delia M. Boylan

Chile's return to democracy in the early 1990s was accompanied by a dramatic shift in mood. Gone were the days of polemical ideological discourse, mutually exclusive global projects, and the political gridlock that twenty years earlier had culminated in the military coup of 1973. In their wake, a process of political learning had taken place across the political

The author would like to thank Andrés Asenjo, Jorge Domínguez, Richard Feinberg, and Terry Karl, as well as the authors and participants at the Technopol conference for their helpful comments on various drafts of this chapter. Special thanks also go to Tomás Duval and Jeanne

spectrum, marked by pragmatism, compromise, and the nearly universal acceptance of market economics and democratic politics.

To date, much of the scholarly attention to Chile has centered around the ideological realignment of the center and left, and their corresponding role in the construction of a consensus.[1] In contrast, little consideration has been given to the corresponding maturing process within the right, and its behavior in the Chilean transition.

This is unfortunate. In fact, one of the most dynamic transformations taking place in the years leading up to the Chilean transition was the emergence of the so-called renovated right. A small group of predominantly young professionals, the Renovados, were strongly identified with the economic legacy of the authoritarian regime but also were deeply committed to democratic politics. While the technopols of the center and left were busily discovering the utility of the market, this new right was shrewdly mastering the tactical use of elections and bargaining.

Evelyn Matthei in many ways embodied the essence of the right's drive to redefine its niche within the Chilean political system. An economist by training, Matthei came to political life following a decade of experience in the academic, public, and private sectors. As a result of such training, she was well versed in the theory and practice of a social market economy. In turn, despite the lack of a formal political past, she had also acquired a keen sense for the art of negotiation and compromise.

This background served her well during her first foray into politics as a deputy in the Chilean National Congress. In her defense of various policy initiatives, Matthei drew upon the technical and democratic strands of her past. In particular, she played a pivotal role in early taxation legislation, where her economic expertise and negotiating skills were crucial to cementing its successful passage.

But if Matthei earned a reputation early on as an effective figure within the legislature, it was in the public realm where she flourished most. At a moment when her party was struggling to articulate a national vision for the future, Matthei stood out as one of its most eloquent standard-bearers. Offering a unique blend of personal charm, economic shrewdness, and a substantive emphasis on social issues, Matthei immediately set herself apart from the

---

Kinney Giraldo. Above all, I would like to thank Marco Riveros Keller, without whose support many of the interviews included in this chapter would not have been possible.
    1. See Chapter 6 in this volume.

strictly technocratic image traditionally engendered by the right. Her ability to move beyond her "technical self" to build an effective dialogue with those outside her own constituency proved to be an invaluable trump card in the sphere of electoral politics. As a result of her demonstrated charisma, she was catapulted overnight to a position of national popularity and recognition.

But like others who come to the world of politics from the halls of academe or private enterprise, the true test of her political savvy would lie in her ability to master the less tangible aspects of political efficacy. And it was here where she would eventually falter. Despite her great promise, Evelyn Matthei came to commit a series of errors that almost terminated her meteoric political career. Although she was subsequently able to recover from this near demise, Matthei's renewal did not come without a cost. Ultimately, she was marginalized from her original cohort, and her visibility in the national political scene reduced considerably.

While the Evelyn Matthei story illustrates the many advantages that *técnicos* bring to politics, it is equally suggestive of their liabilities. As this chapter argues, Matthei's rocky start is intricately related to the hybrid nature of the technopol itself. For despite its other virtues, technical training may deprive the individual of certain fundamental political skills, such as alliance building, a sense of timing, and, above all, political judgment.

In sum, this chapter serves a dual purpose. Through an examination of the ideas and actions of this young politician, we can understand better the right's contribution to the Chilean transition. In turn, by tracing the vicissitudes of Evelyn Matthei's career, we also observe a particularly vivid dramatization of the fate that threatens all technopols who fail to complement their attention to "tech" with the parallel cultivation of "pol." While Evelyn Matthei's particular case ends on a positive note, it also serves as a much needed reminder of the perils and the promise inherent in this new breed of political animal in Latin America.

The Setting

The Rise of the Renovated Right

Amid the tide of literature on transitions to democracy that has surfaced over the past decade, very little attention has been given to the role of the political parties of the right.[2] To the extent that the issue has been raised at all, authors have tended to focus on two related concerns: first, the need to avoid alienating the center-right in the first democratically held elections and, second, the empirical observation that a center-right government seems to offer the safest legitimation strategy for newly established polyarchies.[3]

And yet, while these two insights clearly underscore the implicit importance of the center-right at the moment of the transition, both assume it to be an actor that must be placated or contained. This bias undoubtedly reflects the assumption—frequently borne out in practice—that the parties of the right tend to ally with a variety of other actors—such as the propertied classes, privileged professionals, and the armed forces—who may have less at stake in seeing democracy work.[4] Nonetheless, as Nancy Bermeo correctly points out, there is no reason to exclude the democratic right from our analysis of transitions.[5]

First, an adequate understanding of the process of value change under authoritarian rule would shed light on how democracy comes to be perceived as the most preferable alternative by all actors in the transition, especially the center-right. Second, further research might also unveil a pivotal role for the right in the behind-the-scenes tactics that have been deemed so crucial to the bargaining that takes place once the transition is under way. This chapter cannot hope to address the evolution of the right's pro-democratic thinking. But it does offer some insight into its practical consequences by examining the behavior of the center-right within the Chilean transition and one representative individual within it.

In Chile, the so-called renovation of the right was most closely associated with the rise of a group of politicians within the National Renovation Party (Renovación Nacional, or RN). Under the adept leadership of a "young Turk" named Andrés Allamand, the Renovados sought to put the right back on the

2. Perhaps the most representative work in this regard is the five-volume series edited by Guillermo O'Donnell, Phillippe C. Schmitter, and Lawrence Whitehead, *Transitions from Authoritarian Rule* (Baltimore: Johns Hopkins University Press, 1986). A noted exception to this neglect of the parties of the Latin American right is Douglas A. Chalmers, María do Carmo Campello de Souza, and Atilio A. Borrón, eds., *The Right and Democracy in Latin America* (New York: Praeger, 1992).

3. See Nancy Bermeo, "Rethinking Regime Change," *Comparative Politics* 22, no. 2 (1990): 359–77.

4. Guillermo O'Donnell and Philippe C. Schmitter, *Transitions from Authoritarian Rule: Tentative Conclusions About Uncertain Democracies* (Baltimore: Johns Hopkins University Press, 1986), 62.

5. Bermeo, "Rethinking Regime Change," 369.

political map following seventeen years of military rule. Recognizing that the transition represented an historic opportunity to undertake this task, they used their technopolitical resources to articulate and defend a new project for the right.[6]

In the economic sphere, their project was rooted in a continued adherence to the social market policies initiated under military rule. It placed a premium upon "individual liberty," whereby the market was conceived as the most efficient designator of resources, private property as the principal factor of development, and individual initiative as the primary creative impulse in the economy. In keeping with such a vision, the state was relegated to a regulatory and compensatory role, assuming those tasks that could not be assumed with equal effectiveness by intermediate organizations or individuals, such as the defense of the very poor. Finally, like its predecessor, the project also embraced a staunchly "internationalist" agenda, favoring an open and liberalized economy.[7]

A second defining element of the Renovado's project was the distance it sought to establish between itself and the military government, and, in particular, General Augusto Pinochet. Few members of this younger cohort had actually held positions in the Pinochet government. As a result, they had much less at stake in defending the dictatorship and could even, at times, be critical of it. For example, though the Renovados were willing to justify the military coup of 1973 as necessary for restoring order in Chilean society, they also advocated a strict adherence to the rules established in Chile's 1980 constitution for the transition to a modern democratic political system. More pointedly, they argued that the armed forces should have an apolitical, subsidiary role in this new polity, confined to defending the nation's sovereignty, assuring national security, and guaranteeing institutional stability.

Above all, however, this project was marked by its commitment to representative institutions and consensus building as the means of facilitating a peaceful transition to democracy. Because of their limited political involvement during the authoritarian period, the Renovados were largely divorced

6. A summary of the main ideas associated with the Renovado movement can be found in Andrés Allamand, *Andrés Allamand: Discursos, entrevistas, y conferencias* (Santiago: Editorial Andante, 1987). For an excellent discussion of the evolution of the Chilean right over the course of the twentieth century, see Tomás Moulian and Isabel Torres Dujisin, "La derecha en Chile: Evolución histórica y proyecciones al futuro," *Estudios Sociales,* no. 47 (Trimester 1, 1986).

7. See "Fundamentos de una sociedad libre y responsable," *Renovación* 11, no. 30 (February–March 1989): 9–12. For a description of the original economic program of the military government, see *El ladrillo: Bases de la política económica del Gobierno Militar Chileno* (Santiago: Centro de Estudios Públicos, 1992).

from Chile's pre-1973 ideological divides.[8] As a result, they were much more prone to compromise and willing to seek multipartisan agreements. This moderate attitude was evident in the negotiations following the historic plebiscite of October 1988, in which Pinochet lost his bid to remain in power for eight more years. In these negotiations, RN played a pivotal role in overcoming the impasse between the military government and its political opponents, thereby enabling Pinochet to exit power peacefully.[9] Subsequently, when gearing up for the presidential elections of 1989, RN called for a "Democracy of Agreements," through which different political currents would work to consolidate democracy and win back the confidence of society at large.

In sum, this modern generation marked a decisive break with the more traditional caudillos that had historically characterized the Chilean right, for whom politics was a hobby for the pursuit of personal interests. The Renovados brought a certain professionalization to political life, guided by a notion of public service. Their professional training and exposure to the mechanized age equipped them with a rational and efficient approach to politics, manifested in the way in which they conceptualized and confronted problems. Free of the weight of a compromising past, they arrived on the political scene with a clean slate, well positioned to be protagonists in Chile's democratic renewal.

Evelyn Matthei: The Makings of a Technopol

In order to understand how Evelyn Matthei came to embody this Renovado project, one must first consider a variety of personal, academic, and professional experiences that shaped her evolution as a technopol. A careful reading of her background reveals an individual who at each stage of her technical development also exhibited an active interest in and command over the bargaining and consensus building that underpins democratic politics.

Of particular relevance to her democratic political beliefs was the fact that her father, Fernando Matthei, was commander in chief of the Chilean air force and one of four generals in the country's ruling junta during the second decade of military rule. Despite his high position within the Pinochet administration,

8. The notable exception to this generalization is Andrés Allamand, who was active in politics as a youth leader in the pre-1973 Partido Nacional.

9. Such negotiations included, for example, increasing the number of elected senators, reducing the length of the presidential term, and granting the president power to enact antiterrorist laws.

Fernando Matthei was also a widely recognized "soft-liner."[10] He was adamant that the state apparatus be turned over to civilian control following a period of military rule, as called for in the 1980 constitution. In what was perhaps his boldest and most controversial public defense of these beliefs, General Matthei was the first member of the authoritarian government to concede the victory of the "No" vote to the public on the night of the plebiscite in 1988. Fernando Matthei's consistently independent and critical position with regard to the military regime was an important early influence on his daughter's political beliefs. From him, she learned about the dangers of an excessive centralization of power and the need for an eventual transition to democracy in Chile.

Parallel to this childhood-instilled belief in the need to establish political limits on the reach of executive power, Matthei also learned a similar lesson in the economic sphere. In particular, through her college training in economics at the Universidad Católica de Chile in the mid 1970s she became thoroughly versed in the essentials of the social market economy. The Católica is famous in Chile for its affiliation with a group of economists from the University of Chicago—the so-called Chicago Boys—who developed and disseminated the monetarist prescriptions that revolutionized the Chilean economy during the 1970s and 1980s.[11] During her years at the Católica, Matthei formed part of a select group of technically oriented students that were given privileged access to senior government officials implementing this economic "revolution." The idea was to foster a highly trained, technocratic "youth corps" that would be well positioned to safeguard changes taking place in the country's economic structure at the time. Unlike the other technopols examined in this volume who went abroad in order to acquire their technical expertise, Matthei earned her "international" economic training on her home turf.

With these basic views about the virtues of democracy and the market firmly in place, the next phase of Matthei's career enabled her to put them to practical use. One year after graduating from the Católica, Matthei was appointed director of studies at the Superintendancy of Pension Fund Administrators (Administrador de Fondos de Pensiones Sociales, or AFPS). Established in

10. This term, taken from O'Donnell and Schmitter, *Transitions from Authoritarian Rule,* refers to those members of the outgoing authoritarian regime who recognize the inevitability of democracy and the need to legitimize the regime in the wake of this inevitability.

11. For a description of the Chicago Boys' activities in Chile and the Pinochet economic program more broadly, see Juan Gabriel Valdés, *Pinochet's Economists* (Cambridge: Cambridge University Press, 1995).

1982, this semiautonomous government agency oversaw the overhaul of the Chilean social security system, in which the formerly state-run system was to be thoroughly privatized.[12] In principle, Matthei's was a strictly technical position, hinging on her abilities to identify existing problems in the system, develop alternatives for their improvement, and elaborate an efficient solution. As time wore on, however, Matthei gradually took on new responsibilities of a much more *political* nature.

In particular, she spearheaded the agency's effort to sell the idea of investing in pension funds to the public. At the time, the country was just emerging from a financial crisis of major proportions, and there was a great deal of skepticism regarding the effectiveness of such an enterprise. In order to overcome resistance to the idea, Matthei brought together influential representatives from labor organizations, business groups, and the media to discuss the initiative, listen to their concerns, and ultimately persuade them of its benefits. In light of her demonstrated ability as an interlocutor among different social groups, she was subsequently asked to participate in the Economic and Social Council (Consejo Económico y Social, or CES), a legislative advisory board established by the military government in the mid 1980s. Much like the AFPS, the CES served as a forum where Matthei would meet with political leaders, executives, and other sectors of society to discuss various governmental policy initiatives. In her role in both of these institutions, one could detect the roots of Matthei's latent political persona—someone naturally given to consensus building and the free exchange of ideas.

In the final phase of Evelyn Matthei's pre-political career, she rounded out her technical training with an entirely new set of skills. In 1986, she went to work at Bancard, a credit card administrator in the private sector, where she managed the tourism, insurance, and commercial relations branches. In this position, she gained firsthand experience in product marketing, negotiation, and the administration of resources. By adding this array of management skills to her repertoire of technical expertise, Matthei acquired a hands-on feel for the inner workings of the social market economy. In so doing, she was able to go beyond the sound policy ideas she had learned in government and academia, and actually experience the country's economic model as a working professional within it.

---

12. For a detailed description of the social security reform, see Maria Elena Gaete M., Evelyn Matthei Fornet, and José Pedro Undurraga, "Capitalización individual y reparto en el actual sistema de pensiones chilenas," in *Sistema privado de pensiones en Chile,* ed. Sergio Baeza and Rodrigo Manubens (Santiago: Centro de Estudios Públicos, November, 1988).

During the same period she also showed the cautious first signs of an interest in democratic politics. Although her father's position in the government precluded her from any formal political involvement, Matthei looked on with interest at the reemergence of political parties and the signing of the National Agreement in 1986.[13] Subsequently, a journalist friend invited her to participate in a series of informal lunches where individuals from across the political spectrum got together to exchange views on the economy. Such lunches stimulated Matthei's deeply rooted belief in the need to open up Chile's political system. More pointedly, they served as a venue where she began to meet some of the country's dynamic, young politicians—such as Andrés Allamand—who would be the driving force behind the renovation of the right.

In sum, while the individual background of other Renovados may have stemmed more decidedly from the academic, the technocratic, or the business realm, Matthei's experiences in all three arenas enabled her to borrow from each without being overly influenced by any. They also furnished her with the essential features ascribed to the technopols examined in this volume. On the one hand, she obtained practical experience in the use of realism and efficiency as criteria for making decisions. On the other hand, she also became well versed in the art of persuasion, negotiation, and the exchange of ideas. In the decade leading up to her entry into politics, Matthei thus fused a liberal economic and political outlook with skills conducive to their practical realization, thereby embodying the principal traits of the new cohort of politicians of which she would form part.

Transition to Democracy: Matthei Joins Politics

Before considering Matthei's formal entry into politics, it is important to understand the correlation of forces within Chile's political right at the moment of the transition. On one side, a moderate alliance had emerged between Andrés Allamand and the Renovado cohort, and a more conservative, agrarian-based movement associated with former interior minister Sergio Onofre Jarpa, on the other. Despite their differences over economic policy, these two groups were in fund ental agreement over what they considered to be the major issue of the moment: the need for democratization. On the other side was a more extremist faction, composed largely of

---

13. The National Agreement marked the first attempt at negotiation among Chile's various political parties during in the 1980s.

former ministers from the military government. In addition to its economic orthodoxy, this hard-line faction was wary of a full-fledged transition, favoring instead a "protected democracy" under the guidance of General Pinochet. Although the two sides attempted to join forces in 1987, their would-be alliance collapsed in 1988 in the wake of a bitter feud, leading to the present configuration of right-wing political parties—Renovación Nacional and the Independent Democratic Union (Unión Democrática Independiente, or UDI).[14]

Matthei joined RN at the behest of Andrés Allamand. Allamand had met Matthei during the luncheon seminars in the late 1980s and was impressed with her economic prowess and natural democratic tendencies. She seemed to be a perfect fit with the modern message he was trying to inculcate within his own party. Though Matthei felt more strongly identified with the UDI's economic message, she was also sympathetic to the need for free elections and a more consensual form of politics. Faced with the choice of joining a party whose platform more closely resembled her economic views or a party whose platform more closely resembled her political views, she opted for the latter, convinced that democracy had to be the country's number one priority. To compensate, she vowed inwardly that her principal contribution to RN would be that of upholding the tenets of the social market economy.

Allamand succeeded in convincing Matthei not only to join his political party, but also to participate in an upcoming television program where RN would present its party platform. One week later, Matthei made her first public appearance as a member of RN, seated between the young modern right of Andrés Allamand and the traditional agrarian right of Sergio Onofre Jarpa. Readily displaying her expertise on topics of economic policy and poverty alleviation, it was clear that Chile was witnessing the launching of a new political star. Following her debut on this television program, Matthei was literally converted, from one day to the next, into a household phenomenon. In her own words, "I began my debut on a television program, having recently joined the party, and the next day people recognized me on the streets. They noticed that I was young, a woman, a Matthei, and an economist. It was like a wave that captured me and never left me again."[15] In the

---

14. A detailed description of the events surrounding this split can be found in Katrina Berrier, *Derecha regimental y coyuntura plebiscitaria* (Santiago: Programa de Jovenes Investigadores, Servicio Universitario Mundial, Comité Nacional Chile, 1989).

15. Evelyn Matthei, "No siento ningún miedo de gobernar," interview by Elinor Comandari K., *Cosas,* 9 June 1992, translation by author. Unless otherwise noted, all translations hereafter are by author.

year that followed, Matthei became increasingly involved in RN. She was elected to its Political Commission with a record number of votes and soon thereafter decided to make politics a full-time career.

In her first bid for electoral office, Matthei faced a particularly daunting task. The district in which she was asked to run was an upper-middle-class, solidly right-wing neighborhood in northern Santiago. Her competitor was a former Chicago Boy from the UDI who had already campaigned for a year and a half when Matthei entered the race with six months to go. With the RN-UDI rivalry still fresh in everyone's minds, the outcome of this first election was widely perceived as a test of the relative strength of these two parties within the right's electorate.

Matthei had no trouble rising to the occasion, and her performance in this first election was in many ways indicative of her innate abilities as a technopol. In the words of one of her colleagues, "Evelyn did not choose politics; politics chose Evelyn."[16] From a stylistic standpoint, her principal virtue lay in her ability to strike the right balance between the tough technocrat with training in economics and someone who could communicate in an informal and open fashion. In addition to her sincerity, the skillful use of graphics and colors gave her a softer and more human image and proved quite effective in combating her opponent's strictly technocratic mien.

But while her surname and the effective use of marketing techniques undoubtedly contributed to her victory, much of her success also stemmed from the moderate political message that she transmitted. Her competitor had adopted a very aggressive stance toward the newly elected center-left Concertación government, captured in his slogan, "A Rooster to the Fight." In contrast, Matthei repeatedly emphasized the need to negotiate with the parties of the Concertación, maintaining that "conversing with opposition parties . . . to provide stability for the country does not mean abandoning principles."[17] In addition, she also argued for the depoliticization of the armed forces, the need to try those military officials guilty of human rights abuses, and the importance of reexamining the country's divorce legislation. In short, Matthei struck a chord in this conservative electorate as someone who would bring a more reasoned and peaceful approach to Chilean politics following seventeen years of military rule.[18]

16. Federico Mekis (RN), interview by author, tape recording, Santiago, 14 July 1992.

17. "El asalto de las condes," interview by Martita Fresno, *Qué Pasa,* 3 August 1989, 16.

18. As revealed in private focus groups conducted by a confidential source who worked on Matthei's campaign. Interview by author, tape recording, Santiago, 11 August 1992.

Matthei won the election with 41 percent of the vote, the highest percentage of any member of the legislature elected that year, with the exception of Andrés Alywin, the president's brother. This first election was in many ways a harbinger of Matthei's natural political gift for crafting a message of reasoned moderation that voters could trust. The speed and depth of her success in such an endeavor marked her as one of the most promising of her generation of politicians. As a colleague phrased it some years later, "This was an upward curve. From then on, she never went backward . . . continuing to develop like the crescendo does in music."[19]

In Office: The Technopol Acts

In her first year as parliamentarian, Matthei wove together the knowledge and skills of her technical past with her natural democratic sensibility. On the one hand, she clearly exhibited the facility with economic analysis, independence of position, and penchant for intense detail characteristic of the technocrat. On the other hand, she also demonstrated the astute flexibility of the politician sensitive to delicate political realities and willing to work on a team. Such a synthesis proved decisive in the passage of landmark tax-reform legislation, where Matthei combined technical expertise with political shrewdness in the consolidation of the country's economic and political model.

Principles over Populism

There is no question that Evelyn Matthei's intellectual training as an economist affected the way in which she approached her role as a member of the Chilean Chamber of Deputies. From a substantive standpoint, such training was most germane to her work on the Finance Committee, where she and a handful of economists from other political parties were charged with reviewing all legislation related to government fiscal policy, making recommendations, and proposing alternatives. Though not always in agreement, there was, as one committee member observed, a "common technical language" spoken by these economists that fostered an assessment of a given initiative's impact on the macroeconomic environment at large, rather than just its

19. Federico Mekis (RN), interview by author, tape recording, Santiago, 14 July 1992.

immediate, short-term political advantages.[20] As a result, they often assumed positions that were not necessarily those of their parties but that seemed most appropriate in economic terms.

The economist's rationality was also evident in many of Matthei's interventions on the Chamber floor during her first year in office. She was firmly committed to the efficient allocation of government resources, seeking always to build a lean and competent state. She continually voiced concern over the government's use of its discretionary funds, particularly in its subsidies to state workers in the railroad and mining sectors.[21] For example, when the government sought to subsidize two foreign automobile manufacturers in Chile, Matthei led the attack against this measure, arguing that it was "hardly ethical to spend so much money with so little effect" and providing actual data to demonstrate the negligible positive impact of such a subsidy on the economy as a whole.[22]

In assuming such technocratic positions, Matthei was often at odds with—and even criticized by—many of her colleagues within RN. This points to a second technocratic element in Matthei's behavior—her disdain for easy political solutions in favor of a commitment to deeply rooted beliefs. As she herself said, "I'm in politics for principles—if the cost of following a given policy is not to say what I think, then . . . I'm better off in private enterprise or in academia."[23] Such an independence of mind was not confined to economic issues but, rather, something she demonstrated across other areas as well. In particular, her open and critical stance toward human rights was unusual for anyone on the right, but especially for the daughter of one of the former junta members. While many on the right chose to deny the existence of human rights atrocities, Matthei was very vocal in her belief that individuals associated with such crimes should be tried and held responsible by name.[24] As a result of her candor, Matthei was readily endowed with legitimacy by her peers in other parties, who viewed her as someone willing to assume an uncomfortable position on sensitive themes, even when this might bring "trouble among her own."[25]

20. Andrés Palma (PDC), interview by author, tape recording, Santiago, 14 July 1992.

21. Evelyn Matthei, "Cómo eliminar la pobreza," *La Segunda,* 10 January 1992.

22. Cámara de Diputados de la República de Chile, Versión Oficial de la Sesión No. 55, Legislatura Extraodinaria número 321, 14 May 1992.

23. Evelyn Matthei, interview by author, Santiago, 4 September 1992.

24. Evelyn Matthei, interview by Patricia Politzer, Televisión Nacional de Chile, 18 June 1990.

25. Jaime Estévez (PS), Andrés Palma (PDC), and Jorge Schaullson (PPD), interviews by author, tape recording, Santiago, 14 July 1992.

A final area where one could detect the roots of Matthei's technocratic past was the applied and thorough manner in which she conducted her job as politician. After years spent analyzing the ins and outs of the social security system, Matthei approached her work with an extremely close attention to detail. When preparing to comment on or propose legislation, she would make sure that she had gathered information from a variety of different sources prior to formulating an opinion. For example, when authoring legislation to enable organ transplants in Chile, Matthei held a series of consultations with lawyers, priests, and doctors to discuss the legal, ethical, and scientific ramifications of the project, and followed these with a two-hundred-person seminar where the issue was debated publicly. In keeping with the dedicated follow-through of the technocrat, she went on to promote its study in the legislature and to increase its visibility in the press. Ultimately, Matthei succeeded in elevating the topic onto the legislative agenda, where it was approved in August 1992. As one legislative adviser commented, it "would certainly go down in the records as the Matthei law."[26]

Political Sensibility: Pragmatism, Moderation, Conciliation

But while thus retaining many of her technocratic traits during her first year in public office, Matthei also proved herself capable of meshing these with her democratic proclivities. For although Matthei had earned a reputation as someone committed to certain ideas, she was also sensitive to the need to temper these in accordance with political and social realities.

This political sensibility was perhaps most visible in her dealings with her own party, where the predominantly agrarian electoral base of RN was at times at odds with her more technical instincts. For example, during the negotiations over the 1990 tax reform, a clause was introduced that would have forced agriculture to be taxed like all other sectors of the economy. Although Matthei was a strong supporter of the tax legislation, she was also sensitive to how this clause would impinge upon smaller and medium-sized producers, and—by extension—on RN's electoral fortunes. Accordingly, she renegotiated this politically prickly point for her party and was successful in obtaining a higher cutoff point for those farmers that would have been adversely affected.

The need to find an acceptable middle ground was also at play on the divorce issue, where Matthei had to reconcile her own beliefs about the

26. Maná Luisa Barril (RN), interview by author, Santiago, 21 July 1992.

desirability of a divorce law with the practical recognition of certain societal taboos. In heavily Catholic Chile, divorce had historically been illegal, and marriages could be officially terminated only through a complex series of procedures known as "annulment laws." Despite their widely recognized inefficiency and flagrant violation, few politicians on the left or the right had spoken up against them. Once again, Matthei defied the odds and publicly called for the creation of a divorce law.[27] And yet, recognizing the delicate nature of this issue, she also tied such legislation to a series of religious stipulations that would placate the Catholic Church. In this way, she again sought to craft a practical solution to a very real social problem, but to do so within the bounds of what was politically feasible.

Finally, Matthei's more democratic side was also demonstrated in her work habits: she was not only open to the modification of her ideas but, above all, committed to teamwork. Unlike many technical people who can close in upon themselves and dogmatically defend their views, Matthei was more given to interaction and exchange. Even in those cases where she had a series of well-documented arguments, she was never so wedded to their defense that she was not willing to make her own ideas vulnerable. As one fellow committee member commented, "She always writes in pencil so as to erase should she be convinced by the weight of someone else's arguments."[28]

Finally, Matthei also distinguished herself from the typical technocrat through her willingness to be a team player. For example, during the presidential election campaigns of 1992, she traveled throughout the country in order to support RN candidates in their local election bids. Similarly, when developing the organ transplant legislation, she not only sought the input of deputies from other political parties but also allowed them to share in the credit for this popular initiative. In both of these ways, Matthei demonstrated an early and avid commitment to democratic institution building, whether at the party or the legislative level.

Validating the Economic Model: The 1990 Tax Reform

But in was in the 1990 tax reform that Matthei was best able simultaneously to put her technical and democratic sides to use. As the first legislative initiative of the newly installed Concertación government, the tax reform had tremendous symbolic importance. First, the reform was explicitly

27. *El Mercurio,* 18 August 1992.
28. Patricio Melero (UDI), interview by author, tape recording, Santiago, 22 July 1992.

"pro-equity." It moderately raised taxes on the most economically advantaged sectors and funneled this revenue directly into social spending for the benefit of the poorest 40 percent of the population. In this way, it was advertised by the new government as an attempt to address the legacy of "social debt" inherited from the military regime. Second, the reform was to entail considerable negotiation between the government and various political and social actors. It was thus intended to showcase democratic consensus building in action.

In both respects, this legislation offered a golden opportunity for RN. By supporting the initiative, RN could prove its commitment to fostering a competent but caring state. At the same time, its involvement in the tax-reform negotiations would underscore this party's willingness to play a constructive opposition role.[29]

Matthei played a key role during several stages of the reform's development. First, she and coeconomist Senator Sebastián Piñera served as the RN representatives in the initial negotiations with the government. The successful outcome of these meetings was critical. For the government, it was important to have the opposition on board in its effort to fulfill its campaign promise of providing "growth with equity."[30] For RN, it was important to make sure that the legislation did not step outside the bounds of what would be tolerable to its electorate. Through a process of give-and-take, the two sides were able to arrive at a mutually acceptable agreement.

Although RN came under strong criticism for such negotiations from the UDI and other conservative factions, Matthei was not thrown, arguing: "We are not scared by the accusations of treason that the most self-exalted sectors throw at us every time we arrive at important agreements. . . . These basic agreements allow us to avoid confrontation and achieve a sensible evolution toward democracy."[31] Like Fernando Enrique Cardoso in Brazil, Matthei's involvement in the tax reform proved her to be an opposition figure committed to compromise.

But Matthei's role was not confined merely to securing certain guarantees for her party during these initial negotiations. She also played a pivotal role once the bill reached the legislature, where she not only helped to refine some

29. For more on the substance and process of this reform initiative, see Delia M. Boylan, "Taxation and Transition: The Politics of the 1990 Tax Reform," *Latin American Research Review* 21, no. 1 (1996): 7–31.

30. For more on the actions of key technopols engaged in this reform process on the center and the left, see Chapter 6 in this volume.

31. Evelyn Matthei, "Momento clave," *La Segunda,* 25 May 1990.

of the bill's finer technical points but also became a champion of its merits on the Chamber floor. In particular, she sought to stave off criticism from those—principally in the UDI—who saw the tax reform as potentially destabilizing the country's economic model.

Like Pedro Aspe, Matthei had a deep-seated commitment to the normative goal of social equity, but only insofar as this objective could be achieved within the parameters of what was economically efficient. When defending the tax reform, she was careful at all times to frame it as a social "investment," reminding her audience that "growth will only be produced if we all chip in and assure that in the next few years we will have stability and tranquillity not only in the political realm, but also in the social and economic arenas." In this way, she reassured the bill's opponents: "[I]f we have reached an agreement with the government, it is because we are sure that we will be contributing to the solution of the problems of the poorest families in the country and that we will not be endangering the growth or the development of the country."[32]

But perhaps the most difficult task facing Matthei in the unfolding of the tax-reform legislation was selling the bill to her own party. In effect, she and Piñera needed to explain to their colleagues in RN why a political party that purported to represent business and agricultural interests would enthusiastically endorse a tax increase on those very groups. While the arguments used publicly to defend the initiative were rooted in a socioeconomic rationale, Matthei and Piñera relied upon a much more political logic when making a case to their own party.

In a nutshell, they shrewdly reasoned that if RN refused to endorse this increase in social spending, it would be held to blame over the next four years for the government's inability to fulfill its electoral promises. In turn, by participating in the tax-reform negotiations, RN would also gain democratic legitimacy with the center and the left. In Matthei's words, RN would be seen as "a serious party . . . that is trustworthy, capable of saying no to the government, but also capable of cooperating for what we see as the good of the country."[33] Finally, it was no secret that the UDI had just unilaterally negotiated the composition of the congressional committees with the government, and the tax reform would thus allow RN to get its finger back in the political pie.

32. Cámara de Diputados de la República de Chile, Versión Oficial de la Sesión No. 15, Legislatura Extraordinaria número 319, 2 May 1990.

33. Evelyn Matthei, "Evelyn Matthei: Renovación Nacional es un transatlántico," interview by Isabel Hohlberg, Caras, no. 52 (11 April 1990): 46.

Throughout her participation in this consensus-building effort, Matthei's economic expertise and political prowess proved decisive. Because she had the technical know-how to appreciate the reform's contents, she was able to formulate a tight, internally consistent argument and support it with quantitative evidence. As one fellow member of the finance committee commented, "Ninety percent of her own party probably opposed this reform, but no one had the capacity, either economic or analytical, to throw up an argument against her."[34] At the same time, she was also able to marshal sound political arguments in her favor. Using these multiple layers of economic and political rationale, Matthei thus played a decisive role in securing this piece of socioeconomic legislation at a pivotal moment of political transformation.

Matthei as Opposition Figure: A New Image for the Right

As the initial phases of the transition receded, RN sought increasingly to strengthen its role as an effective political opposition force. In this drive to sharpen its programmatic message, Matthei emerged as one of her party's leading figures. This section of the chapter highlights how Matthei, in her increasingly political role, capitalized on her extraordinary communicational gifts; the following section details the costs that were attendant to her rapid rise to stardom.

Constructing a Viable Alternative: The Right's Challenge

With the passage of time, RN adopted an increasingly critical position toward the Concertación government. This more aggressive stance was undoubtedly triggered in part by criticisms of RN from the country's more conservative sectors as a "weak," "traitorous," and "unconvinced" party following its role in the tax-reform negotiations. There was also some fear that the more consistently hard-line UDI was gaining ground with the right's traditional electorate.[35] But such a shift was also a by-product of the natural evolution of the regime transition itself. As issues previously left out of the national debate

34. Jaime Estevez (PS), interview with author, tape recording, Santiago, 14 July 1992.
35. See "Las intimidades de renovación," *APSI*, 16–19 April 1992, 14–17.

increasingly came to the fore, the right recognized both an opportunity and an imperative to define its niche in the political landscape.[36]

Defining the parameters of this new debate was by no means an easy task. Not only did the Concertación enjoy tremendous popularity, but it did so while embracing many of the policies historically identified with the right. It was thus incumbent upon RN to establish a distinctive identity. Accordingly, in early 1991, RN shifted its party lemma from a "democracy of agreements" to a "democracy of alternatives." In brief, the idea was to portray the Concertación government as a political force of last-minute conviction, while presenting RN as a true believer with respect to the fundamental principles associated with a social market economy and a liberal democratic order.

In order to pursue this strategy, Matthei and others in RN began selectively to criticize the government on a series of social and economic issues. For example, during 1991, they launched a campaign to raise awareness of the degree of violence in Chilean society, contending that the government was fundamentally overlooking this vital social problem. As Matthei wrote, "[I]t is time that we become conscious that security should be seen as a basic service for the community, as basic as electricity, roads, ports, health, and education. Violence does not only fundamentally affect the citizen's quality of life, but can come to destroy our economic and social progress."[37]

In turn, RN also sought to present itself as a more competent economic alternative, criticizing the center-left Concertación for practices that allegedly smacked of its statist past. In an initiative led by Matthei, RN called for the privatization of the country's remaining state-owned enterprises as an alternative means for financing social investment. Arguing that "the privatization of public enterprises is a general trend in the world today," Matthei assailed the government as "little committed to the social market economy. . . . Will it be necessary for Chile to throw overboard the unique opportunity it has had to combine development with democracy so that a few of our leaders modernize their outlook?"[38]

But beyond identifying those weaknesses in the government's current program, RN also began to outline the bare bones of an alternative project for the future. The Renovados sought to demonstrate that the difference between the right and the left lay not so much in contending views about political or

36. See Mark Klugman, "La crisis en la Derecha: Hay una crisis? Hay una 'Derecha?' " *Puntos de Referencia,* no. 100 (Junio 1992): 1–4.

37. Evelyn Matthei, "Causas de la violencia," *La Segunda,* 26 April 1991.

38. Evelyn Matthei, "Privatizaciones de empresas," *La Segunda,* 13 May 1991.

economic systems as in "the ultimate conception of the human being and human social life."[39] Rooted in the ideas in Pope John Paul II's encyclical *Centesimus Annus,* this new vision made the "dignity of the human being" the ethos of their political identity.[40]

Such "dignity" translated into a myriad of policy applications. First and foremost, it implied a host of so-called human issues, including the defense of the unborn, respect for human rights, and attention to the concerns of the poor. In turn, it embodied the defense of the family, as reflected in legislation to protect women and children. Finally, it entailed a subsidiary role for the state, favoring privatization and decentralization to devolve as much decision making as possible to the individual. In an effort to promote this new vision, Matthei in 1992 called for a complete revamping of the country's educational system. The idea was to verse students more generally in Western culture and ethics, the foundation—she argued—of a society rooted in individual imagination and effort.[41]

While these attempts by RN to define itself as an effective opposition force met with varying degrees of success, there is no doubt that Evelyn Matthei was a central figure in this process of programmatic renewal. Much as Cardoso sought to bolster Brazil's opposition parties of the left, so too did Matthei seek to cultivate the right as a viable opposition alternative. But while her input into the development of such a message was significant, her greatest contribution was far and away her role in its effective transmission.

The Economist Turns Politician

Concurrent with this broader shift in her party's platform, Matthei also underwent a parallel transition of her own, as her original economist's identity was gradually supplanted by that of a more political persona. This transformation was above all visible in her changing role within her party. After her first year in office, Matthei was made a vice president of RN and a member of its executive board. During her second year, she competed inter-

39. See Tomás Duval Varas, "Consideraciones sobre la Derecha en Chile," working paper, Instituto de Libertad, Santiago, June 1992.

40. Baron Christoph von Harsdorf, "Temas de hoy de los Partidos Liberal-Conservadores" (speech presented at the seminar "El mundo en la era post-socialista," Instituto Libertad, International Republican Institute, and Fundación Hans Seidel, Santiago, 23–25 April 1992). See also Pope John Paul II, *Centesimus Annus* (Vatican City: The Vatican, 1991).

41. Matthei, "No siento ningún miedo de gobernar."

nally to become its candidate in the national presidential elections of 1994. In this way, the young economist who had cautiously voiced her opinions on income distribution back in 1988 was replaced by an assertive, seemingly mature politician espousing a national vision for the future.

As her responsibilities within RN mounted, Matthei began to shed her reputation as a moderate. This change was particularly evident in her attitudes toward the government. For despite her early enthusiasm for such collaborative endeavors as the tax reform, Matthei expressed increasing skepticism that such a climate could be re-created with respect to pending constitutional reforms, such as the abolition of Chile's nine "appointed senators" and changes in the composition of the judiciary. While Matthei attributed her change of heart to a loss of trust in the Concertación government,[42] others felt that it was due to the more political role she had assumed within her party. As one fellow member of the Finance Committee commented, "What I perceive today is that she can no longer play the rebel with an economist's rationality in benefit of the poorest sectors, because if this has political costs, she's not willing to assume them. . . . A year and a half ago we assumed those costs together . . . today that isn't possible, and I think this changed when she decided to run for president."[43]

Finally, Matthei's more "political" identity also manifested itself in the type of issues she began to promote. Although she came into office focused on the themes of inflation, investment, and macroeconomic growth, she gradually moved away from these classic economic topics to divorce, organ transplants, and educational reform. While in part a reflection of an expanding set of personal interests, this broadening of her substantive concerns from the economic to the social realm was also a shrewd strategic move. By making such non-class-based issues the central thrust of her substantive message, Matthei put herself in a prime position to appeal to voters on the center and the left.

42. Evelyn Matthei, interview by author, tape recording, Santiago, 4 September 1992. Specifically, Matthei claimed that the Concertación government had lost its golden opportunity to bring about such reforms by adopting a short-term "divide-and-conquer" strategy with the parties of the right, negotiating certain key agreements with the UDI, such as the composition of the Senate committees and the national television council, while negotiating others, such as the tax reform, with RN. It is worth noting that certain members of the Concertación government coalition agree with such a critique.

43. Andrés Palma (PDC), interview by author, tape recording, Santiago, 14 July 1992.

The Matthei Advantage: A Kinder, Gentler Chile

There is no doubt that one of the key factors behind the rapidity and intensity of Matthei's political transformation was her unusually effective communication skills. Unlike some of the other individuals considered in this volume whose strengths lay more in their abilities as statesmen, Matthei was remarkably successful at cultivating a popular public image. Thus, while Cavallo's political future might arguably be harmed by his lack of an ample support base and Aspe could stand to augment his "kissing babies" appeal, Matthei suffered no liabilities in this regard.

Such a natural fluidity in the transmission of her message was attributable to a variety of factors. Above all, there was something resoundingly authentic about Matthei when she spoke. She was credited as someone very "human" and capable of transmitting emotion. As one public relations specialist aptly put it, "In this world so saturated with ideas, dogmas, and abstractions, Evelyn came almost unclothed . . . people could look in her eyes and know she was telling the truth."[44] As a fellow party member noted, "her contribution is not primarily conceptual—the ideas are more or less a given. Matthei's strong suit is when she looks you in the eyes and says 'I care.' "[45]

Matthei understood the value of this contribution to her party's electoral fortunes. To improve those fortunes, she continually exhorted her colleagues to abandon the aseptic efficiency-based image so characteristic of the right in favor of a warmer and more human image. In an address to 150 of her party faithful, she noted, "We must recognize that we have a weakness in the way in which we transmit our ideas. We talk about the modernization of the country. About advancement and economic development. About being efficient. But we don't talk about the pain and the impotence that those with low incomes suffer." As she astutely pointed out, "People do not die or vote for efficiency. People die and vote for emotions, for passions, for feelings. . . . For the belief that a candidate will tell them the truth. For an ideal." Matthei's delivery was so moving that at its conclusion, 150 people spontaneously lined up to congratulate her on its content.[46]

In addition to her very direct and personal style, a second source of her popular appeal was her ability to speak in a simple and concrete language about the everyday concerns of citizens. Unlike so many *técnicos* who find it

---

44. Mario Lubert, interview by author, tape recording, Santiago, 23 July 1992.
45. Andrés Allamand, interview by author, tape recording, Santiago, 21 July 1992.
46. Evelyn Matthei, address to RN's national convention, reprint, 14 March 1992.

difficult to move beyond a discussion of macroeconomic flows, Matthei translated discussions of efficiency into solutions to everyday problems. Matthei believed that the things that worry people are not so much the "big-picture" issues of institutional stability and free trade agreements but, rather, having heating in their homes, pavement on their roads, and the opportunity to educate their children. As one journalist noted, "She doesn't bring to mind the social market economy, or democracy, or the military government, like so many other politicians. Evelyn evokes a simple person, who understands human beings and goes straight to their souls."[47]

Finally, some observers attributed Matthei's popularity to the fact that she was a woman. Because she was a woman, they argued, she was more capable of demonstrating human emotion and of establishing a personal bond with the public. As one party member commented, "Matthei can kiss a thousand people a day in her campaign. A man cannot do that."[48] Others claimed that her gender imbued her with a maternal sensibility, calling to mind an image of the home and the family. As one political analyst phrased it, "Evelyn Matthei offers a woman's touch . . . a kinder, gentler Chile."[49] But there were others, most notably the president of her party, who saw Matthei's gender as having a different communicational effect. According to Allamand, Matthei embodied a trend in Chilean society toward the increased professionalization of women that had not yet been fully realized in the political realm. From this perspective, Matthei represented modernity, a professional woman who was both at home and at work—a role model for many Chilean women.[50]

However one chooses to explain it, there is no question that at the close of but one and a half years in politics, Evelyn Matthei had experienced resounding success in the public eye. Her personal popularity went far beyond that of her party's. In a public opinion poll taken in March 1992, she received the highest popularity ranking of any individual in the Chamber of Deputies, earning 5.8 on a scale of 1 to 7, a score matched only by the president of the Chamber. In July 1992, the public ranked her as the most important opposition figure in the country and fourth as a presidential contender.[51] Unfortunately, hindsight suggests that the momentum with which she assumed this

47. Ricardo Silva (*El Mercurio*), interview by author, tape recording, Santiago, 21 July 1992.
48. Cristián Correa (RN), interview by author, tape recording, Santiago, 21 July 1992.
49. Mario Lubert, interview by author, tape recording, Santiago, 23 July 1992.
50. Andrés Allamand, interview by author, tape recording, Santiago, 21 July 1992.
51. See the July 1992 public opinion poll conducted by Centro de Estudios Públicos–Adimark and reprinted in *La Segunda*, 10 September 1992. This poll also provides results from the previous (March 1992) poll.

mantle may have clouded her judgment, costing her and her party a shot at stealing the throne from the center-left.

The Hour of Reckoning: When *Técnico* Is Not Enough

Although Evelyn Matthei unequivocally mastered the skills necessary to be an effective politician in the public sphere, she underestimated the need to establish the same dominance within her own party. To some extent, Matthei's undoing can be attributed to the lack of an institutional grounding prior to entering politics, depriving her of the tutelage, discipline, and security that might have fostered more caution on her part. More pointedly, however, her failure to develop a set of political skills essential to internal party leadership caused Matthei to make a series of ill-conceived political moves that nearly ended her career. While Matthei was ultimately able to rebound from such adversity, demonstrating her resilience as a politician, her downfall and renewal are illustrative of some of the hazards facing all *técnicos* seeking political office.

Moving From Tech to Pol: The Need for Institutional Grounding

As Jorge Domínguez notes in his Chapter 1, one key feature distinguishing Evelyn Matthei from the other technopols considered in this volume was her lack of involvement in an institutional team before joining politics. Although in some sense trained by the Chicago Boys team during her years at the Católica, Matthei never had a formal affiliation with any one institution for any extended period of time. Rather, as noted earlier, her trajectory was more peripatetic, marked by brief but intense stints in various career paths. In this way, unlike the stable, ongoing cadres within which the other technopols evolved, Matthei was the product of a disparate and disjointed series of institutional homes.

This lack of institutional foundation sheds light on why Matthei got into trouble in the first place and why, once in hot water, it was so hard for her to get out. As the histories of some of the other technopols suggest, institutional experience is important both for the technical background it can provide, as well as for its effect on other, less visible aspects of professional development.

Participation in an institutional team offers three advantages that may facilitate the technopol's transition to political life. First, a key component of team-oriented training is often that of mentorship. Tutelage fosters like-minded thinking among teammates over a period of years, yielding more predictable sets of responses to given situations. Second, teams teach discipline. Individuals trained within the cadres of a team are less prone to act precipitately to advance their own careers. Rather, position and advancement come only after years of paying dues, reinforcing caution and patience. Finally, membership in a team offers an institutional safety net in the face of unexpected adversity. Should one get into trouble, there is a ready network of standard operating procedures that can be consulted in crafting solutions.

Evelyn Matthei lacked the fruits of such team membership. Had she benefited from earlier and more formative institutional links, much of the catastrophic spiral that enveloped her career might have been avoided. Lacking this institutional anchoring, she was fundamentally unprepared to handle a series of events that came to pass, and made several rash decisions for which she would pay a high political price.

But while this discussion illuminates a structural weakness of Matthei's not shared by others in this volume, a second set of liabilities that also worked against her *do* have wider relevance. For if it is true that an institutional background helps to ameliorate the disjuncture between the technical and political domains, it does not eliminate it entirely. In addition, any *técnico* who truly wishes to penetrate political life must learn to dominate a party apparatus. This internal leadership hurdle is by no means an easy obstacle for the average technopol to overcome, since it requires certain political skills that do not come with technical training. As the Matthei case reveals, technical and political skills are of a fundamentally different—and, at times, even contradictory—nature. If they are not honed jointly, they run the risk of colliding, with potentially disastrous consequences.[52]

Alliance Formation

One political skill necessary for the assumption of leadership within a political party is the ability to build and maintain a long-term internal support

---

52. I am particularly grateful to Tomás Duval for his help in this section of the paper.

base. While the multiple fiefdoms that tend to characterize political parties make this an inherently difficult task for *any* politician, it is all the more challenging for someone coming to politics with a technical mentality. Alliances hinge first and foremost on the principle of loyalty, a concept that may be at odds with the instrumental logic of the *técnico*. For whether one comes to politics from the academic or the business world, decisions in these spheres are not calculated by considerations of loyalty, but, rather, by facts and knowledge, in the first instance, or the laws of the market, in the latter. As a result, while *técnicos* may be adept at building coalitions for broader political purposes, it is not clear that they are equally skilled at doing so to advance personal ambitions.

Matthei's experience within Renovación Nacional serves to demonstrate this point. From its birth, Renovación Nacional was plagued by a fundamental tension between the two halves that bore it name: the Renovados, on the one hand, and the Nacionales, on the other. The Renovados were the young, technically trained, and pro-democratic cohort who sought to modernize the party's programmatic message. Under the leadership of Andrés Allamand, it was this current—including Evelyn Matthei—that assumed control of the party in the early 1990s. But alongside the Renovados—and not without influence—existed a more traditional faction drawn from the pre-1973 right. Under the imposing command of Sergio Onofre Jarpa, this nationalistic wing distrusted the technical orientation of the Renovados, inclining instead toward economic protectionism. While the two factions needed each other for electoral purposes, this marriage of convenience was tenuous at best.

Given this internal balance of power, a party such as RN offered two alternatives for the politician seeking internal leadership. One strategy was to toe a no-holds-barred, "renovated" line, regardless of the political antibodies that this might produce among the Nacionales. This was the strategy of Piñera, who made no disguise of his Renovado proclivities when seeking the presidential nomination within RN. Alternatively, one might try somehow to bridge the divide—as Matthei seemed initially inclined to do—by maintaining a foot in the Renovado camp while simultaneously courting the Nacionales. To be successful at such a fence-sitting strategy, however, required an innate understanding of how best to manipulate these two factions to one's own advantage. Ultimately, Matthei did not prove agile in such an endeavor.

Indeed, many were shocked by the manner in which Matthei announced her candidacy for the presidential nomination within her party. Pitting herself against the designated Renovado candidate and her longtime ally Sebastian Piñera—Matthei abruptly abandoned the Renovados and formed an alliance with the Nacionales. The legitimacy of this alliance was immediately called into question. Many both inside and outside the party had a hard time squaring Matthei's solidly technocratic past with the more nationalistic rhetoric of the Jarpistas, particularly in light of Jarpa's well-known disdain for *técnicos*. As a result, few interpreted the Jarpa-Matthei alliance as a bona fide decision by Matthei. Rather, most perceived it as an effort by Jarpa to counteract Piñera's candidacy, a strategy in which Matthei served as a pawn for powerful traditional interests.[53]

To be fair to Matthei, it is true that part of the reason she may have been so willing to support Jarpa was that she had been isolated by the Renovados, who no longer included her at the very top levels of party decision making.[54] She was also inevitably blinded by the prospect of presidential power. Nonetheless, whether her decision was based on victimization, alienation, ambition— or a combination of the three—is largely irrelevant. After just three short years in elected office and no prior political experience, the bottom line was that she lacked the leadership skills to manage this high-risk strategy. In this regard, neither Piñera's split from the old guard of his party nor Matthei's split from Piñera bespeaks familiarity with an institutional tradition. Rather, they reflect the short-term calculations of two young *técnicos* who—stripped of ideological differences—became locked in a naked struggle for power.

Timing

A second and related skill necessary for party leadership is a well-developed sense of timing. In order to be an effective leader, a politician must learn how to recognize an opportunity, when to take advantage of it, and how aggressively to push for its realization. Here again, however, a technical background—and, in particular, a business past—can be a political liability. For while the business sphere encourages a high quotient of risk, politics often calls for a much more measured approach to decision making.

At stake here is really a difference in the incentive structure inherent in these two domains. In the business world, the objective is to conquer the market as quickly and as thoroughly as possible, so as to maximize immediate returns and fend off encroaching competitors. But a ready application of business logic to the political realm may be ill-advised. What makes for successful marketing in the business world does not necessarily do so in

53. See, for example, "El varón, la dama y el padrino," *El Mercurio,* 2 August 1992.
54. Based on several confidential interviews by the author with RN party members, Santiago, August–September 1992.

politics. Whereas in the business world the objective is to sell the largest quantity possible of a given product to the largest number of potential buyers, in the political world the individual *is* the product, and one must sell oneself. By transplanting the corner-the-market mentality to the political domain, one therefore courts the danger of being immediately and fully consumed.

In this way, *técnicos* who come to politics from the business world may be inclined to rush their political careers. The knowledge that they can always return to the business world if things do not go well in the next election is only likely to aggravate their inclination toward impulsive behavior.[55] But such an impulsive approach to politics has a high probability of backfiring. For in the political world efficacy is less a function of speed than it is of agility.

Both Matthei and Piñera came to politics with a business background. And both stood out for their unbridled ambition and desire to scale the heights of the Chilean political system: after just three short years in the public eye, each made a formal bid to become president of the republic. Arguably, this was a courageous move. But one must also question the reasonableness of such a proposition. In particular, it was never clear that either of them had bothered first to establish a firm position of leadership within their party. As a result, both rushed headlong into their quest for power without a firm understanding of what was at stake, and were forced to pay the consequences.

Political Judgment

The preceding points are tied to a third and final political skill crucial to effective party leadership: political judgment. In broad terms, political judgment refers to an intangible sensibility that not only entails the careful weighing of alternatives so as to avoid potential problems before they occur, but also the ability to manage a crisis once underway. While the mishandling of internal party alliances or an exaggerated sense of timing may hinder political efficacy, a lack of political judgment can ruin a career.

The amorphous nature of political judgment raises the question whether it can be adequately mastered by someone versed in the technical realm. *Técnicos* are trained to provide concrete solutions to discrete problems. When confronted with a given issue, they are programmed to respond with "a, b, or c." As a result, they may not learn to resolve larger dilemmas with nuances and subtleties. After all, a crisis in the private sector can usually be resolved

---

55. Note that while the future is still uncertain for Matthei, Piñera never left his business practice during his entire tenure as senator and showed no intention of doing so.

through budget cuts, personnel dismissal, or institutional reorganization. Similarly, when confronted with a theoretical anomaly, the economist can always find recourse in a mathematical equation. But the solution to a political crisis is not so cut-and-dried. Rather, a political crisis is a much more elusive phenomenon that may be at odds with the disaggregated problem-solving approach of the technician.

At least so it seemed in August 1992, when a political crisis of major proportions exploded inside RN. The crisis broke out during the heat of the prepresidential race between Matthei and Piñera, when a taped version of a private telephone conversation of Piñera's was publicly broadcast on television. Although the conversation revealed that Piñera had been trying to use his influence to bias a journalist against Matthei, the nexus of the so-called espionage scandal became the violation of Piñera's privacy. Over the course of the four-month investigation that ensued, Matthei repeatedly disavowed any complicity in the scandal. But in the wake of irrefutable evidence, she finally confessed that she had not only known about the illegal tape's existence but had indirectly furnished it to the media.[56]

The espionage scandal was thus the crowning blow in a series of poor judgment calls that clouded Matthei's political career. These began with her precipitate decision to run for president, continued through her unseemly alliance with Jarpa, and eventually led to her tacit participation in an underhanded campaign against a competitor in her own party. But perhaps her biggest error of all was her decision to remain silent during more than sixty days of the criminal investigation, a decision that indelibly tarnished her reputation for honesty and transparency. As a punishment for her behavior, she was suspended from all political activity within RN for the next ten years.

On the Rebound: Evelyn Matthei's Political Rebirth

In the months following the espionage scandal, Matthei disappeared from the public eye. She refused to give interviews to the press and, on those few occasions when she was obliged to make a public appearance, seemed visibly distressed. Over time, however, Matthei gradually reemerged from this hibernation, and was eventually willing to talk about her situation. Part of this

---

56. An extensive account of the "Piñeragate" scandal can be found in "La hora de la verdad," *Qué Pasa*, 9 November 1992, 12.

reversal was undoubtedly facilitated by the Supreme Court's decision to absolve Matthei of any criminal activity in the espionage scandal. In addition, there was a general perception that the RN leadership had been excessively harsh in its treatment of her.[57] More important than these external factors, however, was the fact that during her hiatus from political life, Matthei matured considerably on a personal level.

When speaking about her behavior during her first two years in office, Matthei acknowledged that her rapid success had blinded her judgment. With hindsight, she recognized the absurdity of two individuals—not even forty years of age—competing for a presidential bid while still so new to politics itself. In her own words, "I was not sufficiently mature . . . I hadn't had enough setbacks";[58] she noted that after the scandal took place, she "learned to be much more cautious."[59] But she also saw this immaturity as a problem not unique to her and Piñera, but rather to the right as a whole. As she correctly observed, "We lack a generation of more experienced politicians that have lived more and that know how to resolve conflicts . . . inside the party. This we will learn over time. Discipline is a matter of tradition."[60]

Coupled with this process of personal growth came a gradual rebirth in the political arena. While there had been rumors that Matthei would leave politics altogether and perhaps even go abroad for a graduate degree, she instead demonstrated her tenacity as a politician. Resigning from RN, Matthei announced her decision to run for reelection in the legislative elections of December 1993. Although she was courted by several political parties—most notably the UDI—Matthei chose instead to run as an independent. Relying on the distinctively personal style that had once catapulted her to stardom, Matthei again demonstrated her public appeal. With a campaign team drawn from sympathizers across various political currents, Matthei clinched a victory in a predominantly poor district in which the right had no previous political foothold.[61]

57. Matthei was suspended from all political activity in RN for a period of ten years. See "La jugada de Evelyn," *Qué Pasa,* 20 March 1993.
58. Evelyn Matthei, "Evelyn Matthei: Recuperé la alegría de vivir," interview by Claudia Giner R., *Cosas,* no. 434 (11 May 1993).
59. Evelyn Matthei, "Regresa Evelyn Matthei," interview by María Angélica de Luigi, *Caras,* no. 139 (9 August 1993).
60. "Si somos incapaces de limpiar el espíritu," *Las Ultimas Noticias,* 31 January 1993.
61. "El distrito de San Antonio: En busca del segundo nombre para la cámara," *La Epoca,* 10 December 1993.

Despite her comeback in the electoral arena, it would be a mistake to presume that Matthei was simply able to pick up where she had left off. Rather, Matthei's involvement in the espionage scandal had left some permanent damage. To begin with, her relationship with her former colleagues in RN was severely strained. Some members of RN had objected publicly to her inclusion in the right's "list" for the 1993 elections.[62] In turn, Matthei herself was quite critical of the RN leadership, claiming that her ascent within the party had been deliberately blocked and expressing deep skepticism that such ties could ever be rebuilt.[63] Finally, the crisis also took its toll on Matthei's political aspirations. Although her 1993 victory certainly pointed to her continuing popularity, her days as the rising star of the right appeared to be over.

At the same time, it is not clear that this latter trend was an entirely negative turn of events. No longer viewed as *presidenciable*, Matthei was now obliged to focus her energies on her duties as an ordinary member of the Chamber of Deputies. After having virtually disappeared during the final months of her presidential campaign, Matthei's constituent-related activity increased dramatically following her reelection. She began devoting two full days a week to her district, where she would discuss the problems confronting various communities. In addition, she also became quite active in the Chamber of Deputies' Women's Caucus, where she championed the need to foster greater women's participation in politics.[64]

This more scaled-down and parochial approach to her career also had an effect on the types of issues to which Matthei gave priority. Gone were the internal party disputes and lofty philosophical debates that had dominated her life before the espionage scandal. In their place, Matthei focused instead on solving concrete problems affecting her district and the nation at large. On the one hand, this brought her back to her initial area of expertise— economics. In the course of 1993 and 1994, she played an important role in legislation to modernize the banking system and spearheaded an investigation to expose corruption within the state-owned copper mines. On the other hand, it also triggered a renewed commitment to social policy. Over this two-year period, Matthei continued to fight for organ transplant legislation, an overhaul of the health-care system, and legislation to help single mothers.

62. "Difícil lista con Evelyn," *Las Ultimas Noticias,* 4 March 1993.

63. Evelyn Matthei, "Ella sí sabe hacia dónde va a disparar," interview by María Eugenia Camus, *La Epoca,* 4 September 1994.

64. Ibid.

In sum, it is still too soon to tell how the Evelyn Matthei story will play itself out in the long run. What is clear is that within a year of her involvement in one of the worst political crises in recent Chilean history, Matthei had resurfaced and did not look likely to disappear any time soon. As of March 1994, she had a 37 percent approval rating in national public opinion polls, with many speculating about the possibility of a Senate seat in 1997.[65] As Matthei's story suggests, the *técnico*'s adjustment to political life can be a difficult one. But it is not impossible if undertaken self-consciously and with caution.

Conclusion

Throughout the course of her dramatic career in public office, Evelyn Matthei experienced the entire range of highs and lows that political life has to offer. Entering her vocation as a virtual novice, Matthei's baptism by fire into the Chilean political system is instructive for our broader understanding of the technopol phenomenon.

In the economic sphere, Matthei and her fellow economists on the right made an important contribution to the consolidation of the social market economy in Chile. An expert in the policies that underpin such a model, Matthei used her technical expertise to protect and defend its faithful implementation. In particular, she championed the need for a streamlined but nonetheless competent state that would not fail to be attentive to the needs of the most disadvantaged.

In the political realm, she and her "renovated" cohort also played a crucial role in facilitating Chile's transition to democracy. Through their willingness to cement key agreements with the government, Matthei and her colleagues helped to consolidate the country's fledgling democratic institutions.

But while Matthei was very much identified with this larger, renovation project, she also left it with her own distinctive imprint. At a moment when her party sought to reposition itself for the future, she stepped forth as one of its most articulate and compelling spokespeople. By creating a new, more human image for the right centered around social issues, Matthei broadened her party's appeal among a wider public.

65. "El despegue . . . ," *Que Pasa,* 30 April 1994.

Matthei's technical know-how, consensus-building skills, and public persona won her a national presence that few could claim to have matched in so little time. Unfortunately, with the thrill of victory also came the agony of defeat. Through her drive to take the country's largest political prize at any cost, Matthei committed a series of political errors that had damaging consequences for herself, her party, and the right as a whole.

And yet, while the errors she committed were serious, their exaggerated consequences expose a problem faced by all technopols. While arguably extreme, the difficulties Matthei encountered in navigating her own political party are not unique to her case. With the exception of Cardoso, the other technopols considered in this volume also fell short of cultivating the skills conducive to effective party leadership.

Matthei's is thus a cautionary tale, if not without its own intrigue and drama. As her father, General Matthei, summed it up: "I taught my children to fly far and high, because for me that was what life was all about. I wanted them to fly high even if they fell—better that than a life of stagnation."[66] Clearly, his daughter has not let him down.

66. Fernando Matthei, interview by author, tape recording, Santiago, 14 August 1992.

6

Development and Democracy in Chile

Finance Minister Alejandro Foxley and the Concertación's Project for the 1990s

Jeanne Kinney Giraldo

In March of 1990 Patricio Aylwin assumed office with the stated intention of being "president of all the Chileans" after nearly three decades of political polarization had turned Chile into a "nation of enemies."[1] A government of "national reconciliation" would attempt to heal the divisions left by the Christian Democratic "Revolution in Liberty" (1964–70), the Popular Unity's

This chapter is based on interviews conducted in Chile in July and August of 1992 and archival research. I would like to thank Miguel Angel Centeno and Paul Sigmund for their comments on an earlier draft of this chapter, my fellow authors and Richard Feinberg for their comments at a

"Chilean Road to Socialism" (1970–73), and the military-technocratic "Silent Revolution" (1973–90). One of the most divisive issues of the preceding decades had been economic policy, and this would be the case in the transition to democracy as well.

Although the market-oriented reforms carried out by the authoritarian regime of General Augusto Pinochet created a generally favorable economic situation and contributed to a consensus among experts on the value of macroeconomic stability and export-led growth, the economy still posed a significant challenge for the incoming center-left coalition government, the Concertación. Precisely because of the reforms, the economy was at the center of everyone's expectations for the new government, friend and foe alike. The government would need to meet its constituents' expectations that payments on the "social debt" accumulated under military rule would begin, despite the immediate need for contractionary policies to cool an overheated economy.

The government would also have to prove to a skeptical military, ideological business class, and an overrepresented right in Congress that the successes of the existing economic model would not be undermined by democracy, greater efforts to redress poverty, and an increased role for the state. Most of the key actors in the new government believed that the fate of the new democracy would rise and fall with the management of the economy: economic failure would result, at the very least, in defeat at the polls, and quite likely in an authoritarian regression. Either outcome would foreclose future efforts to democratize the system.[2]

The weighty responsibility of safeguarding Chile's prospects for democracy fell squarely on the capable shoulders of Alejandro Foxley Rioseco, an internationally renowned economist who had been the leading critic of the military government's economic policies. As finance minister, Foxley would maintain a balance of continuity and change with the previous government's economic policy—for example, an austere fiscal policy paired with increased

conference on technopols held at Harvard University, and the technopols who took time out from their busy schedules to be interviewed, especially Alejandro Foxley. I would also like to thank Verónica Montecinos for sharing her insightful work on economists in Chile. Funding for this research was provided by the National Science Foundation and the Inter-American Dialogue. All material quoted from Spanish-language sources was translated by the author.

1. Pamela Constable and Arturo Valenzuela, *A Nation of Enemies: Chile Under Pinochet* (New York: W. W. Norton, 1991).

2. See Angel Flisfisch, "La gestión estratégica de un proceso de transición y consolidación: El caso chileno," *Proposiciones* 25 (1994): 20–33. Flisfisch is a Michigan-trained political scientist who was a central actor in the renovation of the Socialist Party and a political strategist in the Aylwin government.

social spending—in an attempt to legitimize democracy for entrepreneurs and the social market economy for ordinary people. Although this combination of policies was somewhat new in the Latin American context, the real challenge was not in designing the policy package but in securing its passage and successful implementation. This task was preeminently political. Foxley would need to negotiate a tax increase with business and the right to provide the funds necessary for his social programs; at the same time, he would need to "manage" the very legitimate demands made on the government in order to maintain a conservative fiscal policy. The cooperation of labor and the parties of the center-left coalition in moderating demands and negotiating accords was imperative, and although Foxley could depend on the transitional moment to mute many disagreements or criticisms from these sectors, a successful management of the economy and a deliberate policy of consultation, education, and compensation would be important in maintaining their support.

By all accounts, Foxley was successful. Inflation fell from a high of 30 percent at the beginning of the Aylwin administration in 1990 to 12 percent in 1992, and the entire increase in revenues from the tax hike was devoted to social programs. Chile was trumpeted as the leading example of "growth with equity" by the head of the International Monetary Fund, Michel Camdessus, and the country earned a triple-B investment ranking from Standard & Poor's in 1992, identifying it as the country with the least risk in Latin America. The economy boasted a strong balance of payments, a record level of foreign exchange reserves, an average fiscal surplus equivalent to over 2 percent of the gross domestic product (GDP), an investment rate greater than 27 percent of GDP by 1993, an average annual growth rate of 6.3 percent from 1990 to 1993, and increasingly diversified exports, which represented 37 percent of GDP in 1992. Unemployment hovered around 4.8 percent by 1993; real wages increased at an average annual rate of 3.7 percent from 1990 to 1993; and levels of extreme poverty had been reduced from 45 percent of the population in 1987 to 32.7 percent in 1992. *Euromoney* named Foxley runner-up Finance Minister of the Year for 1992, second only to Domingo Cavallo of Argentina.

Foxley's success in adjusting the prevailing economic model to the requirements of equity and democracy rested to a large extent on his activities while in opposition to the military regime. It was then that he developed his understanding of what was necessary to make democracy and development compatible: a political and social system capable of generating a stable consensus with regard to a nationally shared project of development.[3] It was also then

3. According to Eugenio Tironi, a Socialist active in the opposition's process of renovation and

that Foxley and other technopols worked to build a minimum consensus on economic policy and to foster a "culture of cooperation" among polarized socioeconomic and political actors that would be necessary for deepening the "consensus."

From the opposition, Foxley challenged the Pinochet government's radically different solution to the problems of development in Chile. The Chicago Boys, as the military regime's economists were called because a number of them had received their training at the University of Chicago, were devoted to dismantling the state and justified authoritarianism to do so. In contrast, Foxley and renovated sectors of the Christian Democratic and Socialist Parties sought to reconstruct a "competent" state that would be compatible with democracy. The center-left's project not only asserted an important economic role for the state (e.g., promoting exports, investing in human capital and infrastructure, regulating financial flows, spending on social programs) but also reclaimed a central role for the political system in running the economy efficiently. It is this revalorization of politics as much as his personal political skills that makes Foxley a democratic technopol.

The first two sections of this chapter discuss how Foxley's ideas about the conditions for making democracy and development compatible were decisively shaped by the trauma of regime breakdown, his rejection of the authoritarian regime's technocratic approach to economics, and a study of the political science literature on cooperation and consensus building. These ideas are treated at some length because, with few modifications, they influenced his actions as minister and underlay the political and economic strategy of the Aylwin administration as a whole. The middle section discusses the evolution of events in the 1980s that contributed to a convergence on economic policy from both sides of the political spectrum and the emergence of "interlocutors" in political and civil society who would facilitate Foxley's future ministry. Foxley's ability as finance minister to reach accords with Congress, business, and labor and his efforts to shape expectations, cultivate a culture of cooperation, and persuade different sectors of the viability of his project are evidence of the importance Foxley places on politics and the

---

director of the Secretariat of Communication and Culture in the Aylwin administration, Foxley's diagnosis of the breakdown of democracy as the result of a lack of consensus on a national model of development was innovative. Others criticized the lack of compromise in an ad hoc manner, but they ultimately attributed the crisis of democracy to the disequilibrium between a politically overdeveloped system and an economically underdeveloped one. See Eugenio Tironi, "Clases sociales y acuerdo democrático," in *CED Documento de trabajo*, no. 14 (Santiago: Centro de Estudios del Desarrollo, 1984), 25.

political system for the future viability of democracy and development in Chile. This is also revealed in his activities as president of the largest party in Chile, a post he won at the end of his four years in government. As leader of the Christian Democrats, Foxley was less concerned with spreading his economic ideas than with fortifying the center-left governing alliance (by strengthening its base in society and encouraging cooperation among parties and between parties and the government), which was the cornerstone of effective democratic governance in Chile.

The Early Years of a Technopol: The University, the Party, and the Crisis of Democracy

Foxley was born in 1939 into a middle-class family in Viña del Mar, an important port city in Valparaíso. He attended Catholic schools during a period of great vitality in the socially conscious Chilean Catholic Church and participated actively in religious groups. It was then that he was first awakened to the problem of poverty, which would motivate much of his early professional work on income distribution.

Like many intellectuals of the center and left, Foxley was both a party militant and public servant. He was active in the Christian Democratic Party at the Catholic University of Valparaíso, was elected president of the student federation in 1960, and formed the Unión de Federaciones Universitarias de Chile. In 1963, he earned a scholarship to pursue his doctorate in economics at the University of Wisconsin at Madison. There he devised a mathematical model of the Chilean economy that he would later use as head of the Global Planning Division of the National Planning Office (Oficina de Planificación Nacional, or ODEPLAN) during the last two years of Eduardo Frei's Christian Democratic government (1964–70).

By the late 1960s the Chilean political class was becoming increasingly polarized, and these divisions were reflected within the Christian Democratic Party. In 1969, the radical wing of the party splintered off to form two minor parties on the left; the conservative wing began to collaborate with the right in January of 1972.[4] Foxley remained within the party, which moved to the

4. For example, the economists of the Technical Commission of the Christian Democratic Party cooperated with the Chicago Boys on the economic plan they would eventually implement from the military government. The plan was later published as *El ladrillo: Bases de la política económica del Gobierno Militar Chileno* (Santiago: Centro de Estudios Públicos, 1992).

center-left: his economic views and socialization in Christian reformism kept him from succumbing to the revolutionary fervor of the left, while his deeply felt progressive commitments and economic views kept him from collaborating with the right.

Instead, Foxley remained on the margin of daily political battles, operating from the economic think tank CEPLAN (Centro de Estudios de Planificación Nacional), which he had founded at the Catholic University in 1970 after the Popular Unity coalition replaced the Christian Democrats in government. From this institutional base, he cooperated with progressive economists of the center and left on a National Project of Development.[5] Their gradualist plan took a middle position on the growth-versus-redistribution debate of the day, proposing a transition to a model of export-led growth. It spurned both the more extreme industrialization proposals of the governing left and the radical free market plans of the Chicago Boys, who had taken over the economics faculty of the Catholic University beginning in the 1950s.[6]

Foxley's economic views anticipated his later "growth-with-equity" message by arguing that growth *with* redistribution was both necessary and attainable. He opposed the left's plans to redistribute through large wage increases, which he believed would only encourage consumption in an economy historically plagued by low levels of internal savings. In the short and medium run, indirect redistributive measures—government programs in health, education, and housing—would benefit the poor by providing services and creating jobs but without increasing consumption to a level that would damage growth.

5. In particular, Foxley worked closely with Christian Democrat and Chicago-trained economist Ricardo Ffrench-Davis, Christian Democratic sympathizer Oscar Muñoz, and Socialist Sergio Bitar (President Salvador Allende's minister of mines from 1971 to 1972 and future president of the Party for Democracy). Their plan was completed but never published because of the September 1973 coup (Oscar Muñoz, interview by author, Santiago, 10 August 1992). For a partial summary of this plan, see Alejandro Foxley and Oscar Muñoz, "Income Redistribution, Economic Growth, and Social Structure," *Oxford Bulletin of Economics and Statistics,* February 1974, 21–44. The following discussion is based on that article; Alejandro Foxley, "Alternativas de descentralización en el proceso de transformación de la economía nacional," in *Chile: Búsqueda de un Nuevo Socialismo,* ed. Foxley (Santiago: CEPLAN, 1971); and idem, "Opciones de desarrollo bajo condiciones de reducción en la dependencia externa," in *Proceso a la industrialización chilena,* ed. Oscar Muñoz (Santiago: CEPLAN, 1972). The second work centers on Foxley's advocacy of "communitarian socialism," and the third is based on his mathematical model of the Chilean economy.

6. See Juan Gabriel Valdés, *La Escuela de Chicago: Operación Chile* (Buenos Aires: Grupo Editorial Zeta, 1989), for a discussion of the ascendancy of the Chicago Boys in the decades preceding the coup.

In the long run, the solution to the problem of equity was the increase in productive jobs that would accompany a transition to export-led growth. The state would play an active role targeting certain sectors for the development of vertically integrated industries that would meet the following criteria: labor absorbing, technologically sophisticated, and capable of competing in the world market. These objective and transparent criteria would guide the state's industrial policy and prevent it from acting as the granter of favors it had become in the preceding years. Foreign capital would be permitted in areas where it could offer technological assistance or access to markets; in other cases denationalized industries would have to be expropriated or "Chileanized" in some way.

Then, and now, Foxley believed in a role for the state that balanced decentralized efficiency and participation with the centralized authority necessary to guide the nation's development. Objecting to the left's excessive confidence in the state, Foxley argued for restrictions on state action on a variety of grounds. He was concerned with the ability of state enterprises to operate efficiently and flexibly and believed that the state needed to be modernized in its macroeconomic management and more targeted and selective in its industrial and redistributive activities. The state's redistributive activities were adversely affected by groups with privileged access to the state who distorted the development process to serve their own particular interests. This applied not only to business but also to organized workers and middle sectors who prevented state action from being targeted to the poorest. (This theme would resurface with a vengeance twenty years later when Foxley, as finance minister, saw it as his task to resist many of the demands of organized groups in order to safeguard state resources for the poorest.)

In addition to his modernizing plans for the state and emphasis on indirect redistribution, Foxley (along with other economists of the center and left) sought to make economic development compatible with increased popular participation in the policy-making process.[7] Inspired by Christian Democratic ideology, he advocated "communitarian socialism," a decentralized system of social property designed to avoid the concentration of economic and political power in the hands of the state that accompanied the left's plan of traditional, centralized socialism. Under this plan, worker management in factories would constitute one of a plurality of forms of ownership within a mixed economy that would evolve gradually toward a largely self-managed

7. See William Ascher, "Planners, Politics, and Technocracy in Argentina and Chile" (Ph.D. diss., Yale University, 1975).

system. Worker participation was a central plank of the 1970 Christian Democratic presidential campaign platform, for which Foxley served as economic coordinator.

The breakdown of democracy in 1973 led Foxley to revise key elements of his vision of the political economy. While he remained convinced that growth with equity and participation were essential ingredients of democratic development, he felt that he had been too ideological in accepting the left's premise that participation had to involve a change in property relations. He decided that a change in property relations, however gradual, was incompatible with democracy because it created a "perception of threat" among entrepreneurs, which led to economic and political instability. Relatedly, Foxley also reevaluated the conditions necessary for political stability, which he believed was the basis for economic rationality and efficiency. In the 1960s, Foxley believed that political stability would be possible if a commitment to gradual change were combined with a *multiclass majoritarian* consensus (i.e., center-left cooperation); after the breakdown he came to believe that gradual change and a *national* consensus on a model of development were necessary.

Finally, Foxley strongly criticized the Christian Democratic and Marxist minority governments for their claims to have a monopoly on the truth; their exclusionary and ideological projects focused excessively on a change in property relations as the mechanism for social change. This criticism was easily extended to the military-technocratic alliance, which repeated—in a much more extreme and violent form—the same errors as the center and left. Foxley's response to these errors would be to advocate the creation of inclusionary and less ideological projects that focused on politics as the mechanism for social change. The overly ideological intellectuals of the center and left and the equally ideological technocrats of the authoritarian regime would have to be replaced by a new kind of intellectual more inclined to compromise and inclusion.

Foxley as Opposition Technopol

In the aftermath of the September 1973 military coup, which put an end to President Salvador Allende's Popular Unity government and a proud tradition of democracy, many Chileans of the center and left spent their time reflecting on how they might have prevented the breakdown of democracy and what they might do to hasten its return. Foxley was in London when the coup occurred, and he would spend his time in Europe engaged in these labors of reflection on the past and incipient opposition to the military regime. He led a study of the Frei and Allende experiments in income redistribution for the International Labor Organization in Geneva, which confirmed and intensified his previous concerns about the limitations of state action.[8] He also explored the possibility of gaining international funding for an economic think tank in Chile that could operate independently of the authoritarian government. When the military intervened in the Catholic University in 1975, he was ready with a team of lawyers to petition the government to convert his university think tank into CIEPLAN (Corporación de Investigaciones Económicas para América Latina).[9]

With politics outlawed, Foxley and CIEPLAN soon found themselves at the forefront of opposition to the military regime, along with important sectors of the Roman Catholic Church led by Cardinal Raúl Silva Henríquez. A regime that based its legitimacy at least partly on its self-proclaimed roles as defender of Western, Christian civilization and administrator of an indisputable economic rationality was particularly vulnerable to the criticisms of these impeccably credentialed and internationally connected religious and economic experts. Like Cardinal Silva, Foxley was morally indignant and scathing in his criticisms of the authoritarian project.

The economic criticisms made by Foxley and his CIEPLAN colleagues have been widely disseminated, and it is not the purpose of this chapter to offer an in-depth analysis of their technical proposals.[10] Less well known, however, and the focus of much of this chapter is Foxley's broader vision of the political economy, which influenced his technical prescriptions and

8. Alejandro Foxley, Eduardo Aninat, and Juan Pablo Arellano, *Redistributive Effects of Government Programmes: The Chilean Case* (Oxford: Pergamon Press/ International Labor Organization, 1979). Coauthor Aninat noted that the study was based on very sound and advanced empirical work, though he admitted that the conclusions on public enterprise were still slightly ideological (Eduardo Aninat, interview by author, Santiago, 21 August 1992). Aninat and Arellano joined Foxley in the Aylwin government, the former as foreign debt negotiator and the latter as budget director. Aninat succeeded Foxley as finance minister in the next administration.

9. Jeffrey Puryear notes that CIEPLAN was the first independent think tank to be formed outside of the auspices of the Catholic Church. Without church protection, Foxley took extra precautions to guarantee the institute's viability, including attaining legal status in Colombia (should they be forced to leave Chile) and naming a "prestigious international advisory committee." See Jeffrey Puryear, *Thinking Politics: Intellectuals and Democracy in Chile, 1973–1988* (Baltimore: Johns Hopkins University Press, 1994), 47.

10. See CIEPLAN, *Modelo económico chileno: Trayectoria de una crítica* (Santiago: Editorial Aconcagua, 1982), and idem, *Reconstrucción económica para la democracia* (Santiago: Editorial Aconcagua, 1983), for the technical critiques and proposals of CIEPLAN members.

informed the activities of the center-left coalition both from the opposition and later from the government.[11] Foxley's dispute with the government was much more than a technocratic critique; it was a conflict between one vision of the political economy that justified authoritarianism and another vision that justified democracy.

Two Visions of the Political Economy

The economic prescriptions advocated by the Chicago Boys and by Foxley were closely linked to their understandings of the breakdown of democracy in Chile. The Chicago Boys viewed Chilean history from the prism provided by their version of neoclassical political economy.[12] They believed that forty years of excessive state intervention in the economy had created a populace of economically irrational and unfree individuals and an ill-functioning economic system that propagated inflation. Their solution was to dismantle the developmental state, submit economic actors to the discipline of the market, and reduce the role of political institutions, which were believed to distort individual interests. Economically, the market was better than the state under *all* circumstances; politically, a "strong and courageous" state was needed to control vested interests.

The Chicago Boys advocated radical, comprehensive programs that needed to be imposed from above without vacillation. Economics was a science that should not be contaminated by politics or values.[13] If policies did not elicit the desired response, the irrationality of economic agents (rather than the unsuitability of policies) was blamed; the solution was to maintain or even intensify the heretofore ineffective policy. Authoritarianism was necessary for policy continuity and effectiveness: military backing would allow policies to be applied for as long as necessary and would make their package credible, and, in the long run, the Chicago Boys' economic policies and Pinochet's

11. The most complete statement of Foxley's political economy is his *Para una democracia estable: Economía y política* (Santiago: CIEPLAN, 1985), consisting of pieces written between 1982 and 1984.

12. For a general account of neoclassical political economy, see Merilee S. Grindle, "The New Political Economy: Positive Economics and Negative Politics," in *Politics and Policy Making in Developing Countries: Perspectives on the New Political Economy,* ed. Gerald M. Meier (San Francisco: International Center for Economic Growth, 1991).

13. On the Chicago Boys' ideology, see Pilar Vergara, "Auge y caída del neoliberalismo en Chile: Un estudio sobre la evolución ideológica del régimen militar," in *FLACSO Documento de trabajo,* no. 216 (Santiago: FLACSO, 1984). Valdés, *La Escuela de Chicago,* provides an account of the "economics-as-science" ideology prevalent among Chicago Boys in the Catholic University in the 1960s.

politics would refound Chilean society and provide the conditions for policy continuity even after Pinochet's departure from office and a return to (a restricted) democracy.

In the short run, the military-technocratic alliance solved the problem of ideological and populist politics by repressing politicians, especially leftists and unions. In the medium term, the dismantling of the state apparatus would preclude demand making and prevent any proponents of a statist ideology from implementing their plans should they accede to higher office. In the long run, the benefits of the market economy would trickle down and win converts among the people. Economic competition would replace ideological conflict as the new principle of associational life. Workers would be reabsorbed into the system on the basis of freedom of association and economic benefits. Authoritarianism was not only a tool for implementing stabilization policies, it was also necessary to bring to Chile the economic freedom that was a prerequisite for political freedom. A military-technocratic alliance independent of politicians and vested interests would be in the best position to refound Chile economically and politically.

Foxley, on the other hand, had different ideas about how to "refound" Chile so that democracy and development would be compatible. Whereas the Chicago Boys believed that the fundamental problem in Chile was a lack of markets, Foxley traced it to a lack of consensus. The Chicago Boys traced the "beginning of the end" of Chilean democracy to the creation of a developmental state in the 1930s; Foxley saw it in the breakdown of consensus on this so-called Compromise State in the late 1950s. Disillusioned by coalitional politics and economic "stagnation," increasingly ideological intellectuals and politicians had proposed wholesale changes in the rules of the political and economic game.[14] The resulting political and economic instability led to uncertainty for capital, short-time horizons for economic decision making, and a decrease in investment, which in turn forced the state to intervene even more in the economy and "crowd out" private capital.

This crisis of consensus, though it had important economic implications, required a political, more than an economic, solution—a political and social system capable of ensuring stability and generating consensus. For Foxley, "inefficiency is not only, not even mainly, an economic problem. Inefficiency is the result of the inexistence of political and social institutions capable of

14. For a discussion of these beliefs in the Popular Unity government, see Robert L. Ayres, "Economic Stagnation and the Emergence of the Political Ideology of Chilean Underdevelopment," *World Politics* 25, no. 1 (1972): 34–61.

processing demands or structuring society . . . the most important problem is one of the governability of society, not of too much government."[15] Like the Chicago Boys, Foxley sought to overcome the ideological and populist past. Unlike them, he believed that Chile should solve its "problem of governability" not by repressing politicians but by creating a pragmatic and responsible "leadership class" animated by a spirit of cooperation.

Both the Chicago Boys and Foxley believed that policy continuity would ultimately be ensured by a national consensus on the model of development that transcended the whim of any one government. The difference lay in how they believed this consensus would be reached and then maintained. The Chicago Boys saw consensus as the result of the success of their market policies imposed by force; it would be maintained by rational individuals acting in a market situation to maximize their economic benefit and in a political system that depoliticized most decisions. Foxley, on the other hand, believed that a "new way of doing politics"—consensus seeking—was necessary to create, maintain, and deepen a consensus on a national model of development.[16]

In contrast to the Chicago Boys, Foxley believed that economic policies should meet criteria originating in the political and ethical spheres: "If one considers an open democratic society to be a superior and more desirable political environment than that of any authoritarian regime, the challenge to design policies adequate for that environment has to be met." Most elementally, "if a political system is going to be a democratic one, economic policies must necessarily be a reflection of a basic underlying consensus." From this perspective, "economic policies that weaken consensus, that add to the fragmentation of society, and that seriously accentuate conflicts, should be as carefully weighed as those that create inefficiencies in the allocation of resources."[17]

15. Alejandro Foxley, "Crisis económica y democratización: Transiciones en América Latina," in *Para una democracia estable*, 159–60.

16. While a post hoc analysis might show that both economic and political processes contributed to the current consensus, the point here is that the two views resulted in different approaches to politics and economic policy making.

17. Alejandro Foxley, "Stabilization Policies and their Effects on Employment and Income Distribution," in *Economic Stabilization in Developing Countries*, ed. W. Cline and S. Weintraub (Washington, D.C.: Brookings Institution, 1981), 225; idem, *Latin American Experiments in Neoconservative Economics* (Berkeley and Los Angeles: University of California Press, 1983), 206; and idem, "La relación entre ideología y política en el cambio democrático," in *Para una democracia estable*, 89.

This meant that a belief in correct technical prescriptions had to be mediated by a consideration of what was consensual. Foxley hoped that this approach to policy making would help overcome the polarization of Chile's democratic past and authoritarian present. He believed that the central and most conflictual issues in Chile—the proper roles of the state, business, and labor—ought to be the subject of dialogue. The only conditions were that the role of the state be discussed nondogmatically and that neither labor nor business be excluded.

With respect to the role of the state, Foxley identified an emerging middle ground between what he saw as the "inefficient statism" of the democratic past and the "naïve free-marketism" of the authoritarian present. In this spirit, he advocated a state that would intervene more selectively in the economy than in the past but also more decidedly. The challenge was not just to eliminate the state but to redesign it—as Albert Fishlow put it, "not simply [to take] the state out, but [to] bring the private sector, and civil society, back in more positively."[18]

Based on the lessons he had learned from the breakdown of democracy, Foxley believed that business must not be excluded as a legitimate actor in a model of development; respect for private property and an emphasis on stability were key requirements for their productive contribution. Foxley argued that the inclusion of labor was a sine qua non of a democratic society, but he largely left open to debate the contours of this participation. For Foxley, as for the political economy literature as a whole, the requirements for "bringing the private sector back in" were more clear and varied less from country to country than the means for "bringing civil society back in."

Foxley believed that participation could contribute to efficient and lasting policies by increasing their social acceptance and by helping to establish rational expectations. The exchange of information between government, business, and labor would help in the formulation of policy and in maintaining clear rules of the game. Foxley criticized the military regime's exclusionary politics not only for being morally wrong but for contributing to inefficient and unstable policies. The lack of feedback from society only exacerbated the dogmatism of the Chicago Boys, and the use of force and lack of consultation in imposing policies was likely to cause tensions that could undermine the model, either by generating popular protests or through

---

18. Albert Fishlow, "The Latin American State," *Journal of Economic Perspectives* 4, no. 3 (1990): 73.

rejection at the polls in a future democracy. Participation was not only legitimate in its own right, but it had the added benefit of being legitimizing.

Roles of Different Actors in the "New Way of Doing Politics"

For economists, the politics of consensus seeking advocated by Foxley meant that they would need to be students as much of politics as of normative economics so that they could play a central role in forging a consensus on a national model of development, becoming "activists of accords" and "mobilizers of public creativity." The politics of ideological imposition "from above," which characterized the Frei, Allende, and Pinochet governments, should give way to pragmatic discernment in consultation with those "from below" (i.e., outside of the government). This consultation would allow policy makers and politicians to respond to the concrete needs of the people rather than an ideological view of what these might be.

Economists would have to help politicians and socioeconomic actors reach a minimum consensus on the rules of the economic game. Without such an agreement, any increase in participatory mechanisms would merely mean a multiplication of the arenas for ideological conflict. A political coalition of the center-left was needed to provide the difficult combination, necessary for democracy, of commitment to change *and* the ability to impose limits on change. Just as the free market was indispensable but insufficient in the economic sphere, so too was a political free market necessary but insufficient for the reconstruction of democracy.

Socioeconomic actors, like politicians and intellectuals, would need to behave more responsibly and less ideologically. This change in behavior would be accomplished in two ways. First, Foxley and other technopols would urge social and political actors to understand that with participation comes responsibility (acting as "teachers to the nation," in Domínguez's terms). The Latin American tradition of state paternalism would be replaced by a new concept of partnership in which actors were asked to share with the state a national perspective on issues in addition to their own "narrow" interests. Second, the relationship of actors to the state needed to be structured in a way that favored this national perspective, avoided undermining state authority, and encouraged cooperation among actors.[19] The participation of labor and business, for example, should not constitute a parallel

19. Foxley left open the exact mechanisms that would accomplish this mix, but he did establish the principles that they should satisfy. See his "Condiciones para una democracia estable," in *Para una democracia estable*, 45–57.

legislature that would challenge state authority and lie outside of democratic control (as Foxley believed was the case in some instances of corporatism in Europe). As minister, Foxley settled on a formula in which matters of national concern (such as a minimum wage or labor legislation) were handled by government, business, and labor but in which other matters were left to bipartite negotiations between the relevant sectors of business and labor. Foxley believed that all social conflicts should not fall upon the state, but should sometimes be handled by the actors themselves. Cooperative business-labor relations would be a key to modernization.

Despite efforts to expose actors to a national perspective, Foxley realized that organized groups would still press for their own interests and that this would result in a bias in favor of the middle and upper sectors. When all else failed, it would be up to the statesman to act on behalf of the (unorganized) poorest sectors and the national interest, to be "somebody who tends not to think along partisan lines or in terms of partial interests, but always looks at the interrelationships for consistency."[20] Foxley felt that a state acting on behalf of the "common good," with active consultation of all actors, was a more effective and more democratic alternative than a state captured either by technocrats or interest groups.

The Development of a "Leadership Class"

Foxley's diagnosis of the need for a national consensus on a model of development meshed with the evolving views of chastened sectors of the center and left who were examining their role in the breakdown of democracy and renovating their political doctrines and practices in the direction of greater moderation and intellectual tolerance. The political opening that accompanied the crash of the economy in 1982 provided the opportunity for a greater dialogue and the establishment of personal relationships of trust among intellectuals, politicians, and labor leaders, relationships that contributed to the emergence of Foxley's renovated "leadership class."[21]

The basis for these dialogues had been established after the coup, when intellectuals and politicians became less ideological as a result of self-criticism and contact with their increasingly moderate counterparts in Europe, either

---

20. Foxley, interview by Richard Feinberg, 28 September 1992, *The State of Latin American Finance* (Washington, D.C.: Washington Exchange, 1992), 22.

21. See Puryear, *Thinking Politics,* for a comprehensive discussion of the influence of intellectuals on politics during the 1973–88 period.

through exile or the activities of think tanks.[22] Think tanks had become the main forums for opposition activity, and their reliance on international sources for funds contributed to research that stressed empirical work rather than ideology.

Independent processes of partisan renovation also contributed to a center-left convergence in the 1980s.[23] On the left, Socialists reevaluated their rejection of reformism, liberal democracy, and markets. In the renovation of the center, Foxley played an important role, mainly through his writings on reconciling development and democracy. As a member of the Christian Democratic Party's National Council in the 1980s, Foxley advocated party unification, a reevaluation of the uncompromising behavior that had contributed to the breakdown of democracy, and cooperation with the moderate left rather than the right. His harsh public criticisms of the military regime and his support for social mobilization during the protests of the 1980s made him a particularly effective interlocutor with the left and the more progressive wing of the Christian Democratic Party.

In addition to his interactions with politicians and intellectuals on the center and left, Foxley began to increase his contacts and those of his colleagues with civil society. With the support of the Ford Foundation, he sponsored "Dialogues with the Community" starting in 1985, a program that sought to make technopols out of CIEPLAN economists through trips to the provinces, universities, and unions. Economists would present their ideas and learn what the people thought, which in turn would guide their decisions about feasible policies. CIEPLAN economists also provided technical and

---

22. For example, the Centro de Estudios del Desarrollo invited an Austrian social scientist to speak on the social pact in his country and sponsored a trip of entrepreneurs, workers, academics, and politicians to Italy and Spain. CIEPLAN hosted a 1986 forum featuring Adolfo Suárez, architect of the Spanish transition to democracy.

23. On the renovation of the left, see Patricio Silva, "Social Democracy, Neoliberalism, and Ideological Change in the Chilean Socialist Movement, 1973–1992" (paper presented at the Congress of the Latin American Studies Association, 1992), and Brian Loveman, "The Political Left in Chile, 1973–1990," in *The Latin American Left: From the Fall of Allende to Perestroika,* ed. Barry Carr and Steve Ellner (Boulder, Colo.: Westview Press, 1993). For a longer account, see Ignacio Walker, *Socialismo y democracia: Chile y Europa en perspectiva comparada* (Santiago: CIEPLAN-Hachette, 1990). On the renovation of the Christian Democrats, see Carlos Huneeus, "Aprender del pasado para construir la democracia: El caso del Partido Democrático Cristiano de Chile," in *Reforma política y consolidación democrática: Europa y América Latina,* ed. Dieter Nohlen and Aldo Solari (Caracas: Editorial Nueva Sociedad, 1988), and Ignacio Walker, "Political Alliances and the Role of the Centre: The Chilean Christian Democratic Party," in *The Legacy of Dictatorship: Political, Economic, and Social Change in Pinochet's Chile,* ed. Alan Angell and Benny Pollack (Liverpool: Institute of Latin American Studies, University of Liverpool, 1993).

moral assistance to union leaders in their struggle against the dictatorship; this generated between technopols and social actors trust and understanding that would benefit the first government.[24]

The Emergence of Interlocutors on the Right

The economic crash of 1982 not only accelerated the debate and forging of ties among the opposition that would be important for the future government, it also led to changes on the right that offered the potential for an understanding with the center-left on economics. With the crash, many of the Chicago Boys' policies and much of their style of governing were discredited, and Foxley and the CIEPLAN Monks were at least partially vindicated:[25] as they had predicted, the Chicago Boys' dogmatic adherence to flawed policies (like the fixed exchange rate) and their ideological refusal to use the state (e.g., to regulate financial flows and the banking industry) had deprived them of the flexibility and the tools necessary to be good managers of the economy even within an authoritarian setting.[26] The Chicago Boys' policies and policy style contributed to the collapse not only of their economic project but nearly of the government as the people took to the streets in a series of monthly national protests and business dissent increased.

Pinochet was able to ride out the popular protests with increased repression and an offer to negotiate that divided the parties on the center and the left. He defused business opposition by dismissing the Chicago Boys and replacing

24. For example, Foxley was able to form a personal relationship of trust with the president of the Central Unitaria de Trabajadores (CUT), Christian Democrat Manuel Bustos, through visits and public shows of solidarity during Bustos's internal exile at the end of the Pinochet regime for his role in a 1987 general strike. Labor Minister René Cortázar worked with the Christian Democratic Workers' Front during the 1980s and conducted economic classes for Bustos during his imprisonment. See Ascanio Cavallo, *Los hombres de la transición* (Santiago: Editorial Andrés Bello, 1992), 146–47.

25. A collection of critical articles written for Chilean journals by CIEPLAN researchers between 1977 and 1982 was published at this time, fueling the debate over the causes of the crash. See CIEPLAN, *Trayectoria de una crítica*. Whatever the technical merits of the debate, a 1983 survey of Chilean citizens of all classes demonstrated that virtually everyone blamed the government for the economic crash. See Carlos Huneeus, "From Diarchy to Polyarchy: Prospects for Democratization in Chile," in *Comparing New Democracies: Transition and Consolidation in Mediterranean Europe and the Southern Cone,* ed. Enrique Baloyra (Boulder, Colo.: Westview Press, 1987), 138.

26. Even economists sympathetic to government policies acknowledged that the Chicago Boys' dogmatic refusal to change mistaken policies exacerbated the crisis. See, for example, Sebastián Edwards and Alejandra Cox-Edwards, *Monetarism and Liberalization: The Chilean Experiment* (Chicago: University of Chicago Press, 1991).

them with ministers who implemented short-term countercyclical measures to fight the recession and created mechanisms for business participation in the policy process. Although these policies kept business from defecting to the opposition, the neoconservative project was not consolidated under military rule until after Hernán Büchi Buc, an engineer with graduate studies at Columbia University, was appointed finance minister in February of 1985. Büchi's program combined some of the pragmatic and interventionist short-run policies of the 1982–84 interlude with a long-run vision closer to the neoliberal Chicago Boy model.[27]

Büchi eschewed a good part of the dogmatism that characterized the previous incarnation of the Chicago Boys in government, as one of his close advisers, Cristián Larroulet, avers: "In the early days, we believed too much in science. With Hernán, we learned the art of the possible."[28] Büchi scrapped much of the macroeconomic policy of the first model, instituting a crawling-peg exchange rate (as advocated for decades by CIEPLAN economist Ricardo Ffrench-Davis) and using a combination of high exchange rates and low tariffs to provide protection. He modified the rapid and unprotected opening of the Chilean economy that characterized the pre-1982 Chicago Boys' model by establishing a Copper Stabilization Fund and by providing protection for agriculture through price-support systems (a measure that was supported by opposition economists but not by those in the government).[29] In addition, Büchi's focus on investment and savings, regulation of business and banking, increase in public works spending, use of a state agency to promote nontraditional exports, and maintenance of mechanisms for the participation of entrepreneurs solidified the shift to a more pragmatic, activist, and inclusionary state.

Thus the "second incarnation" of the neoliberal model moved a step closer to Foxley's political economy and its prescriptions for effective and lasting policies: a greater reliance on the state, increased flexibility and pragmatism, and the consultation of socioeconomic actors (albeit limited to business).[30]

---

27. For a good overview of this period, see Barbara Stallings and Philip Brock, "The Political Economy of Economic Adjustment: Chile, 1973–1990," in *Political and Economic Interactions in Economic Policy Reform: Evidence from Eight Countries,* ed. Robert H. Bates and Anne O. Krueger (Cambridge, Mass.: Blackwell Publishers, 1993).

28. Quoted in Constable and Valenzuela, *Nation of Enemies,* 214.

29. A 1986 survey showed that several of Büchi's more pragmatic policies were supported by a majority of opposition economists and opposed by government economists. See Jorge Marshall and Felipe Morandé, "Propuestas económicas, consensos y conflictos," in *Propuestas políticas y demandas sociales,* vol. 2, ed. Manuel Antonio Garretón (Santiago: FLACSO, 1989), 111.

30. In *Boloña and Büchi: Estrategas del cambio* (Lima: Agenda 2000 Editores, 1991), Büchi repeatedly stresses the importance of pragmatism and flexibility in his ministry, which he

With Büchi's changes the economic model shifted from being a mostly divisive force to one that could *potentially* provide the basis for a future consensus among policy elites.[31]

In addition to the softening of the government program, the crash and the political opening it created contributed to the emergence of an interlocutor on the center-right that was more moderate and more willing to compromise than the government (as Delia Boylan shows in Chapter 5).[32] Although Büchi was hailed in 1985 for his pragmatism and flexibility (in comparison to his predecessors), by 1990 his policies and uncompromising stance were seen as overly ideological and rigid (in comparison to the more moderate center-right).

Toward a Convergence on Economic Policy

As government policies became relatively less ideological and more flexible under Büchi, CIEPLAN's criticism of the government's economic model became correspondingly less homogeneous, less global, and more conjunctural (e.g., criticizing low taxes and the inequitable way in which privatizations and debt-equity swaps were carried out).[33] Foxley continued to denounce the "unilateralism" of government policies, which he argued undermined the

---

contrasts to the previous style of the Chicago Boys. In another, much briefer account, he offers the more standard "Chicago Boy" explanation of his success: a coherent team, a comprehensive radical program, and the political backing of a "leader with vision" (see "Lecciones de mi experiencia como Ministro de Hacienda," *Instituto de Libertad y Desarrollo* [1992]: 10–12). Revealingly, but not surprisingly, Büchi makes little mention of the importance of consulting business when reflecting on the lessons of his ministry.

31. As economist David E. Hojman notes, "[T]he most pragmatic economic policies of the Pinochet regime . . . reflect thinking and attitudes much wider than the Chicago circle"; "fundamental policy continuities . . . link together the Frei government [of 1964–70], the most enlightened measures applied by Pinochet after the 1982–83 crisis, and Aylwin's [government]." Hojman, *Chile: The Political Economy of Development and Democracy in the 1990s* (Pittsburgh: University of Pittsburgh Press, 1993), 26, 202.

32. With respect to economic policy, for example, politicians and economists from National Renovation (RN) on the center-right to the moderate Socialists on the center-left believed that unemployment was the result of a structural deficiency and that the government should act to train workers ("invest in human capital"). The government and the far right, on the other hand, believed that unemployment was transitory and as such called for a government response of either passivity or emergency programs (Marshall and Morandé, "Propuestas económicas," 70). See also Jorge Marshall, "Los consensos de los programas económicos," *Revista de CIEPLAN* 12 (April 1988): 33–36.

33. Oscar Muñoz, interview by author, Santiago, 10 August 1992, and Manuel Marfán, interview by author, Santiago, 7 August 1992. This assessment was confirmed by a review of CIEPLAN and opposition criticisms reported in the press during this period.

process of dialogue and reconciliation necessary for the success of a future democracy. As evidence, Foxley noted that conflict was greatest in areas where the regime had most concentrated its unilateral innovations (e.g., health, education, justice, and labor).[34]

Despite these criticisms, during this period Foxley began to accept certain aspects of the government's economic program. He did so for three reasons. First, parts of the economy had recovered. By 1987 Foxley was promoting among his CIEPLAN colleagues the view that the transition from import-substituting industrialization to export-led growth was largely complete, a significant sector of entrepreneurs had absorbed the new rules of the game, exports were growing, and investment had recovered.[35] Though still a critic of the high social, economic, and political costs generated by how the transition had been carried out, Foxley would work to maintain stable rules of the economy because he now saw it as his mission to ensure that the price the country had paid was not in vain.

Second, Foxley wished to initiate an ongoing dialogue that would be important for a future democracy. As he told Jeffrey Puryear: "We were convinced rationally that this country had to learn to get along with itself, and we had studied game theory, and the theory of cooperation. . . . Thus [we sought deliberately] to initiate a game of cooperation in which we recognized more positive points than we had previously, *more even than we really thought were positive*. . . . And we defined it in terms so that the other side could say, 'Those guys have recognized our positive points. Now we are obliged to seek a greater understanding with them.' "[36]

Finally, in the mid-1980s Foxley's understanding of the public "mood"—based on public opinion surveys and his contacts with the people—converted his belief in gradual change into a kind of minimalism that would lead him to emphasize more continuity in economic policy than he would have recommended from a purely "technical" perspective. Foxley interpreted the failure of the protests as evidence that the people's fear and their desire for

34. Alejandro Foxley, "En defensa de lo social," *Hoy* 531 (21–27 September 1987): 28–29.

35. Oscar Muñoz, interview by author, Santiago, 10 August 1992.

36. Quoted in Puryear, *Thinking Politics*, 115–16; italics added. According to Foxley, he stumbled upon Robert Axelrod's *The Evolution of Cooperation* (New York: Basic Books, 1984) in a Washington bookstore, read it in two hours, and declared, "That's it. That's how politics works" (Foxley, interview by author, 13 August 1992). In addition to these two references to game theory, a survey of Foxley's written works and conferences shows that much of Foxley's study of cooperation focused on social pacts and the Spanish transition.

stability were as strong as their desire for change. In a 1985 interview, he noted that after the constant revolutionary efforts of the previous quarter century, the "fundamental demand" of the people was for stability and certainty.[37] He cited surveys that showed a demand for negotiation and consensus, even among the supposedly radicalized youth and marginal sectors. As a result Foxley concluded that the government should "do a few things but do them well" and "stimulate only those changes that have a good chance of success (i.e., that arouse the most consensus)."[38] This would become the unofficial mantra of the Aylwin government. These minimalist conclusions would only be reinforced by the failure of the intellectuals in Raúl Alfonsín's Argentine government, who, Foxley believed, attempted to accomplish too much.[39]

Foxley as Minister-to-Be

During the fourteen-month delay between the opposition's victory in the October 1988 plebiscite and the presidential and congressional elections in December 1989, Foxley essentially operated as the finance minister-to-be, given the likelihood of the Concertación victory and his undisputed leadership among opposition economists. It was then that he finalized the coalition's policy platform and began to establish rational expectations among business and the public about what government policy would be.

37. Alejandro Foxley, interview by Raquel Correa, *Revista de CIEPLAN* 1 (August 1985): 20–27. Foxley's view was confirmed three years later by focus groups that the opposition conducted as they prepared their strategy for the plebiscite. See *La campaña del NO vista por sus creadores* (Santiago: CIS/Ediciones Melquíades, 1989), especially the contributions by Carlos Vergara, Javier Martínez, and Ignacio Walker.

38. See especially Alejandro Foxley, "Reflexiones sobre los cambios en la democracia," in *Democracia en Chile: Doce conferencias* (Santiago: CIEPLAN, 1986), and idem, "Los tareas de la democracia," *Revista de CIEPLAN* 17 (January 1990): 4–15.

39. See Alejandro Foxley, "La política económica para la transición," in *Transición a la democracia: Marco político y económico,* ed. Oscar Muñoz (Santiago: CIEPLAN, 1990), 117, for Foxley's description of the general situation facing intellectuals who come to power after a long period of authoritarian rule. He argues that, despite the creativity and competence of the new officials, their overly ambitious plans run up against the officials' own lack of experience, the inexperience of Congress, and a state apparatus weakened by the preceding government's efforts to dismantle the state.

The Concertación's Economic Policy

The key moment in defining government policy came in March of 1989 as the Concertación prepared its detailed socioeconomic program. Foxley did not participate in the original internal negotiations over the program, but the draft document that was crafted by the heads of the technical committees of his own party and the Socialist Party reflected the convergence on economic policy generated by discussions in opposition think tanks and the lessons learned from the economic failures of neighboring democracies. It acknowledged the need to retain the positive aspects of the military's economic model, such as an emphasis on exports and macroeconomic equilibrium, and it stressed the need to address social problems without falling into "populism." Representatives from each party made it clear that they understood they could propose only the minimum of their ideal projects.[40]

Despite this positive general orientation, the actual program left much to be desired from Foxley's point of view. As economic coordinator for the Christian Democrats, Foxley wanted to change the draft in favor of a less regulatory role for the state on twenty different points. He felt that the proposed program was ambiguous in such key areas as foreign investment, deregulation of the internal market, the participation of private capital in mining, the maintenance of low and equal tariffs, the tax system, and privatizations of public enterprises.[41] These ambiguities reflected historical points of disagreement between the Socialists and the Christian Democrats that Foxley felt should be resolved (at least for the next four years); failure to do so at the draft stage would likely lead to disputes later that could have disastrous consequences for a center-left government, which, after the paralyzing divisiveness of the Frei and Allende administrations, needed to prove its competence to govern.

Foxley also advocated changes in the draft because some policies violated key precepts of his political economy, such as the need for clear and stable rules and protection for private property (for example, it advocated a review of pre-plebiscite privatizations that lacked in transparency and the annulment of all privatizations occurring after the plebiscite). Although he was not certain about retaining certain aspects of the model, such as low and equal tariffs and the direct foreign investment laws, Foxley opted to err on the side of stability.

Foxley met privately with his Socialist Party counterpart (and future minister of the economy), Carlos Ominami, to discuss the matter, and after a day-long

---

40. For a discussion of the draft document, see *Hoy* 608 (13–19 March 1989): 39–41.
41. Cavallo, *Los hombres,* 150.

discussion Ominami agreed to the changes Foxley had proposed. By virtue of their joint authority as economic coordinators for the two major parties of the opposition, Foxley and Ominami won acceptance for their modifications in the Economic Commission of the Concertación. Once this accord went to the parties for approval, however, the Socialists insisted on the original twenty points in a document signed by Jorge Arrate, then president of the Socialist Party and "one of the most technically qualified economists on the left," the economist who had headed the draft committee and who was also a member of the party's political commission, and, much to Foxley's surprise, Ominami himself.[42] An outraged Foxley quit the commission, arguing that if the two parties could not cooperate now, it would be impossible to govern together. The future secretary-general of the presidency (and Christian Democrat) Edgardo Boeninger and Christian Democratic party president Andrés Zaldívar backed Foxley, and work in all the committees of the Concertación, involving some fifteen hundred *técnicos,* came to a standstill. The Socialists relented, and Foxley and Ominami assumed office with their modified program.

An understanding of this incident adds an important dimension to prevailing interpretations of the Concertación's economic policy and highlights the fact that situations described by "consensus" and "consensus seeking" often involve a degree of imposition and uncertainty that is not suggested by the terms. Explanations of the Concertación's economic policy generally point to some combination of consensus and constraint; the most common combination identifies a consensus among technopols on economic policy (as a result of center-left dialogues in the 1980s and the economic recovery engineered by Büchi) that politicians (more or less reluctantly) accepted because of the constraints of the transition (i.e., the presence of Pinochet, the strength of business, and the dominance of neoliberalism internationally).

The incident described above, however, reveals that the level of consensus on economic policies, even among technopols, still permitted a great deal of debate and almost resulted in an economic program (e.g., review of privatizations) that would likely have led to a very different transition scenario.[43] The final

---

42. The description of Arrate, who had done graduate work in economics at Harvard, is from Puryear, *Thinking Politics,* 117. The economist who wrote the draft argued on behalf of the original over the revised version, but Ominami's behavior and views as minister suggest that he signed the document because of an uncomfortable situation within his own party. For Ominami's views, see Carlos Ominami, "Promoting Economic Growth and Stability," in *From Dictatorship to Democracy: Rebuilding Political Consensus in Chile,* ed. Joseph S. Tulchin and Augusto Varas (Boulder, Colo.: Lynne Reinner Publishers, 1991).

43. It would be more accurate to speak of a "convergence" on economic policy that offered the

program was less an example of the hegemony of technopols over parties (after all, technopols were on both sides of the debate) than an "imposition" of the Christian Democratic Party on the Socialists.[44] Similarly, the constraints of the transition did not prevent the advocacy and near adoption of "confrontational" economic policies; human agency was important in determining the outcome even in a transition as constrained as the Chilean. While a political logic did explain the ultimate outcome, it was the threat to the existence of the center-left coalition (posed by Foxley's resignation), rather than the constrained nature of the transition, that led to an agreement.[45]

Establishing Expectations

The early establishment of an economic program was designed to minimize the uncertainty associated with the political transition; the fulfillment of these "contractual obligations" as minister would be important both for legitimizing democracy and for ensuring the smooth functioning of the economy. This represented a break with the democratic past, when campaign platforms represented vague promises that raised expectations that could usually not be fulfilled.

In this campaign, Foxley and the opposition sought to counter the expectations of change—both positive and negative—that were associated with the transition to democracy. The Concertación had to convince entrepreneurs, who remembered the massive expropriations and hyperinflation of the Allende period, that a return to democracy was not a return to chaos. Though

---

possibility for compromise; technopols reduced the range of differences enough to provide a necessary but not sufficient condition for reaching agreements.

44. See Edgardo Boeninger, "Desafíos económicos para la construcción de la democracia," in *Orden económico y democracia* (Santiago: CED, 1985), for a comparison of Christian Democratic, Socialist, and liberal views on the political economy circa 1985. Christian Democrats placed less faith in the state and had a more rigid understanding of the conditions necessary for entrepreneurs to make a positive contribution to the economy. These differences between the parties persisted: for example, by 1987, the Christian Democrats indicated that they would not make a wholesale challenge of privatizations carried out by the Pinochet regime in the 1980s, whereas the Socialists advocated a thorough review (Marshall and Morandé, "Propuestas económicas," 61).

45. Similarly, important sectors of the Concertación, led by Socialist technopol Ricardo Lagos, advocated a more confrontational approach on the political side as well. They wanted Aylwin to introduce a package of constitutional reforms and to refuse to send any additional legislation to Congress until it was passed. Aylwin refused, feeling that the need to take quick measures to address the social debt could not be sacrificed to such a maneuver. Even more important, Aylwin felt that this ploy risked a return to the polarization of the past; he did not want to gamble the future of democracy on such a power play. See Cavallo, *Los hombres,* 211.

outside observers sympathetic to the government's neoliberal policies were quick to identify the "conceptual separability" of the economics of the Chicago Boys and the politics of Pinochet, business was not as ready to accept this distinction. They doubted both the commitment and capacity of the new government to follow responsible policies.

Foxley also had to convince the public, with their long pent-up demands, that the new government would be constrained in its ability to address their very legitimate grievances. He believed it was essential to the survival of the new democracy that the Aylwin administration avoid the fate of other newly democratic governments in Argentina, Brazil, and Peru, which had succumbed to what Foxley called the "populist cycle" of trying to fulfill demands beyond their economic capacity. This led to a hyperinflation that was most harmful for the very groups the initial spending had been intended to benefit.

Business

As finance minister, Foxley would be confronted with a dynamic, aggressive group of entrepreneurs who, along with the army, constituted one of the few groups to come out of the authoritarian experience more ideological than it went in. He would have to teach these entrepreneurs that democracy was a viable system, while making changes in the tax structure and labor legislation that they opposed.

In addition to ideological opposition, Foxley had to deal with business's fear of democracy, and especially of the center-left, which was rooted in the experiences of the 1960s and 1970s.[46] As noted earlier, this distrust had important economic implications. Business fear of state intervention in the 1960s had become what Foxley called a self-fulfilling prophecy—distrust led to decreasing investment, which forced the state to intervene even more in the economy. As one observer noted: "The role played by business confidence cannot be exaggerated. It may be argued that the policies of the reformist

46. There is a debate over how fearful business really was of the Concertación. Eduardo Silva regards hostile business statements in Chile as a purely political ploy and downplays business fear. See Silva, "Capitalist Regime Loyalties and Redemocratization in Chile," *Journal of Inter-American Studies and World Affairs* 34 (Winter 1992): 77–117. In contrast, I would agree with Guillermo Campero's characterization of business as "torn between their ideological optimism and their fear of the social powers represented by the opposition." Campero, "Entrepreneurs Under the Military Regime," in *The Struggle for Democracy in Chile: 1982–1990,* ed. Paul Drake and Ivan Jaksić (Lincoln: University of Nebraska Press, 1991), 149. This combination of fear and hope introduced a potential for volatility (as well as for stability) into the transitional situation.

Christian Democratic Frei administration in the late 1960s were better designed and implemented than those of the conservative [Jorge] Alessandri administration in the early 1960s, but the fact remains that the rate of gross fixed capital formation as a share of GDP was always over 20 per cent in the first half of the 1960s, and always under 20 per cent in the second half."[47]

Foxley tried to build credibility and trust by meeting with business and outlining the Concertación's plans after the plebiscite victory, but he made little progress initially. A confrontation in one of their more public and important meetings occurred seven weeks after the plebiscite, when Foxley was a keynote speaker at the annual national conference of entrepreneurs (ENADE '88).[48] As Foxley began to sketch the Concertación's economic project for consolidating Chile's insertion into the international economy, one gentleman stood up in the middle of the room and shook his finger at Foxley, declaring: "Sir, I do not believe a word you are saying." This incident reinforced Foxley's conviction that the building of trust would be a central task of the new democracy.[49]

Foxley's relationship with business, however, would not be based only on giving guarantees of continuity but also on establishing in advance rational expectations about *changes* the new government planned, including a tax increase and a reform of labor legislation. He encouraged business to seek a preelectoral compromise with unions on a new labor code as a means to minimize the uncertainty of leaving those changes to a newly elected Congress. This was not a new message from Foxley, who had long told business that it should not ask for guarantees but rather should take the initiative and make changes that would guarantee its own legitimacy.

The Public

In the midst of the presidential campaign, the Concertación and other groups launched a civic education crusade stressing the political value of democracy and emphasizing that the new democracy would not be able to solve immediately the innumerable economic problems that had accumulated under military rule. Unlike Presidents Alberto Fujimori in Peru, Fernando Collor de Mello in Brazil, and Carlos Menem in Argentina, Aylwin would not campaign on one (populist) platform and govern with another.

47. Hojman, *Chile: The Political Economy*, 183.
48. For the text of Foxley's speech, see "Bases para un desarrollo de la economía chilena: Una visión alternativa," *Colección estudios CIEPLAN* 26 (June 1989): 175–85.
49. Alejandro Foxley, interview by author, Santiago, 18 August 1992.

While the Concertación's discourse of constraints might be a useful theme in all new democracies, it was particularly necessary in Chile to counter the military government's triumphalist message about the economic "miracle" and the accompanying expectations that a government with the will to do so would be able to solve the economic situation of the poorest sectors. The officials of the future government wanted to create a feeling of constraint appropriate to the crisis situation that their economic calculations predicted for the first years of the new democracy: the external debt would come due in 1990; excess capacity was exhausted, and growth would depend on new investments; high prices of copper were projected to decline; and the economy was overheated and experiencing 30 percent inflation (partly a product of two years of electoral spending by the outgoing Pinochet regime).[50] As a result of these economic conditions the center-left was likely to post less favorable macroeconomic numbers than its predecessor and would have to restrict its spending in the difficult context of a new democracy. This made it even harder for the government to satisfy business's demand for proof of economic capability and the public's desire for change. The Aylwin campaign made it clear that it would deal with social demands but only within the context of continued macroeconomic responsibility.

This concern with the need to moderate demands in the wake of regime change was certainly not a new one for the opposition—Foxley emphasized it immediately after the economic crash in 1982, when transition seemed imminent—but its centrality was reinforced by a visit that a decimated Juan Sourrouille paid to the CIEPLAN offices shortly before the Chilean transition. Sourrouille, a center-left intellectual like Foxley and his colleagues, was the former Argentine minister of economy whose failed program had driven the economy to ruins and forced President Alfonsín to leave office before his term had expired. The future economic officials of the Aylwin government sat around the CIEPLAN conference table and listened to Sourrouille, now a mere shadow of the man he had once been, tell the tale of his rise and decline—from a successful first year riding on the shoulders of the crowd to a final year in which he was spit upon by his own neighbors if he dared show his face at the door.[51] Foxley dubbed this syndrome of initial success and eventual disaster the "populist cycle" and vowed to keep it from happening in Chile. As

50. Foxley, "La política económica para la transición," 109–10. The constraints of the authoritarian legacy were a theme throughout the first year of the new government. See, for example, Foxley's first "State of the Budget" address to the Congress, October 1990.

51. Alejandro Foxley, interview by author, Santiago, 18 August 1992.

minister he would deny demands with the same vigor and sense of moral righteousness that he once used to criticize Pinochet; in both cases he felt motivated by his dedication to the poorest sectors of society and the cause of democracy.

The ongoing educational drive to instill a "culture of government" in social and political actors during the campaign and after was a clear effort to limit the number of demands made on the state. In addition to these demand-side efforts, Foxley also recognized the need to address the supply side—the government.

A Governing Team

As minister, Foxley would exercise a great deal of authority over economic matters while at the same time consulting with the president, the cabinet, and the parties. He had the strong backing of his president, a decision-making structure that centralized authority, and a coherent team—all of the ingredients typically identified by the economic reform literature as necessary for government autonomy. In addition, links to parties and other social groups "embedded" this autonomy in society.[52]

President Aylwin, who had participated in opposition workshops on the economy, gave Foxley working control over the nation's purse strings and did not accede to requests without consulting his finance minister—a crucial difference from the experience of many failed finance ministers in Latin America. Foxley fought to make sure that institutional arrangements reinforced his control over government spending. He successfully opposed a proposal to put the Ministry of Planning in charge of coordinating the social-sectors ministries (Health, Education, Housing, etc.), a move that he feared would divide the government into two opposing camps—a "spender's Chile" and a "saver's Chile." Instead, Foxley headed both the Committee of Economic Ministries and the Committee of Social-Sectors Ministries.[53]

In addition to this centralized control and presidential support, Foxley had a coherent economic team: he filled key positions throughout the economic

52. See Peter B. Evans, "The State as Problem and Solution: Predation, Embedded Autonomy, and Structural Change," in *The Politics of Economic Adjustment,* ed. Stephan Haggard and Robert R. Kaufman (Princeton: Princeton University Press, 1992).

53. Alejandro Foxley, personal correspondence with the author, 1 September 1992. Such an internal division is common. See, for example, Peter Cleaves's discussion of the Christian Democratic administration of 1964–70, "Coalition Formation for Short-term Planning in the Economic Committee," in *Bureaucratic Politics and Administration in Chile* (Berkeley and Los Angeles: University of California Press, 1974).

policy-making apparatus with his colleagues from CIEPLAN. However, Foxley's "team" extended far beyond his economic collaborators. The government's key political strategist, Edgardo Boeninger, and Foxley had very similar views on the political economy, a coherence that was nourished by government decision-making procedures that coordinated the economic and political strategies of the government.[54]

Most important, the politicians, economists, and social scientists who had cooperated in think tanks in opposition to the military regime constituted a like-minded network that cut across the leadership strata of the parties, as well as an extremely coherent governing corps (known as the *partido transversal*, or "horizontal party"). This group was significant for its combination of internal coherence and "embeddedness" in political and civil society. Most ministers were technopols—active party members whose partisan affiliation mattered in their selection, although all were picked according to "criteria of excellence." They represented their parties' concerns in government discussions and had to answer to their parties for their actions, but their primary loyalty was to the "mission of the state."[55] Aylwin treated his ministers as political leaders and not as technocrats; each was asked to give his opinion on political matters. This two-way flow of information between parties and the government bolstered all government policies, including Foxley's handling of the economy. In a similar fashion, the ties that many government actors (e.g., those formerly labor consultants and activists in nongovernmental organizations) had forged with labor and social organizations during the dictatorship facilitated consultation and economic policy making.

In addition to these favorable circumstances, Foxley understood that "to do a good technical job in managing the economy, you have to be a politician. If you do not have the capacity to articulate your vision, to persuade

---

54. Compare Boeninger, "Desafíos económicos para la construcción de la democracia," and Foxley, *Para una democracia estable*. For a description of the "three-tiered" decision-making procedure established for all important economic measures, see Edgardo Boeninger, "Governance and Development: Issues and Constraints," in *Proceedings of the World Bank Annual Conference on Development Economics, 1991* (Washington, D.C.: International Bank for Reconstruction and Development/ World Bank, 1992), 282–83.

55. Parties and their representatives in the cabinet were very conscious of the need to avoid excessive party intromission in the affairs of the state (i.e., "co-government"). Both the Frei and Allende administrations had been undermined by divisive party debates that paralyzed government activity. For an account of the problematic relationship between the Allende government and the parties in the Popular Unity coalition, see Sergio Bitar, *Chile: Experiment in Democracy* (Philadelphia: Institute for the Study of Human Issues, 1986). For divisions within the Frei government, see Paul E. Sigmund, *The Overthrow of Allende and the Politics of Chile, 1964–1976* (Pittsburgh: University of Pittsburgh Press, 1977).

antagonists, to bring people around on some unpopular measure, then you are going to be a total failure."[56] Whereas a technocrat may need insulation, technopols thrive as long as arenas for this kind of direct confrontation exist. Foxley benefited from a number of such arenas: decision-making channels that linked him to others in the government, weekly meetings with members of Congress from the Concertación, frequent encounters with party members, consultations with labor leaders, and so forth. By all accounts, he was persuasive.

Foxley as Minister (1990–94): Fulfilling Expectations

As minister, Foxley combined a "progressive social policy with an austere, some would say conservative, fiscal policy" that was designed to address the concerns of the two major constituencies he had targeted during the campaign—the public and business.[57] By giving concrete expression to the new "norms of equity" that would prevail in the economy under democracy, Foxley hoped to legitimize a social market system for the people and to show them that "democracy works." As Foxley commented, "The effort in social policy, I think, was very important in providing wider acceptance and legitimacy for our prudent macroeconomic policies."[58] Foxley's policy blend also sought to legitimize democracy for business by demonstrating that a center-left government can address social equity demands responsibly and that the concessions necessary in a democracy need not undermine economic growth.[59] The first significant measure of the new democracy—a four-year increase in taxes, with the revenues earmarked for social spending—was a key to this package and was personally masterminded by Foxley.

56. Alejandro Foxley, interview by Richard Feinberg, 21.
57. Foxley repeatedly characterized his policy combination in this way.
58. Alejandro Foxley, "The Future of U.S.-Chilean Relations," in *The Heritage Lectures*, no. 323 (Washington, D.C.: Heritage Foundation, 3 May 1991). Even before becoming minister, Foxley had been impressed by the patience and understanding generated among social sectors by the government's commitment to the tax reform. See Foxley, "La política económica para la transición," 131–32.
59. Foxley argued that once a government passed the "fiscal test," business would be less confrontational and start investing. See Alejandro Foxley, "Surprises and Challenges for a Democratic Chile" (speech at the Helen Kellogg Institute for International Studies, panel titled "Prospects for the Hemisphere," Notre Dame, Ind., 13 September 1991).

Knowing he could rely on the support of his own political coalition, Foxley focused most of his attention on selling the tax reform to opposition politicians. Although the nine senators appointed by the 1980 constitution denied the government a majority in the upper house of Congress, Foxley felt he could have passed the tax reform, without seeking a compromise with the opposition parties, by winning over the votes of a few of the more moderate designated senators. He chose to negotiate instead, in keeping with his desire to build consensus as the first and the best approach to policy making. Foxley believed he could take advantage of the center-right's eagerness to prove its commitment to democracy and social equity; he focused on Evelyn Matthei and Sebastián Piñera, two economists of the National Renovation Party who were on the Finance Committees of the House and Senate, respectively. As Boylan shows in Chapter 5, Matthei and Piñera, with their technocratic and business backgrounds, were instrumental in convincing their reluctant fellow party members to vote for the reform. This deprived business hard-liners of the possibility of an alliance with the center-right to oppose the reform.

Also central to Foxley's success in the tax reform and in his ministry as a whole was his use of the mass media. After Pinochet's defeat in the plebiscite, a consensus developed that the failure of the economy to address the social needs of the poorest sectors was a key reason for the electoral loss.[60] Consequently, during the presidential campaign every significant political and social actor expressed a rhetorical commitment to addressing the social debt. Foxley sought to convert this politically profitable sloganeering into a real consensus on the tax reform. Daily he appeared on television to mobilize public opinion against politicians of the right and business, pressuring them to act consistently with their promises by citing public opinion polls that showed 75 percent of the population supported the reform. Those who supported social measures but opposed the tax reform that would finance them were charged with demagoguery and lack of seriousness.[61] The reform passed after only thirty days in Congress by a vote of 61–10 in the House and 30–2 in the Senate. Sixty-seven percent of the 1991 budget was devoted to social spending, for a total of 14.5 percent of GDP, or approximately $800 million.

60. A public opinion poll the month before the 5 October 1988 plebiscite showed that 72 percent of those who opposed Pinochet did so primarily for economic reasons. Augusto Varas, "The Crisis of Legitimacy of Military Rule in the 1980s," in The Struggle for Democracy, ed. Drake and Jaksić, 76. This economic interpretation of the government's defeat was widely accepted by both opposition and regime actors. See, for example, Foxley, "La política económica para la transición," 106.

61. Alejandro Foxley, interview by author, Santiago, 18 August 1992.

The tax reform represented the first test of Foxley's ability to negotiate accords in a democratic setting. However, despite the successful outcome, Foxley's methods received criticisms from various sectors of his own coalition. In order to maintain the greatest degree of flexibility in bargaining with the right, Foxley did not consult labor and parties of the Concertación until *after* he had reached an agreement with National Renovation, thus vitiating the impact of any input on their part. Even some cabinet members reportedly felt uneasy with what they thought was Foxley's excessive use of extraparliamentary negotiations before sending the project to Congress, a strategy that they saw as privileging corporate actors over democratic institutions. After the muted criticisms of this project, Foxley and the government took efforts to treat Congress as the privileged place for negotiating accords.

The renewal of the tax reform took place in Congress, after business agreed in principle to the idea of making the reform permanent. Initially, when taxes were shaping up as the centerpiece of the December 1993 presidential campaign, business and the right repudiated the government's efforts to make the tax reform permanent. In addition to publicly insisting on the need to maintain the reform, Foxley launched a private campaign aimed at business leaders. (The hardening of the moderate right's stance on compromising with the government deprived Foxley of this potential interlocutor, at least initially.) He eventually persuaded business leaders that in order to reduce the uncertainty associated with the elections, they should not oppose making the reform permanent.[62] Business privately communicated their decision to the National Renovation Party and Foxley then publicly started a round of meetings with the opposition. The details of the reform were hammered out in Congress, resulting in what was perceived as a clear success for the government. In this case, Foxley's gradualist philosophy of "expanding the boundary of the possible" had worked[63] — it was more difficult in 1993 for business and the right to oppose renewal of a tax reform that had been proven not to harm profit or investment levels than it was for them to oppose a permanent tax increase in 1990.

62. "Reforma tributaria: Los empresarios dicen que sí," *Hoy* 803 (7–13 December 1992): 46–47. Business's desire to reduce uncertainty was such that there was even support for Aylwin to stay in office.

63. Foxley, "La política económica para la transición," 118–19.

High Grades for Foxley

Foxley's ability to facilitate an agreement on the tax reform at a time when the outgoing government is usually a "lame duck" is testimony to the sustained success of his ministry. A Centro de Estudios Públicos-Adimark poll taken just months before the end of the Aylwin government (June 1993) shows that a majority of the population agreed with this assessment: Foxley was the political personality with the third highest approval rating, behind only President Aylwin and future president Eduardo Frei. His disapproval rating was extremely low, and 72.4 percent of the respondents had a positive or very positive opinion of him.

Part of this approval was surely attributable to the relative well-being of the Chilean economy, but Foxley's personal characteristics also contributed to his popularity and, what is more important, to his ability to legitimize the Aylwin government's project of "growth with equity under democracy." While numerous other economists within the center and left had the technical skills to be finance minister, Foxley's personal history of strident opposition to the military regime paradoxically made him best suited for the task of national reconciliation that motivated the new government. Though his past initially hindered his relationship with business, the eventual understanding between the two was all the more significant because of the original distance between them. Despite disagreements on a variety of policies, business praised Foxley's control of inflation and his frank public declarations that the government would not cede to social pressures.

As important, Foxley's long-standing concern with social justice gave credibility to his message that the government was doing all it could in the face of constraints. Foxley's television appearance, before the plebiscite, in which he refuted the military's economic "miracle" and decried the existence of "five million poor people" in Chile caused a controversy among elites but was recalled frequently by ordinary Chileans. As minister, he projected an image of sober competence and seriousness of purpose that the Chileans demand of their politicians. He was perhaps the person best suited to muster the particular mixture of firmness and concern necessary to adapt the economic model to the demands of democracy and equity.

Despite his enormous pride in Chile's macroeconomic success, Foxley realized that the social action of the state, its apparatus hindered by years of disuse, was slow in affecting the lives of the people. As a result he consciously adopted a nontriumphalist discourse that recognized there was still much to be done. This reinforced Foxley's credibility with the people by demonstrating that he was in touch with them and cared about their problems, even if he could not solve them right away. After the first two years of the government, over half of the population demonstrated their patience by acknowledging in polls that though the government was not solving economic problems, it needed time.[64] Though Foxley believed that legitimacy was ultimately a matter of performance, in the short and medium run many other elements were important in shaping the people's perceptions of the government.

For this reason, Foxley worked hard to ensure that the government's image reflected its efforts to be efficient and honest. The speed with which the tax reform was accomplished and the foreign debt was renegotiated (in a one-week trip to New York) was designed to project an image of center-left competence and to show that democracy works.[65] The success of the center-left in projecting a capable image is suggested by an April 1992 poll that showed that a great majority of the people thought a government of the Concertación would do a better job than a government of the opposition not only in the traditional strongholds of the center-left—addressing poverty, unemployment, housing, and health—but also in managing the economy and controlling inflation.[66]

In addition to his concern that the public understand the government's efforts to pay the social debt, Foxley worked hard to generate a consensus on Chile's integration into the international economy, a project that for many had meant only impoverishment. Like Carlos Menem in Argentina and Carlos Salinas de Gortari in Mexico, Foxley invoked nationalist sentiment on behalf of the internationalization of the economy.

Internationalization of the Economy

Foxley had always favored international integration, but as minister he assigned a much greater political role to this aspect of economic policy than he

64. This survey was conducted in the Greater Santiago area. See Centro de Estudios de la Realidad Contemporánea (CERC),"Informe de prensa," June 1992.

65. The formal negotiating period for the debt—when Foxley and his team headed by Eduardo Aninat made a much publicized trip to New York to meet with bank officials—was purposely postponed until months of preparatory talks had resolved the majority of issues (Aninat, interview by author, Santiago, 21 August 1992).

66. Centro de Estudios Públicos–Adimark poll, April 1992, cited in Ignacio Walker, "Democratic Transition and Consolidation in Chile" (paper presented at the Helen Kellogg Institute for International Studies, Notre Dame, Ind., 1992), 11. The Concertación beat the opposition by at least 36 percentage points on every issue except inflation, where 55.6 percent believed in the ability of the Concertación (vs. 23.1 percent for the opposition).

had previously. Drawing on the example of Spain's entrance into the European Economic Community after the Franco regime, Foxley hoped that Chile's integration into the international economy would serve as a shared national project to mobilize and unify Chileans—the kind of project that Chileans had been missing for decades.[67] He invoked nationalistic pride in Chile's ability to claim space in world markets, to compete "in the first division." As Foxley noted in 1985, Chile's comparative advantage was its people, and continuing investment in human capital would be necessary for the health of the Chilean economy.[68] Conversely, he worked to "make the common people see that their future is tied to how well we do in our international bid."[69]

Foxley believed a project of internationalization could help transcend competing ideologies without nullifying them. For example, he exhorted regional elites to overcome ideological barriers in order to cooperate in forging a collective regional identity and in creatively planning the productive structure of the region that would best enable it to participate in and contribute to Chile's national project of insertion into the world economy. This "association in creativity" and cooperation in a national project, not economic competition among individuals as the Chicago Boys envisioned it, would be the new principle of associational life in Chile. International integration would provide Chileans with an external rationale for political efficiency (i.e., cooperation) that would last long beyond the transitional moment.

This rationale operated in the short run because flexible and cooperative relations have been necessary for Chile to defend itself from potentially destabilizing international fluctuations. In one instance, Congress quickly and almost unanimously approved Foxley's proposals to lower tariffs from a uniform 15 percent to 11 percent in an effort to counter reserve buildup and peso appreciation. When confronted with an oil price shock caused by the Persian Gulf War, Foxley was able to secure the cooperation of Congress,

67. As Eugenio Tironi noted, "[A]n inorganic and strongly differentiated society, with social actors of diffuse identity, tends to find the absent principle of national integration in politics (and culture); in fact, the destruction of Chilean democracy in 1973 originated in the erosion of this integrating principle" (Tironi, "Clases sociales y acuerdo democrático," 37). Writing in 1984, Tironi agreed with Foxley's analysis of the breakdown of democracy but argued that the solution had to involve more than the socioeconomic "concertation" that Foxley, as an economist, stressed at that time. Foxley seems to have taken Tironi's words to heart: after 1985, many of his writings centered on the cultural and political side of reconstructing a national model of development (see, for example, *Chile y su futuro* and *Chile puede más* [Santiago: Editorial Planeta, 1988]), and his actions as minister reflected this emphasis.

68. Alejandro Foxley, interview by Raquel Correa, *Revista de CIEPLAN* 1 (August 1985).

69. Alejandro Foxley, quoted in *El Diario,* 3 October 1991.

unions, and the Central Bank in enacting a variety of measures, including an agreement by the Central Unitaria de Trabajadores (CUT) and the public employees' union to accept less than the traditional 100 percent readjustment of public-sector wages. Finally, Foxley gained the cooperation of Congress, business, and even labor in promoting Chile's image abroad (through lobbying trips and export-promotion tours) in an effort to secure market access for Chile's exports.

Foxley and Labor

Labor's cooperation with Foxley in the face of the oil price shock was typical of its overall cooperative stance, which contributed to the government's efforts to maintain macroeconomic stability. The main labor confederation, the CUT, assumed the "national perspective" that Foxley desired of it from the start, largely because of its commitment to democracy and its normative, partisan, and personal ties with the government, nurtured during the years of struggle against the dictatorship. (Its general weakness worked against, but did not preclude, a more confrontational approach.)

From the opposition, Foxley had stressed the importance of reincorporating labor into national life as part of a responsible "leadership class" and establishing cooperative relations between business and labor. (The minister of labor, economist René Cortázar, came to the government from CIEPLAN and shared Foxley's views.) Within the first two months of the Aylwin administration, the government was able to point to a largely symbolic demonstration of a new era in business-labor relations: an agreement on national matters signed by labor, business, and the government. Formal tripartite accords would be signed annually during the Aylwin administration, and in 1992 permanent working groups for conducting negotiations between the government, the CUT, and the main business confederation were created.

The Aylwin government pursued a policy of consultation and "compensation" toward labor: they established a minimum-wage law, devoted resources to the training of workers, increased social spending, provided CUT with offices in Santiago, and consulted with the unions on a variety of matters. (The importance of consultation for cooperative government-labor relations became most evident when it was gone: labor lamented the Frei administration's different governing style and cited this as one of their reasons for a more hard-line stance.)

Despite improvements in its situation, the CUT announced from the start its unhappiness with what it saw as Foxley's *continuismo*; reform of the labor legislation established by the authoritarian government was a continuing source of tension between the two. After government talks with business and labor had failed to find a workable compromise solution, an opposition-controlled Senate limited changes to the law, which retained significant restrictions on collective negotiation and the right to strike. The consensus-seeking approach of the Aylwin administration as well as its own interests in the development of "cooperative" business-labor relations led to only incremental changes in labor legislation; it remains to be seen if this gradualist approach will yield future changes, as occurred in the case of the tax reform.

Democracy as a Process

Most of Foxley's actions as minister (and indeed those of the government as a whole) were guided by the belief that the country's "future rests in the first place, in the very first place, on the capacity that we have to develop and strengthen a political system in which the underlying political culture is one of cooperation."[70] This emphasis resonated with Aylwin's vision of reconciliation and a government commitment "to search for an agreement that is broader than a simple majority and that considers the introduction of social change in a gradual, incremental way through negotiation and compromise."[71]

After having spent years in the opposition working out their differences and learning to trust one another, Foxley and other key government actors believed it was essential to extend this principle to their long-hostile relations with the right and business (and the military). The cooperation of these actors was essential to avoid an authoritarian regression and to permit the economic successes that would contribute to the consolidation of democracy and the permanency of the Concertación in power. Foxley felt that the first four years of the new democracy would be particularly important as a rare moment of "plasticity" during which lasting patterns of interaction would be set.

In keeping with this principle, the government sought the backing of the center-right National Renovation Party in Congress on the first two major initiatives of the new democracy—the tax reform and the reform of labor

70. Alejandro Foxley, speech, 11 June 1992. Foxley shared this emphasis with Boeninger, whose beliefs are described by Puryear (*Thinking Politics,* 93): "He was convinced . . . that Chile's fundamental political problem was the lack of trust among social and political actors, and that reestablishing that trust was a prerequisite to reestablishing democratic rule. . . . The process of meeting and establishing trust became more important than achieving specific policy outcomes."

71. Walker, "Democratic Transition and Consolidation in Chile," 7.

legislation. While some within the Concertación (including technopols) criticized this approach for the concessions to the right it entailed, Foxley and the government felt that this was preferable to the polarization of the very near past.[72] As long as a culture of cooperation prevailed, ongoing negotiations could yield additional changes in a gradual fashion: the tax reform was made permanent in 1993, and a second reform of the labor legislation was submitted to Congress by the Frei government.

After three decades of polarization, Foxley and key government strategists saw compromise and cooperation as the sine qua non of democracy, and they worked hard to maintain the conditions necessary for dialogue, employing many of the approaches that had worked for them during their years in opposition.[73] They focused on points of agreement rather than differences (a tactic of "conflict avoidance") and employed a common language that would permit debate.[74] They emphasized the importance of words and symbols in maintaining the "culture of cooperation," or "culture of optimism," that would permit the resolution of differences. Whereas the Chicago Boys saw political institutions as distorting individual interests, the technopols of the center-left blamed conflict, ideology, pessimism, and fear. Far from representing a technocratic denial of the conflictual nature of politics, these strategies were designed precisely to address the polarization remaining in Chilean society and to permit at least a gradual resolution of differences. Instead of a technocratic faith in the power of reason to find the optimal solution to any problem, the Chilean technopols place their faith in a reasoned debate to find a compromise solution.

72. Critics acknowledged that a broad consensus is necessary for "foundational pacts" (i.e., an agreement on the "rules of the game"), but they objected to the government's application of this principle to the tax reform and many other legislative packages. See Manuel Antonio Garretón, "Discutir la 'transición': Estrategias y escenarios de la democratización política chilena," *FLACSO Serie de estudios políticos* 15 (October 1991). Garretón, a noted political scientist and Socialist, held a post in the Ministry of Education in the Aylwin administration.

73. In particular, government actors seemed to draw on the strategies that proved successful for them in the 1988 plebiscite. (For an excellent discussion, see Puryear, *Thinking Politics,* 141–45, 156–59.) For example, a "minimalist" approach was crucial to center-left cooperation in the plebiscite. When politicians could not agree on a common candidate and platform, a group of technopols suggested focusing on their point of agreement (a vote for the "No"). Successful cooperation on the "No" vote led to agreement on a common candidate and platform just months later.

74. Enrique Correa, a key figure in the Aylwin administration as secretary general of the government, noted that "probably the deepest legacy of the Aylwin government was the emergence of a community of language that permitted politics to establish itself in the world of reason and to regain its lost respectability" ("La política de consensos: Más que un estilo," *Hoy* 875 [25 April–1 May 1994]: 11).

Foxley and other technopols had good reason to believe that this less confrontational approach was supported by a majority of the population. Recall the events and survey evidence of the mid 1980s that had convinced Foxley (and other technopols) of the need to attempt only those changes that aroused the most consensus. Under democracy, that trend continued. A poll taken in October of 1990 showed that the public felt it was "important" or "very important" that the government consult the opposition (72.9 percent), the banks (72.3 percent), the unions (81.7 percent), and business (80.7 percent) when making economic decisions.[75] Consensual politicians have been consistently ranked the highest in public opinion polls.[76] In Chile, the population's desire for efficiency and competence led to an appreciation for politicians who are able to reach accords, rather than a preference for outsiders or autocrats.

This emphasis on the primacy of creating a culture of cooperation (as opposed to pursuing an immediate democratization that might be destabilizing) explains why Foxley could come to value authoritarian limitations on democratic institutions, such as designated senators, which denied the Concertación a legislative majority: "[They] forced us to reach broad agreements across the political spectrum instead of taking the narrow view of the parties in power. The new political landscape has also served to modify the more radical elements in the government coalition. . . . When you are forced by the rules of the game to play moderate politics, the process itself transforms people into moderate politicians."[77] He also noted that the authoritarian legacy can "do an unexpected service for political leaders of all the parties in the search for and support of moderate solutions. I would almost dare to say that it gives them an excuse when facing their party bases, to be able to select solutions different from those that were possible under the old antagonistic ideological schemes that still are alive in many sectors of the national life."[78]

The preceding passages illustrate not just Foxley's concern for cooperation but also his understanding that "many sectors of the national life" are not part of the "consensus" that one so often hears about in international circles. Foxley

75. Pablo Halpern, Edgardo Bosquet, and Marcelo Henríquez, "Opinión pública y política económica: Análisis de la formación de percepciones económicas," *Apuntes CIEPLAN* 98 (April 1991): 9.

76. Alejandro Foxley, interview by author, Santiago, 18 August 1992. His observation, important in itself, was supported by a review of available polls.

77. Foxley, "Surprises and Challenges," 5–6. The government valued the forced consensus-seeking so much that the constitutional-reform package it sent to the legislature did not change the quorum of 60 percent necessary to reform the constitution (Walker, "Democratic Transition and Consolidation in Chile," 12).

78. Alejandro Foxley, speech at CEPAL, 29 October 1991.

(and other important actors) realized that the key decisions of the transition and the first government had been made by a very reduced number of political and technopolitical elites and that a great deal of work remained in order to consolidate democracy. As president of the Christian Democratic party, Foxley would attempt to strengthen the culture of cooperation that he believed was central to the future of Chilean democracy.

Foxley as Party President

At the end of the Aylwin government, Foxley turned down a post in the Frei government in order to devote himself to politics (what he called, in very untechnocratic fashion, "the highest form of public service"). Six months later, he was elected to the presidency of the Christian Democratic Party (Partido Demócrata Cristiano, or PDC) by a universal vote of party members on a platform of "renovation." Foxley sought to fortify the Concertación through a collegial relationship with other parties, and he participated in the search for a new way for parties to cooperate with, and participate in, the government. He also set out to redress what he saw as a central deficiency of the party system: the distancing of parties from their social bases and the people's lack of trust in politicians.

For a variety of reasons, the role of the Concertación and of the parties under the Frei government was less clear than it had been under Aylwin. In response, Foxley tried to recreate the *partido transversal* at the level of party presidents and in this way fortify the alliance, but he has had little success. While he enjoys a very good personal and working relationship with Socialist Party president Camilio Escalona (representative of the party's hard-line faction), he has been unable to establish a similar relationship with the "renovated" leader of the Party for Democracy.

Also in response to the different situation under the Frei government, Foxley and his counterparts in the Socialist Party and Party for Democracy tried to find new ways to balance the demands of the alliance (to support the government), their natural desire to demonstrate clear party identities and protagonism (in order to retain and increase their share of the vote), and their emerging efforts to act collectively and propose initiatives to the government rather than just respond to the executive agenda. These conflicting pressures are greatest for the PDC, since, as the largest single party in the nation, its members expect it to play the premiere role both within the government and on the national political stage. However, since the president comes from their party, leaders of the PDC (especially Foxley, who benefited from party loyalty as finance minister) feel more compelled than the left to show their loyalty and to mute public criticisms of government policy. When Foxley was able to assume a leadership role and at the same time contribute to the government's project, the party's (and Foxley's) approval rating soared. This was the case when the party intervened to negotiate disputes between the Christian Democratic heads of the public-sector unions and Christian Democratic ministers of health and education and when it participated in the promotion of a second labor reform. Such opportunities are infrequent, however, and Foxley has been criticized by some in the party (and punished in the public opinion polls) for lacking influence within the government and for failing to establish a clear profile for the party in national affairs.

Despite the unavoidable need for a party president to project his or her organization's image on a national stage, Foxley was primarily concerned with reorganizing the party internally and expanding its presence at the local level. He sought to renovate a party that was divided at the national and provincial levels and plagued by a lack of participation (especially by younger voters). Internal statutes were changed in an effort to improve the party's presence at the municipal level and to open it to widespread participation at the base, making it more than just the meeting place for a small circle of militants. Foxley urged local party groups to get more involved in the community—to engage in dialogue with community organizations and local governments in pursuit of common tasks. These efforts represented a return to a key theme of his days as an opposition technopol—the need for politicians to be open to the "real" demands of the people—and echoed the interests of other technopols seeking to "modernize" party politics.[79]

As a technopol, Foxley has brought many positive attributes and one major liability to his difficult new job. On the positive side, Foxley's candidacy attracted a large number of *técnicos* to the party and to public service at the lower levels of government, where their expertise is much needed. The party flourished when Foxley and his team had the opportunity to act as a negotiator of accords with the opposition or social groups (a familiar task from his days as

---

79. The work of Verónica Montecinos on the participation of economists in Chilean parties represents one of the first efforts to understand the nature and origins of this phenomenon. See Montecinos, "Adjusting to Democracy: Economists as Party Leaders in Chile" (paper prepared for the Conference on Technocrats and the Politics of Expertise in Latin America, Amsterdam, September 1995), and idem, "Economists, Parties, and the Modernization of Chilean Politics," in *Deepening Democracy in Latin America*, ed. Kurt von Mettenheim and James Malloy (Pittsburgh: University of Pittsburgh Press, forthcoming).

minister). The organizational skills that Foxley had displayed as a student organizer (founding a national federation) and throughout his career as an academic (founding CEPLAN and CIEPLAN) were put to good use in the reorganization of the party and in Foxley's internal campaign for the party presidency (he had an organizational structure in place throughout the country before the other candidates). Repeating the experiences of his days as an opposition technopol, he traversed the provinces, meeting with the people to find out what they thought and at the same time promoting his ideas for reform. And at Christian Democratic congresses, the general debating hall has given way to brainstorming in small groups, an approach typical in think tanks. (Although these were created in 1991, Foxley seems to have embraced the methodology with renewed vigor.)

Finally, Foxley's status as a "newcomer" to party politics (a status that possibly only Chileans, with their strong party backgrounds, could bestow on a man who had been a devoted militant for over thirty-five years, a student leader, twice a government official, and a member of the party's National Council) was both an asset and a liability. Like most technopols, Foxley had "constructed [his] political identit[y] outside the traditional channels of party machines."[80] Although he was elected to the National Council in 1985 and 1987 with the support of the progressive wing of the party, he was not part of that group, and his political identity rested on the ideas he advanced in his books and seminars. This position "above politics" (i.e., above the currents in the party) contributed to his election on a platform of "renovation" and permitted the promotion of reform without too much of his own interest being imputed to his efforts, but his distance from internal groups and the lack of experience in the "nitty-gritty" of politics that this implied were also the greatest obstacles to his success as a party politician.

As party president, Foxley remained true to the political style he had developed in the opposition and employed as minister—the promotion of change through a consensus-seeking inclusionary strategy. Toward this end, Foxley picked representatives of the major party factions for vice presidential positions, but he offended the factions by eschewing negotiations with them in making the selections. In running the party, Foxley consulted these factional representatives but allegedly did not encourage their real participation, thus creating additional resentment.[81]

---

80. Montecinos, "Economists, Parties, and the Modernization of Chilean Politics," 25.
81. "Directiva DC: El poder light," Hoy 907 (5–11 December 1994): 9–11.

Thus Foxley's major problem as president stemmed from an element of politics for which none of his previous experiences had prepared him: the need to manage and maneuver through the personal rivalries and ambitions that sometimes seem to be at the heart of politics. As Boylan suggests in Chapter 5, technopols may be well suited to building coalitions for broad political purposes, but they are less adept at the murky and often personalized nuances of internal party politics. While this is certainly not inherent to technopols (Mexican technopols, after all, are crafty bureaucratic politicians), it does seem to be a problem for technopols whose previous political experience is primarily at the level of promoting compromise on substantive matters. Foxley himself, who before his plunge into party politics had said that he expected it to be no different from the politics he practiced as finance minister, soon was lamenting what he called the "quicksands" of politics and the "jungle" of personal struggles for power within parties.[82] Personal differences and rivalries (many stemming from Foxley's status as *presidenciable*) have caused Foxley some problems in his relationship with the government, with the Party for Democracy, and within his own party. (Previous to this, Foxley had been saved from missteps in internal party politics by his immense technopolitical skills; for example, although he backed Eduardo Frei, rather than Aylwin, for the presidency in 1989, Aylwin overlooked this and selected him as finance minister.)

Foxley was certainly not unaware of the problem of the personalization of politics when he entered the presidency; after all, his stated goal was to solve internal factional divisions by working to identify a common party goal that would transcend these differences. The need to focus on ideas over personal political struggles only intensified as Foxley got his first real taste of internal party politics and saw the negative effect this had on the public's image of politicians and politics. Although technopols are often blamed for the personalization of politics—the "dull pragmatism" of "consensual" politics is said to substitute personal disputes for ideological debate—they may also be a central part of any effort to put ideas back into politics. Foxley's case suggests that technopols are especially inclined to do so; the articulation of ideas, after all, represents their comparative advantage over those politicians who control the party machinery.

---

82. Alejandro Foxley, interview by María Irene Soto, "El perseguido," *Hoy* 880 (30 May–5 June 1994), 15.

Conclusion

Unlike Domingo Cavallo in Argentina, who is a self-declared state builder, Foxley saw his role in Chile as that of a nation builder. First from the opposition and then from the government, he set out to restore a sense of "nationhood" by building on the successes and failures of the past and looking to the future for a common vision to unite Chileans in a national project of international integration. Most important, he employed an inclusionary style that relied on consultation, compromise, attention to symbolism, and evocation of national projects—talents that are usually thought to be the exclusive preserve of politicians.[83]

Foxley's policies and policy style have met with a good deal of success: the first government avoided an authoritarian regression and established the center-left's competence as a governing force. It left office with high approval ratings in the polls, and the Concertación actually increased its percentage of the popular vote after four years in power. The culture of cooperation nurtured by the government holds the potential for the gradual depolarization of Chilean society and the future democratization of the system.

In all of his activities, Foxley's primary loyalty has been not to the economic model per se but rather to the culture of cooperation that he believes is the guarantor of both economic development and democracy. Foxley is a democratic technopol because he believes that democracy is necessary for successful economic management and that flexibility on policies is necessary to avoid the kind of excessive social conflict or political polarization that had undermined Chilean democracy in the late 1960s. This approach belies a common view of technopols and the policy process, in which the techno is seen as useful for judging what institutions and policies are necessary and the pol is only used to persuade others to accept these policies.[84] Foxley's approach to political

83. Patricio Silva, for example, in writing about the roles of technocrats and politicians in post-1990 Chile, argues that "the politicians time and again have demonstrated their special artistic talents (pragmatism, the ability to reconcile the irreconcilable, etc.) which, almost by definition, the technocracy simply does not possess." Silva, "Technocrats and Social Change in Chile: Past, Present, and Future Perspectives," in *The Legacy of Dictatorship,* ed. Angell and Pollack, 213. Verónica Montecinos was one of the first to recognize the multifaceted contributions that economists could make to democratic governability. See her "Economists and Democratic Transition: The Quest for Governability in Chile," in *Democratic Transition and Consolidation in Southern Europe, Latin America, and Southeast Asia,* ed. Diane Ethier (London: Macmillan, 1990).

84. See, for example, John Williamson, "In Search of a Manual for Technopols" (background

economy highlights the importance of political considerations in the selection of policies. To give but one example, it was Foxley's *political* vision—the importance he places on developing a culture of cooperation, his belief that protection for private property is a requirement for political stability, his interpretation of the people's desires—more than his *technical* assessment of specific policies that influenced his views on the appropriate economic program for the new democracy.

The role for politics in Foxley's approach is not limited to the calculations of policy makers, however. Instead, the political class and intermediary organizations are given an important role, in sharp contrast to the projects of neoliberal authoritarians and "neoliberal populists."[85] Whereas the Chicago Boys rejected politicians and organized groups, Foxley's vision of the political economy depends precisely on the ability of the "leadership class" drawn from these groups to reach agreements on policies. This leadership class, rather than a populist leader or an authoritarian state, is responsible for the pursuit of the "common good."

In keeping with this logic, a primary goal of Foxley's (and of the Aylwin administration) has been the fortification of the political system—establishing a working relationship with the opposition, striving to strengthen the center-left alliance, searching for ways to increase the protagonism of parties relative to a strong executive, and renovating parties so that they are closer to their bases in society. The work of Alejandro Foxley in these areas is typical of the efforts of a whole class of technopols who operate not just from the commanding heights of the state but, increasingly, from the legislature and the parties. The presence of technopols outside of the executive branch and their cooperation with traditional politicians contribute to the strengthening of the political system as a whole and not just the state.

Organized groups have also found that they are legitimate actors in the new democracy, especially to the extent that they behave as part of Foxley's responsible leadership class. They are consulted by the government, and their groups have received some measure of material compensation. This is a significant advance over neoliberal models, which treat the ability to resist demands from labor and other organized groups as a sign of political strength. Although there is a certain degree of this resistance in Foxley's

85. Kenneth M. Roberts argues that there is a certain affinity between neoliberalism and populism because both tend to centralize power and bypass intermediary organizations. See Roberts, "Neoliberalism and the Transformation of Populism in Latin America: The Peruvian Case," *World Politics* 48 (October 1995): 82–116.

approach (perhaps inevitably given the need for macroeconomic stability), there is also a much greater emphasis on education, persuasion, consultation, and compensation as a means of reducing demands. Generally, the government treats organized interests as "respectable but biased"; their demand making is seen as "legitimate but inopportune." Lobbying is preferred to traditional forms of collective action, which the government tends to associate with polarization and unreasonable demands that do not permit the "rational" resolution of differences.

If conflict should occur despite the government's best efforts to moderate and channel demands, the state might use all legal means at its disposal to resist. However, Foxley's approach offers an alternative to this "neoliberal" solution. Neoliberals tend to see compromise with "rent-seeking" groups as a sign of weakness because they focus on the "crisis of state authority" as the obstacle to development. Foxley, however, understands that state authority is linked to the functioning of political and social institutions; it is the inability of the political and social system to generate a stable consensus on a national model of development that undermines both democracy and development. To put it another way, "neoliberals" stress the importance of state autonomy, whereas Foxley emphasizes the importance of "embedded autonomy." From the latter perspective, negotiations with demand-making groups (even those who take to the streets) are frequently seen as a sign of political-system strength (the ability to resolve conflict) rather than state weakness. Policies that are likely to be too conflictual are either avoided temporarily or addressed in a more gradual fashion than is the case in the "political-will" approach to organized groups.[86] So far, this seems to be a workable middle ground between a fully autonomous state and a "captured" state.

In sum, the technopols' vision of how to make democracy and development compatible and the way it has been put into practice in Chile represent important advances over historical and contemporary solutions to the problem. The future of this project depends largely on the ability of the political elite to devise ways to institutionalize the "culture of cooperation" that so far has relied primarily on ties forged between political and technopolitical elites in opposition to the military regime. Foxley's "leadership class" must meet the

---

86. For example, President Aylwin noted that his administration did not undertake the immediate modernization of the national copper company (CODELCO), because they did not want to challenge the workers (and because there was a national consensus on the importance of state action in the copper industry). See Patricio Aylwin interview in *Proposiciones* 25 (October 1994): 16.

challenge of connecting to their bases and encouraging participation. Or, to put it in terms of "embedded autonomy," the ability of the state to continue to act effectively depends on the existence of "valid interlocutors." A first step in that direction has been taken by the political class in Chile, as exemplified by Foxley's efforts as party president to fortify parties as valid interlocutors for the government and to ensure his party's representativeness by increasing its contacts with society. The participation of technopols in the conceptualization of these tasks and their implementation in Chile—in a somewhat tense but nonetheless fruitful cooperation with traditional party elites—holds hope for the future of democratic governance in that country.

Index

Tables are denoted by page numbers in italics.

Jorge I. Dominguez is the Frank G. Thomson Professor of Government at Harvard University and a past president of the Latin American Studies Association. His most recent book (co-authored with James McCann) is *Democratizing Mexico: Public Opinion and Electoral Choices* (Johns Hopkins, 1996). He is also series editor of "Essays on Mexico, Central and South America: Scholarly Debates from the 1950s to the 1990s" (7 vols., Garland Publishing, 1994).